The Complete Travel Marketing Handbook

The Complete Travel Marketing Handbook

37 industry experts share their secrets

Andrew Vladimir

NTC Business Books
a division of National Textbook Company • Lincolnwood, Illinois U.S.A.

This book is dedicated to the memory
of my father, Irwin Alfred Vladimir,
who taught me to search the world for answers
and to my mother, Geraldine Sarah Vladimir,
who has helped me to find them.

1989 Printing

Published by NTC Business Books, an imprint of
National Textbook Company, 4255 West Touhy Avenue,
Lincolnwood (Chicago) Illinois 60646-1975 U.S.A.
©1988 by National Textbook Company. All rights reserved.
No part of this book may be reproduced, stored in a retrieval
system, or transmitted in any form, or by any means, electronic,
mechanical, photocopying or otherwise, without the prior written
permission of National Textbook Company.
Manufactured in the United States of America.
Library of Congress Catalog Card Number: 87-82612
9 0 ML 9 8 7 6 5 4 3 2

Acknowledgments

I first started thinking about the need for a book of collected wisdom on travel and tourism marketing in 1981. At that time, however, I didn't know enough about the industry to put it together. Over the years I've had input from a great many people and this book is as much theirs as it is mine. Here are some of the people I'm deeply in debt to:

All of the contributing authors for their willingness to share their wisdom and knowledge. I know many of them contributed long hours to putting their thoughts on paper and I am deeply grateful.

Their secretaries who endlessly relayed messages and correspondence and typed and retyped material.

The following people for their assistance in researching and editing manuscripts: Karen Cardran, Ewin Gilles, Eileen Golub, Sue Haberle, Essie Landsman, Beatrice Lund, Jack MacBean, Tracy O'Rourke, Tim Palmer, Joe Russo, Lois Tilles, and Dave Treitel.

Many of my past and present clients, business associates, and friends who have helped me to understand this business and shape the concepts in this book. They include Rance Crain, Kirk Cooper, Reggie Cooper, Duncan Farrell, Roger Everingham, Carl Helgren, Mike Hoynes, Bill Hunt, Paul Leseur, Rod McLeod, Steve Norton, Ray O'Donnell, John O'Toole, Peter Osgood, Frangiskos Stafilopatis, David Sutherland, Chuck West, Mike Winfield, Jimmy Williams, and Jim Wooldridge.

The people of Bermuda for according me the honor of serving as their Director of Tourism. In particular, Governor and Lady Dunroissil, Premier John Swan, Tourism Minister Irving Pearman, and Secretaries to the Cabinet Kenneth Richardson and Donald Pudney, all of whom went out of their way to make me feel comfortable.

Dean Anthony Marshall, Associate Dean Rocco Angelo, and my other colleagues in the School of Hospitality Management at Florida International University for sharing their ideas with me. Also Dr. Richard Still of F.I.U.'s College of Business Administration.

My editor, Harry Briggs, who has helped me think through ideas, encouraged me, and most importantly believed in this project from the start.

Finally, I owe a special debt to Ginny and Ellis Rolett, Donna Vladimir, and my children, Alex, Tom, Jenny, Andrea, and Allison, for serving as my cheering section and keeping my days bright and sunny while I have been working on this book.

Andrew Vladimir

Preface

The difference between selling and marketing is that selling is getting rid of what you have, while marketing is having what people want.

Theodore Levitt, Harvard Business School

The travel and tourism business perfectly exemplifies the chicken and egg paradox. Do people flock to Mexico because Mexico has what they want or because the Mexican government has been successful in selling what it has? Do we continue to fly the friendly skies of United because they are offering a $99 seat to Los Angeles which is too good a deal to pass up or because we want to go to Los Angeles and United happens to fly there? If the equation "People wanting to go (X) plus United having flights (Y) equals visitors to Los Angeles (Z)," what then are the relative value of X, Y, and Z? Is the number of visitors to Los Angeles more a function of the number of movie stars and studios in Hollywood or the number of seats United sells for $99? Which is the chicken and which is the egg?

The problem we face in answering these questions is that we are dealing with a complex set of systems and subsystems that comprise the tourism and travel industry. All of these systems have the same objective — creating customers. A system is a single enterprise or a group of enterprises that are in the same business or after the same customers. Delta Air Lines by itself comprises a system, but it is part of the larger airline system.

The airlines in turn are part of the transportation system, which is still only a single part of the tourism and travel system. Each of these systems has its own boundaries and interacts with the economic and social environment independently; but, because they are interrelated and depend upon each other for both input and output, they are constantly striving for a state of equilibrium or *dynamic homeostasis*, as it is referred to by system theorists. This equilibrium is achieved when supply and demand are matched in each of these subsystems or when newer and more elaborate systems are created to replace older, obsolete ones. For a system to achieve this equilibrium it must address and fill the needs of the marketplace. Filling needs is a complex undertaking. If the Smith family flies to Hawaii on American Airlines, rents a Hertz Car, and spends a fabulous week at the Maui Marriott, then American, Hertz, and Marriott have all contributed to the Smiths' need for a relaxing vacation. Could any of them have done it alone? No. Could any one of them have spoiled the Smiths' holiday? Easily.

There is a symbiotic relationship that exists in the travel and hospitality industries. Various business entities live and work in close association to one another which may be, but is not necessarily, beneficial. They are all part of the same system and yet often they tend to operate as if that were not so. Nevertheless the sum of their relationship constitutes the product that consumers buy and unless the total product successfully fills a need, then there can be no economic success. Miami Beach still exemplifies a leisure product that has been unable to get its act together. There are some first-class hotels, a few good restaurants, alluring beaches, and a splendid convention center. But there is no synergism between them, no real affinity; so while visitors admire the Fontainebleau Hilton and the food at Joe's Stone Crabs, the reputation of Miami Beach as a resort remains somewhat confusing.

This is a book, then, about the relationships between systems in the field of travel and tourism. It explores the implications of those relationships and how to manage them. If each system can obtain a better understanding of the inner workings of neighboring systems, they will ultimately be more successful in achieving their own goals. I first came to this conclusion while serving as the Director of Tourism for the government of Bermuda in 1984 and 1985. Because Bermuda has always operated as a carefully controlled environment, my responsibilities included the regulation of hotels, airlines, cruise ships, tour operators, and some attractions. Relations between the government and the hoteliers are particularly crucial to the overall success of the tourism industry, as one article in this volume points out. The hotels, which include several large international chains, did not always empathize with the government's aim to promote growth in all sectors of the economy. There were misunderstandings about how airlines set fares between Bermuda and the United States, how tour operators and other wholesalers attracted business, what the role of travel agents was and how much money and effort ought to be devoted to wooing them, and whether or not and to what extent cruise lines contributed to the social and economic welfare of the community.

Bermuda's situation is in no way unique. That these misunderstandings occur universally can be seen in the weekly pages of the travel trade press. The American Society of Travel Agents tried desperately to explain to Congress what it perceived its role to be in the distribution and marketing of travel products, and failed. The traditional travel agency system in America was subsequently deregulated and is in a state of siege. Airlines, too, have suffered from the same malaise, perhaps to a greater degree than any other enterprises dealt with here. Consumer activists accuse them of capriciously setting fares, of overbooking, and of not maintaining their equipment. Corporations that have established their own travel management facilities are now seeking commissions and rebates and have little sympathy for the lack of enthusiasm their proposals have received. Flight crews want more money and the general public wants lower fares. Clearly this is a misunderstood industry if there ever were one.

This book, however, shall not focus on explaining the inner workings of the various industry subsections to the public. This is a text for professional practitioners and for students who wish to enter the field as sales and marketing executives. It compiles advice written by people who understand the key concepts of the system theory and marketing. By putting their contributions in a single volume, a clearer picture will emerge of the marketing management practices needed for success in travel and hospitality enterprises.

Many of our contributors are legends in their own time. In particular, I am grateful to Dick Ferris, Bill Marriott, and Bob Tisch for supporting this undertaking. Their willingness to participate inspired me and helped stimulate interest from other important leaders in the industry who also contributed articles and made helpful suggestions. I want to thank Donna Tuttle for agreeing to write the forward; she is America's "First Lady of Travel" and deserves recognition for stimulating travel not only to the United States but internationally.

It needs to be noted that because this book deals with a highly dynamic and volatile industry in which mergers, acquisitions, and management changes occur almost weekly, some of the titles and positions of our contributors are bound to change during the life of the book. I have made every effort to be current as of the date of publication, but positions are bound to change with the passing of time. I therefore caution the reader who may wish to use this volume for teaching or training purposes to be aware of this inevitability, and regret that these inaccuracies cannot be avoided.

This book has a second purpose. I have spent all of my life in marketing and advertising. I have helped McDonald's sell hamburgers and Sonesta sell hotel rooms. I have worked for airlines, tour operators, cruise lines, car rental companies, and travel agencies. I believe that many of the techniques that have been successfully employed in the package goods area are just now coming into use in service enterprises. Marketing is less developed and less innovative in these areas and I know the contributing editors who have made this book possible share my view that cooperative marketing by entities that understand how to give people what they want, rather than get rid of what they have, have made a major step toward achieving growth and stability for the travel and tourism industry.

A word about the organization of this material. Because this is a book about marketing, I have organized the material in the manner of a traditional text. The first parts contain contributions that define the industry quantitatively and qualitatively and focus on understanding the consumer. Then there are a series of articles on different systems and subsystems that represent the bulk, though not all, of the products and services that require travelers to generate a major source of revenue. The last of these, the travel agencies, form the core of the distribution system. Finally there are some articles on promotion and public relations. For students studying hospitality and travel marketing, this book provides excellent supplementary reading to regular marketing texts. For professionals who wish to use it for reference, this organization makes the important concepts easily accessible.

Andrew Vladimir

Foreword

Donna Frame Tuttle
Under Secretary, U.S.
Department of
Commerce

*As Under Secretary for the United States Travel and Tourism
Administration, Mrs. Tuttle is the highest-ranking woman in the U.S.
Department of Commerce and one of the most senior-level women
appointees in the Reagan Administration. She has been named The
Travel Industry of America's Woman of the Year for her contributions
to the promotion of travel and tourism and the National Tour
Association's Travel Industry Leader of the Year. She was inducted into
the American Society of Travel Agent's Hall of Fame in October 1987.*

Travel is as old as civilization. While the ancients may have traveled for
survival and explorers of old charted their courses in anticipation of
discovery and riches, they are not too different from present-day
travelers. We, too, travel for various reasons: business, study, health, relaxation, and new experiences. Through travel we gain renewed understanding
of other cultures and people. Tourism, in its highest form, is a quest for
knowledge. Touring is an information-gathering process; it has the ability to
inform and instruct — to teach Americans about the civilization to which
they belong and about other civilizations that share this planet.

Tourism is a subject worthy of study for that reason alone, but also
warrants our attention for other reasons. Tourism is growing. It has an enormous impact on national economies, both developed and developing. It causes
and effects rapid change in the world and we must know more about it.

Since the voyages of Columbus, escalating technological change has compressed our world and created new tourist markets. Commercial jet aircraft
introduced in the late 1950s brought the travel markets of Europe, South
America, Asia, and Australia hours closer to U.S. tourist attractions and
services. Transmissions from communications satellites have stimulated public interest in developments in distant countries and thus, in international
travel. Computer reservation services, new pricing and marketing concepts,
and the rising standard of living in industrial and developing countries have
all served to expand and change the tourism marketplace.

Similar innovations have changed and expanded — and will continue to
expand — domestic tourist markets. In the United States, Individual Retirement Accounts (IRAs) are generating more discretionary funds that can be

used for travel. Monday holidays, shorter workweeks, job-sharing opportunities, and flexible work schedules are creating more leisure times. The trend toward smaller families is freeing disposable income for purposes other than child rearing. Longer life expectancies and pensions are giving senior citizens the time and means to travel for pleasure.

These same developments and innovations are symptomatic of a profound change in the world economy. Individuals with more disposable income and more free time create more effective demand for personal services. Consequently, since the 1960s, such services as tourism have accounted for an increasing share of the Gross National Product of nations. In the United States, in 1985, services accounted for 50 percent of U.S. personal consumption expenditures, and tourism accounted for 20 percent ($269 billion) of personal consumption expenditures ($1,308 trillion) on services.

In its broadest sense, tourism encompasses all expenditures for goods and services by travelers. It includes purchases for transportation, lodging, meals, entertainment, souvenirs, travel agency and sightseeing tour services, and personal grooming services. In addition, tourists make use of the goods and services of other industries, such as insurance, credit cards, advertising, data processing, automobiles, luggage, and laundry and dry cleaning. The full scope of international travel and tourism, therefore, covers the output of segments of many industries.

These are just a few of the reasons why we must understand the causes and effects of tourism, but these are not the only reasons. The fluctuating value of the U.S. dollar on principal foreign markets together with fluctuating resource and commodity prices and world political events can affect the volume and compositon of the U.S. visitor market. Countries that were not important sources of tourism business for the United States even five years ago are emerging as promising new markets. They include Hong Kong, South Korea, India, Saudi Arabia, Kuwait, and Malaysia. We must be prepared to provide the unique and special language, currency, and food services these visitors require.

Technological changes will continue to revolutionize the infrastructure of the travel industry as well as its operational procedures, productivity, and product. We must be alert to and aware of those changes so we can adapt to them.

There will be intensified competition for a share of the world travel market in the coming years. New independent countries emerged during the 1960s and 1970s, and today those countries must earn foreign exchange. More than 70 developing countries have established national tourism offices. The developing country share of the market is already growing and we must be prepared to meet the competition.

In the future we must enlarge the existing "VISIT USA" coalition by bringing more of the U.S. travel industry's one million businesses together in joint marketing endeavors, especially in the rapidly emerging markets. Uniting the components of this industry in an effective marketing coalition that can compete on an equal footing with often publicly owned foreign tourism conglomerates and multinational consortia must be a high priority as the United States struggles to maintain and expand its share of a rapidly changing global market.

The U.S. share of the tourism market has remained virtually unchanged since the mid-1970s. U.S. private sector companies need more and better knowledge about foreign markets, foreign cultures and traditions, and more expertise and financial commitment in promoting U.S. services abroad.

This country has always been a leader. Its tourism industry, too, must lead. That is another reason why we should study tourism.

Contents

The Market

IT MAY BE USEFUL TO BEGIN HERE BY TAK-ing a new look at some definitions that will be familiar to many of the readers of this work.

In their well-known book on tourism, McIntosh and Goeldner define their field as: the science, art, and business of attracting and transporting visitors, accommodating them, and graciously catering to their needs and wants (*Tourism: Principles, Practices, Philosophies*, John Wiley & Sons). Now compare that definition with the definition of marketing by Phillip Kotler, a professor at Northwestern University and the author of many texts on the subject: Marketing is human activity directed at satisfying needs and wants through exchange processes (*Marketing Management*, Prentice-Hall). How curious that three well known authorities from different academic disciplines should define their fields in almost precisely the same terms!

It can be argued that both definitions are so broad and generalized that they are bound to overlap, but it is more likely that the subjects of these definitions overlap, that they may indeed be one and the same or at least close relations. There is much support for this argument in the marketplace. When the government of Bermuda was seeking a Director for the Ministry of Tourism in 1974, the key skill identified by management consultant Warren Keegan as necessary to do the job was an expertise in marketing. Thus Andrew Vladimir, a non-Bermudian with little product knowledge, was hired. Many other contributors to this book established their track records in sales and marketing before taking over the reins of their companies and it is obvious by reading their articles that they see their roles primarily through marketing eyes, although they are responsible for operations and profits as well. Management theorists such as Theodore Levitt have written that it should be the first priority of any business to create customers, not to make a profit. Before you can reap a profit you must have customers. If an enterprise creates customers efficiently it will make a profit; otherwise it will fail. While this may seem patently clear to even the most novice manager, many businesses do not succeed because they tend to be more concerned with making profits than creating customers. Graduates of business schools with M.B.A. degrees are often criticized for being too short-term and bottom line oriented, but it may be that this is true only of those that are product oriented rather than market oriented.

Marketing Begins with the Market

How then do marketing oriented professionals think about the marketing process? It almost invariably starts by defining and quantifying the market. The first questions that need to be answered are:

- ☐ Who are our customers?
- ☐ How many of them are there?
- ☐ Where do they come from?
- ☐ What are they like?
- ☐ What do they want to buy?
- ☐ What do we have to sell?
- ☐ What are they willing to pay for it?
- ☐ How do we communicate with them?

The answers to these questions are usually classified under one of four categories that are popularly referred to as the four Ps of marketing. These four categories are:

1. *The Product or Service:* For airlines this would be routes and schedules. For lodging facilities it might be the complete physical plant or simply all of the amenities that are to be included in a honeymoon or a golf package. For a restaurant, the product is the decor, the menu, the presentation, and the service. Even travel agencies have a range of products and services including free ticket delivery, travelers checks, and computerized analysis of travel costs and savings for commercial accounts.

2. *The Price:* For many enterprises in travel and tourism, pricing strategies have become the most important element of their marketing mix. This is not desirable because it severely limits their ability to utilize the other parts of the mix effectively. Wholesale and retail prices are only one part of this marketing decision. Margins are equally important and most definitely a marketing decision since competitive pressures are involved. Seasonal and group pricing policies are equally important.

3. *The Place:* Place refers to the distribution system. Credit cards and 800 numbers have revolutionized the place at which reservations are made in the hotel business. Ticket printing machines for consumers and satellite ticket printers for commercial accounts are changing the places where airlines distribute their tickets. The importance of location for service businesses such as travel agencies is evolving as a result of these new technologies.

4. *The Promotion:* The sales force may be the most important part of the promotion category because of the nature of the mass distribution system that utilizes wholesalers, hotel representatives and travel agencies; however, because of the elasticity of demand that clearly influences travel patterns, the job of communicating directly with consumers cannot be left entirely to these middlemen and retailers, whose resources include very limited promotional dollars. Therefore, the role of advertising, public relations, and sales promotion to create consumer demand and pull the products and services through the distribution system is paramount. Moreover, in the long-run, companies can make more profits by increasing the effectiveness of their promotion rather than by cutting the profit margins.

In the first two articles in this book, authors Douglas Fretchling of the U.S. Travel Data Center and Don Wynegar of the Department of Commerce assess the impact of tourism on our economy and analyze the various sources of revenue. Fretchling looks at the size of the industry in America and the nature of the American traveler. Wynegar adds to this a carefully quantified analysis of international tourism to the United States—who comes here, where they come from, and what they do. Together the two articles provide an excellent overview of the marketplace in which enterprises that depend on travelers for their revenue operate.

Chapter 1
The Travel Industry Today

Dr. Douglas C. Frechtling
*Former Director, U.S.
Travel Data Center,
President, Guest Plus*

Dr. Douglas C. Frechtling has served as Director of the United States Travel Data Center since its establishment in early 1973. As CEO of the national, nonprofit center for travel and tourism research, he was responsible for directing the Data Center's economic and market research programs. Dr. Frechtling holds a Ph.D. in economics from George Washington University, and is past president of the Travel and Tourism Research Association (TTRA). At press time, Dr. Frechtling had left the U.S. Travel Data Center and started a new venture, Guest Plus.

Travel and tourism comprise one of the most ubiquitous activities in the United States. More than two of every three Americans take an overnight trip or a day trip to a place 100 miles or more away during the year. U.S. Travel Data Center studies of more than half of the nation's 3,400 counties and county equivalents have found that all but three demonstrate measurable effects of travel spending in a given year.

Despite its pervasive nature, travel away from home, as a human activity and as an industry that serves it, is not self-defining. Marketers differ on the scope of travel and tourism as an activity. For example, those operating an urban theme park that draws 90 percent of its attendance from within a twenty-mile radius consider themselves predominantly in the tourism business, while airline and resort hotel marketers disagree.

Similar problems arise in trying to define the travel industry. Most agree that resort hotels, national air carriers, Amtrak, rural parks and attractions, and campgrounds receive the preponderance of their business from travelers. The issue is not as clear-cut for restaurants, drug and department stores, night clubs, sports facilities, gasoline stations, and urban parks.

In short, there is no distinctive group of goods and services that clearly constitute travel and tourism, and only travel and tourism, in most minds. There is no standard "tourism product." Rather, the consumer combines a group of goods and services to create his or her vacation trip.

For the marketer, it is like trying to market an auto chassis while someone else sells the motor to a consumer who wants a shiny new car. The leisure traveler, for instance, is buying an experience comprised of transportation, lodging, meals, entertainment, and other items. His or her judgment of the value/price relationship, either before or after the fact, depends upon the whole, yet a marketer sells only one component of this experience.

To succeed, the marketer must view the product as the customer does—part of a total experience—and act accordingly. This includes developing marketing relationships with the other components of the trip and surveying the value/price relationships of these components along with his own.

The marketer must always keep in mind that the consumer wants a rewarding travel experience, not just an airplane ride or a night in a hotel.

The Industry

While I can't describe the travel industry in traditional terms, I can define it for effective use. The travel industry is nontraditional, limited by the goods and services travelers demand rather than the nature of the supply. For example, restaurants are a component of the travel industry, not because they serve meals but because they serve meals to travelers. The consumer purchases the different items the industry offers because together they constitute his leisure or business trip.

Something attracts an individual out of his home area and causes him to take a trip. This attraction might be a site or a sight, an activity, or people, including friends, relatives, and business contracts. To reach this attraction, the traveler must purchase transportation, either operating his own vehicle and servicing it or paying a fare to a common carrier. Enroute to or at the destination, most travelers require lodging, including hotels and motels, rental second homes, campgrounds, or their own second home. In addition, most travelers require meals from retail food service establishments. Finally, travelers make use of various auxiliary services to assist in the trip.

The typical traveler purchases all or most of these goods and services on the trip. The providers of these are linked by the common needs of consumers. Consequently, the travel industry is the collection of organizations and establishments that derive all or a significant portion of their income from providing these goods and services to the traveler.

In its economic impact studies, the Data Center focuses on the following as representing most of the businesses selling directly to travelers away from home, that is, the travel industry.

An implication of this end-use definition is that the same individual may seek one set of components for a leisure trip and a different set for a business trip. His value/price calculus changes because trip motivations and payment responsibilities change. Indeed, someone else may make his business travel choices for him. The travel marketer must vary the marketing message depending on this change in end use.

Despite these complexities, a number of statements can be made with confidence about the U.S. travel industry. For one, it is big. The Data Center's estimates for 1985 rank the aggregation of businesses that sell directly to the traveler as the third largest U.S. retail or service industry in receipts, and the second largest private employer in the nation.

Transportation	**Lodging**
Airlines	Hotels/motels
Taxicabs/limousines	Campgrounds
Automotive operation	Second homes
Auto rental	
Bus/motorcoach	**Meals**
Amtrak	Eating and drinking places
Cruise lines	
	Auxiliary services
Attractions	General merchandise and miscellaneous
Amusement and recreation services	retail stores
	Travel agencies

Many operators comprise the travel industry. The 1982 censuses of service industries and retail trade provide counts of the following travel-related firms (business organizations or companies) and establishments (single physical locations where business is conducted):

Type of business	Firms	Establishments
Amusement and recreation services (excluding motion pictures)	46,860	49,966
Eating and drinking places	258,314	319,873
Gasoline service stations	85,684	116,188
Hotels, motels, other lodging places	36,956	41,231
Passenger car rental, w/o drivers	NA	3,286

Source: U.S. Bureau of the Census

Small businesses dominate the travel industry. According to the standards of the U.S. Small Business Administration, more than 95 percent of the above firms are classified as small. The healthy implication of this is the absence of explicit barriers to entry and growth. The disadvantage is that many operators in the industry lack management and marketing skills for survival, and capital for expansion.

By anyone's definition, travel away from home requires transportation, which gives rise to two singular sources of instability for the industry.

One is the long history of government regulation of intercity transportation. Relatively recently, the federal government withdrew from regulating the nation's air carriers and intercity bus companies, and these sectors are still adjusting to more competitive environments. The uncertainties are compounded by state and local agencies who do, or seek to, regulate, license, and tax these operators. The occasional cries for reregulation heard from federal legislative and administrative officials add to the uncertainty the marketer encounters.

The other source of industry instability arises from its dependence on petroleum fuels for transportation. The two oil supply shocks in the 1970s devastated many operators and destinations. With hindsight, it is clear that the federal government aggravated the initial effects of shortages by attempting to hold prices down and allocating scarce supplies among competing tourism and non-tourism demands. The marketer should be prepared for the effects of fuel shortages and resulting price inflation and should argue strenuously against government interference with petroleum flows and consumer demand. Otherwise he will watch helplessly as his markets are needlessly agitated by arbitrary and capricious allocation policies.

One other characteristic of the travel industry must give the thoughtful marketer pause. This is the simultaneous tendencies toward excess industry capacity and limited tourism infrastructure in this country. The periodic airline fare wars, surges in the number of air carriers and intercity bus companies, and hotel overbuilding and lackluster occupancy rates in many areas testify to an enthusiasm among suppliers not matched by customers.

At the same time, movement into or out of many of the nation's airports is hampered by poor roads, inadequate baggage handling, a shortage of gates, and limited air traffic control facilities. The situation is not much better for many traveling by roadway. Highway construction and maintenance fall short of reducing demand-killing delays on routes to and from major tourist meccas.

The travel marketer is often in the position of a store selling flashlights in the middle of a hurricane. There is a great demand for the product, but customers can't get there to make the purchase. This requires careful positioning to increase sales without overpromising and guaranteeing customer dissatisfaction. It also demands day-to-day familiarity with supply conditions affecting the demand.

The Market

The U.S. market for travel away from home is big, heterogeneous, and changing.

The Data Center estimates that Americans spent nearly $250 billion traveling away from home in their own country during 1985 and another $17 billion visiting foreign destinations. They spent nearly 5.8 billion nights away from home on more than one billion person-trips (counted each time a person goes on a trip).

One hundred fifty million Americans take one or more trips away from home each year, according to the Data Center's National Travel Survey. While this comprises 63 percent of our population, some groups are more active travelers than others. The following table shows groups with high and low tendencies to travel away from home in 1985:

Relatively high tendency to travel	Relatively low tendency to travel
Married	Widowed
Male	Female
35-44 years of age	65 years and older
Graduate studies	Did not complete high school
Professional/managerial	Blue collar
Own their home	Rent their home
$50-75,000 family income	Less than $10,000 a year
Two wage earners	No wage earners

Source: U.S. Travel Data Center, National Travel Survey

Of course, any such enumeration may oversimplify. For example, those over 65 years of age do not take as many trips per year as their younger counterparts, but stay away from home 50 percent longer when they do travel. The point is that the U.S. travel market is not a monolith, but a complex combination of segments that vary in desire and ability to take a trip. Savvy marketers segment the market to concentrate their messages on those most apt to choose their tourism product. They do not market to everyone.

The behavioral regularity closest to a law in tourism is that the farther a person lives from a destination, the less likely he or she is to visit it, all things being equal. The most important corollary is that the farther a population concentration is from a destination, the smaller the proportion of that population that will visit. The following table summarizes this tendency.

Distribution of U.S. Domestic Person-trips by Destination Distance from
Origin, Personal and Business Travel, 1985.

Straightline distance	Personal	Business
100 to 149 miles	20%	16%
150 to 199 miles	15	13
200 to 249 miles	12	10
250 to 299 miles	7	7
300 to 499 miles	16	17
500 to 999 miles	14	18
1,000 miles or more	16	19

Source: *U.S. Travel Data Center, National Travel Survey*

Geographic segmentation is the most productive segmentation a travel marketer can do, for personal or business trips. Indeed, more than half of all personal trips are within a 300-mile radius of travelers' homes. In short, your best markets are usually in your own backyard.

Changing Travel Patterns

The structure of the market is changing as well. A comparison of the Data Center's most recent travel surveys with the U.S. Census Bureau's 1972 National Travel Survey suggests the following variations from 15 years ago.

A higher proportion of vacation travel is by air now than 15 years ago, and less is by personal motor vehicle. As the leisure travel market matures, people direct more of their expanding discretionary dollars to traveling by the faster but more expensive mode of transportation.

Trips have become shorter. Now more than one-third of trips are to places within a 150-mile radius of the vacationer's home, and 43 percent are now less than three nights' duration.

Americans travel in smaller parties than in 1972, reflecting the change in household structure. Forty percent of travel parties now are just two people, not just because there are few large households, but also because the husband and wife often vacation without their offspring.

We now find considerably less seasonality in vacation travel these days. Looking at the traditional four quarters we see there is relatively more travel in the second and fourth quarters and less in the third than in 1972.

Americans 45 years of age and over account for a smaller share of pleasure travel than they did 15 years ago. To some extent this reflects demographic change, as the number of Americans under 45 years of age has grown rapidly. But as the Baby Boomers grow older, the growth balance will tip in favor of the older generations once more.

We note regional shifts among origins of travel as well. New England and the far west have become relatively less important in generating vacation travel. The south and southwest have become more important. In terms of destinations, New England's share of the national vacation market is down, while the south's is up.

There are relatively fewer vacation trips to visit friends and relatives and fewer outdoor recreation trips. People are traveling to a much greater extent for sightseeing and entertainment than they used to.

There is also an increasing tendency to append leisure activities onto business and convention trips. Approximately 15 percent of business and convention trips include vacation activities. This opens up new opportunities for leisure and business/convention marketers.

These changing patterns emphasize the importance of approaching the travel market as a collection of segments, not a single mass that responds equally to all forms of promotion and other influences. The travel marketer must segment the markets, assess opportunities, evaluate alternative strategies, and carefully target promotional resources if he or she is to succeed in the years ahead.

Marketing Challenge

Prospects for growth are not as favorable as they were in the 1950s and 1960s when the market was expanding rather rapidly. During that period family formation rose rapidly in this country. Passenger travel technology reduced travel costs through faster, larger, and more comfortable planes, buses, and automobiles.

The nation also enjoyed a major expansion of its surface and air transportation infrastructure. It built our interstate highway system. Many airports and bus terminals were built and expanded. Resort and lodging plants were improved as well.

During this period there were very few close-to-home leisure alternatives to vacation travel. If we wanted a beach vacation when I was a child in Washington, D.C., we drove to Cape Cod or Maine, the closest developed resort areas. There were few major recreational facilities near urban areas.

Since the late 1970s, the leisure travel market has shown signs of maturity; the rate of growth trend equals that of the overall economy. This is because no major new markets have opened up. The major mass markets that developed in response to cost-reducing innovations, such as jet transports and the interstate highway system, expanded vacation travel substantially. There have been no major cost-reducing advances in transportation or any other sector recently.

There are also many more competitors for leisure time and discretionary dollars now around home. We have seen an explosion in home entertainment equipment ownership: video cassette recorders, improved audio systems, cable TV, and home computers. Americans are investing heavily in home exercise equipment as well and the do-it-yourself market is expanding vigorously.

An explosion in attractions and recreation opportunities available in urban areas has occurred. People do not have to travel away from home as they once did to enjoy recreation, sightseeing, entertainment, and the other benefits vacations afford.

Leisure travel has also become much more fragile in recent years. Since there are now more substitutes for it, pleasure travel demand is more sensitive to economic changes such as super-inflation and recession. The market has also demonstrated extreme sensitivity to terrorism, nuclear accidents, and even the threat of crowding and congestion.

We have also found that consumers may turn to heavy purchases of major durable goods after a recession. The automobile- and housing-related items Americans postponed buying during the long and harsh recession in 1981-1982 soaked up many discretionary dollars in the ensuing recovery at the expense of increased travel activity.

In short, it is harder to market successfully to travelers in the modern age. There is no reason to believe travel markets will return to the halcyon 1950s and 1960s. The days of riding a rapidly expanding travel market are gone. The days of the professional tourism marketer are at hand.

Chapter 2

The Impact of International Tourism on the United States

Don Wynegar
Director, Office of
Research, USTTA

Don Wynegar is the Director of the Office of Research of the U.S. Travel and Tourism Administration. He is responsible for developing and managing USTTA's research activities and evaluating the agency's program performance. He is currently a member of the Board of Directors of the Travel and Tourism Research Association and also serves on the Program Advisory Council of the U.S. Travel Data Center. As an Adjunct Professor, he teaches graduate tourism classes at George Washington University.

International travel to the United States represents an important growing segment of our domestic tourism industry. In 1985 for example, 21 million foreigners visited this country, contributing more than $14 billion to the American economy. Indeed, visitors from abroad accounted for approximately 5 percent of total travel expenditures in the United States.

Another way to look at these figures is to measure our share of the total global travel market. One guide to that measurement is a count of international arrivals worldwide. In 1985 our 21 million visitors represented 6.4 percent of a total of 325 million international travelers. While in the United States, however, these travelers spent a disproportionate share of money — that $14 billion in expenditures translated into 11.1 percent of all foreign tourism receipts ($105 billion). The bottom line is that our tourism receipts represent a major source of export earnings — one-third of the total for all business services.

Foreign visitors, because of their huge numbers, generated an impressive number of jobs as well. A study conducted by our office showed that in 1983, 313,000 American jobs were created directly as a result of these visitors, with a payroll of $3.1 billion and tax revenues of nearly $1.7 billion, of which $850 million went into Federal tax coffers.

A significant fact to keep in mind when examining these figures is that the expenditures mentioned here were spread all across the travel industry and not concentrated just in one sector. Here's how the figures break down:

Lodging	28%
Domestic transportation	15%
Purchases and incidentals	27%
Entertainment	11%
Food and beverages	19%

Let's take a closer look at some of these industry sectors and the way foreign visitors impacted on them:

The Lodging Industry

We estimate that nearly two-thirds of all foreign visitors spend at least part of their visits in hotels or motels. Fifty percent of these visitors were Canadians, 46 percent were from overseas countries, and the remaining 4 percent were Mexican air travelers. Because many Canadians tend to visit friends and relatives or camp when they come South, only 60 percent of travelers from that group stay in commercial lodgings at all, which makes them the lightest user group of all visitors, despite their high numbers. Compare this with 80 percent of our overseas visitors and 75 percent of Mexican travelers who stayed in hotels and motels.

Another difference that is worth noting between the various groups is their length of stay. For all visitors the average American visit lasts 13 days, but there is a significant difference in duration by market as you might expect. Canadian visitors spend an average of only 7.7 nights here, while overseas visitors stay 22 nights. Mexican air visitors stay 14 nights. Of course, not all of that time is spent in commercial lodgings. We found that overseas visitors spent slightly less than half of those nights (9.4 to be exact) in hotels and motels, while Mexicans stayed almost as long — 8.6 nights. Comparable data for Canadians were not available.

The Transportation Industry

Of the 21 million visitors that came to the States in 1985, slightly more than half (10.7 million) arrived by air. Approximately 67 percent of these came from overseas destinations, 28 percent from Canada, and the remainder from Mexico. For U.S. flag carriers those visitors represented revenue of $2.5 billion according to the Department of Commerce. Domestic airlines also received some business from these travelers; about half of them flew domestically during their visit here.

The Rent-A-Car Industry

We have found that about 40 percent of overseas and Mexican air travelers rent cars while they are here. In absolute numbers that translates into 2.9 million overseas and 290,000 Mexican rentals.

The Changing Composition of the Inbound Market

As marketers concerned with predicting an uncertain future, we need to be especially alert to new trends that may affect the allocation of our resources, such as promotional dollars. The structure of the inbound visitor market, like a chameleon that changes its colors to match new environments, has changed substantially over time. In the 1960s and early 1970s, our foreign visitors were predominantly Canadian tourists. In 1960 Canadians accounted for 86 percent of our international arrivals while overseas countries supplied only 11 percent and Mexico 3 percent. Fifteen years later, we had already experienced a significant change. In 1975 Canadians had decreased to only 63 percent of our foreign visitors, overseas residents had climbed to 23 percent, and Mexicans had increased to 14 percent. The same trend has been more or less continuing. By 1985 our Canadian visitors accounted for only 52 percent of the market, overseas visitors continued to climb to 36 percent, and Mexican arrivals had almost plateaued at 12 percent. The key fact, however, is that this shift in market shares is not a result of a correlating decline in visitors. Canadian arrivals have actually remained relatively unchanged over the past decade, which indicates, I believe, a mature, yet changing market. The shift in market composition is a result of the rapid growth in arrivals from overseas countries, which more than doubled from 1975 to 1985. In this same period Canadian visitors increased only 10 percent and Mexican arrivals rose only 18 percent.

I would now like to discuss the changes in and characteristics of the three major market segments we've identified and tracked:

Canada

Although the Canadian tourist market to the United States (of one night or longer) has not changed substantially in volume over the past decade, the characteristics of this market have undergone significant changes. Canadians visiting America by air have increased by 72 percent over the past decade, while those traveling by auto have actually declined slightly, by 6 percent. Consequently, in 1985, auto travel represented 64 percent of total Canadian tourists to the United States, compared to a 74 percent share in 1975. The share of arrivals accounted for by air travel rose from an 18 percent mark in 1975 to 28 percent in 1985.

The shift in modes of transportation has correlated with a smoothing of seasonal demand among Canadian visitors. In 1975, Canadians visited this country most often during the warm-weather months of the third quarter (41 percent) and second quarter (22 percent) of the year, while fewer visited during the colder periods of the first (19 percent) and fourth (18 percent) quarters. By 1985, a somewhat different seasonal distribution was seen: first quarter arrivals, 21 percent; second quarter, 24 percent; third quarter, 37 percent; and fourth quarter, 18 percent.

Following is a profile of Canadian tourist travelers (overnight or longer) to the United States in 1985:

- [ ] 46 percent were residents of Ontario; 20 percent were from Quebec; and 15 percent were from British Columbia.

- [ ] 53 percent were males and 47 percent were females.

- [ ] Age groups were: under 20, 15 percent; 20-34, 22 percent; 35-54, 33 percent; and 55 and over, 30 percent.

- [ ] 63 percent were on pleasure/recreation/holiday trips; 27 percent were visiting friends/relatives; 12 percent were on business trips.

- [ ] 64 percent traveled to this country by auto; 28 percent by air; 5 percent by bus; and 3 percent by other means.

- [ ] 60 percent stayed in hotels/motels during their visit; 19 percent in private homes; 12 percent used camping facilities; 7 percent stayed in private apartments.

- [ ] The average length of a visit was 7.5 nights.

- [ ] Per capita expenditures in this country were $218, for a daily average of $29 per traveler.

Longer-haul, usually warm-weather destinations in the United States have benefitted most from the increase in air travel from Canada, especially during the winter months. In 1985, Florida, California, Arizona, and Hawaii accounted for fully half of all visitor-nights spent in this country by Canadian tourists. Florida alone accounted for nearly one-third of Canadian visitor-nights in the United States, as well as one-fourth of total tourists' spending. Table 1 illustrates the distribution of Canadian tourist travel by the main states visited in 1985.

In the Canadian *vacation* travel market in the United States (that is, non-weekend, nonbusiness), which comprises about 46 percent of all tourist arrivals from that country, shifts in market demand have been even more pronounced. In terms of vacation trip motivations, there has been a shift toward more vacations in major U.S. cities and resorts and fewer rural sightseeing/outdoor activity vacations. Canadians strongly view the United

States as a more (relative to Canada) upbeat, exciting vacation option, offering a variety of vacation choices. This country is not rated as well, relative to Canada, as providing a relaxing, outdoor-oriented, family vacation in quiet, scenic surroundings.

Table 1
CANADIAN TOURIST TRAVEL TO THE UNITED STATES IN 1985
Main States Visited

State Visited	Person- Visits	Person- Nights	Total Spending*
	(000)**	(000)	($ mils)
Florida	1,459	26,498	622
California	660	6,780	222
New York	2,026	6,005	208
Hawaii	308	4,935	208
Maine	767	3,853	84
Washington	1,358	3,724	79
Arizona	171	3,146	65
Michigan	880	2,243	56
Massachusetts	380	1,891	64
Nevada	441	1,839	117
Vermont	601	1,725	42
Texas	155	1,431	44
New Jersey	285	1,357	40
South Carolina	250	1,199	36
Montana	407	1,188	32
Total United States	10,881	81,964	2,370

Source: Statistics Canada.
*Spending data exclude international transportation fare payments.
**Multiple visits (one traveler can visit more than one state); figures reflect number of visitors spending at least one night in the state.

The move toward increased dependence on air travel has been even more evident in the vacation market. For the first time, in 1984, Canadian vacation trips to the United States by air equaled vacation trips by car, with each accounting for 44 percent of total vacation arrivals. Additionally, there are now proportionally more winter and spring vacation trips to the United States and less summertime vacations; 56 percent of all 1984 Canadian vacation trips to this country took place during winter and spring months, while less than one-fourth occurred during the summer months. This reflects the move toward a more seasonal spread of consumer demand for such trips, as well as more multiple vacation trips (of shorter duration) being taken each year. Lastly, there has been a steady increase in usage of travel agencies by Canadian vacation visitors, reflecting the shifts in modes of transportation, trip purpose, and destination patterns.

Mexico

Mexico is the second largest single country source of foreign visitors to the United States. Hard times befell this tourist market in the early 1980s. Inbound arrivals from that country peaked at nearly 3.6 million in 1981, only to contract substantially in the following two years as massive devaluations of the Mexican peso, under- and unemployment, and weakened consumer buying power cut into the market. After rebounding somewhat in 1984, 1985 saw Mexican visitors return to their previously average level, slightly over 2.5 million Mexican tourists, representing 12 percent of the total inbound arrivals.

Inbound Mexican air travel has been more resilient than the overall market to America. In 1985, approximately 697,000 air arrivals accounted for 27 percent of total Mexican arrivals. Seasonal demand for this segment in 1985 was: first quarter, 20 percent; second quarter, 26 percent; third quarter, 34 percent; and fourth quarter, 20 percent.

Following are the characteristics of Mexican air travelers to the United States, based on the USTTA report, *In-flight Survey of International Air Travelers*, covering 1984:

☐ Nearly two-thirds (64 percent) were residents of Mexico City.

☐ 54 percent were on vacation/holiday; 24 percent were on business; 18 percent were visiting relatives, and 9 percent were visiting friends.

☐ 88 percent had visited the United States before.

☐ 62 percent booked their air trip through a travel agent; 25 percent made their own bookings.

☐ 54 percent used travel agencies as a source of U.S. travel information; 28 percent relied on friends and relatives; 22 percent got information from airlines.

☐ 77 percent flew economy class; 12 percent first class; and 6 percent executive/business class.

☐ 35 percent visited on some type of prepaid inclusive package.

☐ 51 percent traveled with a family group; 31 percent traveled alone; the average party size was 1.8 persons.

☐ 58 percent were male adults (average age of 40); 31 percent were female adults (average age of 38); 11 percent were children under 18.

☐ More than half were white-collar workers; 20 percent were homemakers.

☐ Average annual household income was slightly over $27,000.

☐ The average visitor spent 15.8 nights away from home, of which 13.9 nights were spent in the United States.

☐ 74 percent stayed in U.S. hotels/motels (for an average of 8.6 nights); 32 percent stayed in homes of friends/relatives (for an average of 13.4 nights).

☐ 42 percent rented a car in the United States; 39 percent used private autos of friends/relatives; and 20 percent used domestic air transportation.

☐ 74 percent visited only one state; 16 percent visited two; and 10 percent visited three or more.

The favorite destinations of Mexican air travelers to the United States are California, Texas, New York, and Florida. Table 2 details the pattern of visitation among this group in 1984.

Table 2
U.S. DESTINATIONS VISITED BY MEXICAN AIR TRAVELERS IN 1984

U.S. Destination Visited	Estimated Visitors*	Share of Total Air Visitors
	(000)	(%)
California	235	36
Texas	201	30
New York	81	12
Florida	70	11
Nevada	38	6
Illinois	35	5
Puerto Rico	25	4
Washington, D.C.	24	4
Arizona	23	4
Georgia	22	3
Hawaii	11	2
Louisiana	7	1
Total United States	652	100

Source: U.S. Travel and Tourism Administration.
*Multiple visits (more than one destination could be visited on a single trip).

Overseas Countries

As mentioned earlier, the most significant expansion in inbound arrivals over the past decade has occurred in the overseas visitor market. Since 1975, overseas countries have sent nearly 4 million additional tourists to the United States, more than doubling the number in 1975. This segment was also the most resilient during the early 1980s, when reductions in the number of foreign visitors were registered in most markets.

Over the years the composition of the inbound overseas travel market to this country has changed considerably. Arrivals from Asia and the Middle East have grown more rapidly than any other group, growing by a factor of 45 over the past 25 years, by 2.4 times over the past decade, and by 21 percent from 1980 to 1985. Understandably, the Asia/Middle East share of total overseas visitors has correspondingly increased, from 9 percent in 1960 to 31 percent in 1985. Most other areas have either maintained or declined in relative market share. Europe, although still the largest source of visitors from overseas countries, declined in market share from 44 percent in 1960 to 39 percent in 1985. South America dropped from a 17 percent share of the total overseas market in 1960 to a 10 percent share in 1985; the Caribbean from a 21 percent share to 10 percent in 1985. Table 3 summarizes these shifts since 1960, in terms of volume, percent, and market share changes.

The largest individual country sources of overseas visitors to the United States are Japan, the United Kingdom, West Germany, France, and Australia, in that order. The Japanese inbound market has displayed the most dynamic growth over the years, doubling in volume over the 1975-1985 decade and supplying almost 1.5 million more visitors in 1985 than in 1960. The Japanese share of total overseas arrivals has similarly gone up, from only 3 percent in 1960 to the largest market share, 20 percent, in 1985. The countries accounting for significantly lower market shares during this span of time were the United Kingdom (with a 16 percent share of the total overseas market in 1960 and an 11 percent share in 1985) and Venezuela (with 7 percent and 2 percent shares, respectively). The trends in arrivals from the top ten overseas market countries are illustrated in Table 4.

The seasonality of U.S. visitation from overseas countries has remained quite consistent over time. In 1985, the following quarterly distribution of arrivals was recorded: first quarter, 21 percent; second quarter, 25 percent; third quarter, 31 percent; and fourth quarter, 23 percent. It should be noted, however, that the seasonality is different according to the different regional and country markets. Additional information concerning the characteristics and travel patterns of individual visitor markets is available from the USTTA.

The following items profile total visitors to the United States from overseas countries in 1984, according to USTTA research data:

Table 3
CHANGES IN THE INBOUND MARKET FROM OVERSEAS COUNTRIES
1960 - 1985

Overseas Area	1985 Arrivals	O/S Mkt. Share	1975 Arrivals	O/S Mkt. Share	1960 Arrivals	O/S Mkt. Share
	(000)	(%)	(000)	(%)	(000)	(%)
Europe	2,905		1,478	40.8	263	43.8
Asia/Middle East	2,363		1,002	27.6	52	8.7
South America	782	10.4	431	11.9	100	16.6
Central America	286	3.8	138	3.8	23	3.8
Caribbean	727	9.6	338	9.3	125	20.8
Oceania	342	4.5	185	5.1	31	5.2
Africa	131	1.7	53	1.5	7	1.2
Total Overseas	7,537	100.0	3,624	100.0	601	100.0

	1980-1985		1975-1985		1960-1985	
	Volume Change	% Change	Volume Change	% Change	Volume Change	% Change
	(000)	(%)	(000)	(%)	(000)	(%)
Europe	−495	−15		+97	+2,642	+1,005
Asia/Middle East	+403	+21		+136	+2,311	+4,444
South America	−408	−34		+81	+682	+682
Central America	+16	+6	+148	+107	+263	+1,143
Caribbean	+137	+23	+389	+115	+602	+482
Oceania	+2	+1	+157	+85	+311	+1,003
Africa	−34	−21	+78	+147	+124	+1,771
Total Overseas	−378	−5	+3,913	+108	+6,936	+1,154

Source: U.S. Travel and Tourism Administration.

☐ 46 percent were on vacation/holiday; 35 percent were visiting on business; 19 percent were visiting relatives; 12 percent were visiting friends; 9 percent were attending a U.S. convention; and 4 percent were studying in this country.

☐ Only 18 percent were visiting the United States for the first time; 82 percent had been here before.

☐ 73 percent booked their air trip through a travel agency.

☐ 63 percent used travel agencies as an information source; 22 percent relied on friends or relatives for information; and 19 percent obtained information from airlines.

☐ 75 percent flew on an economy/tourist class ticket; 16 percent used an executive/business fare; and 7 percent flew first class.

☐ 29 percent visited on some type of prepaid inclusive package.

☐ 41 percent were traveling alone; 39 percent were part of a family group; the average party size was 1.6 persons.

☐ Male adults (average age of 40) accounted for 63 percent of all overseas arrivals; female adults (average age of 37) represented 30 percent; and children under 18 made up the remaining 7 percent.

☐ 67 percent were employed in white-collar occupations; 10 percent were homemakers; 7 percent were students; and 4 percent were retired.

☐ The average annual household income of visitors was $36,655.

☐ The average trip lasted 26.5 nights away from home, of which 22 nights were spent in the United States.

☐ 80 percent stayed in U.S. hotels/motels (for an average of 9.4 nights); 39 percent stayed in private homes (for an average of 21.7 nights); only 2 percent used campsites.

☐ 48 percent used domestic airline transportation during their visits; 39 percent rented autos; 38 percent used private autos of friends/relatives; and 20 percent used intercity bus travel.

☐ 47 percent visited only one state; 23 percent visited two; and 30 percent visited three or more states.

☐ The average overseas visitor spent $1,155 while in the United States, for a daily per capita expenditure of $54.

Visitors from overseas countries travel extensively throughout the United States, as indicated in Table 5. The most-often-visited destinations are New York (New York City and Niagara Falls), California (Los Angeles, San Francisco, San Diego, and Yosemite National Park), Florida (Miami and Orlando/DisneyWorld), Washington, D.C., and Hawaii. Again, destination patterns vary significantly between visitors from different countries, and additional research data concerning these variances are available from the USTTA.

Table 4
CHANGES IN INBOUND TRAVEL FROM THE TOP TEN OVERSEAS COUNTRIES
1960 - 1985

Overseas Country	1985 Arrivals	O/S Mkt. Share	1975 Arrivals	O/S Mkt. Share	1960 Arrivals	O/S Mkt. Share
	(000)	(%)	(000)	(%)	(000)	(%)
Japan	1,496	19.9	746	20.6	20	3.4
United Kingdom	861	11.4	438	12.1	94	15.7
West Germany	509	6.8	298	8.2	37	6.1
France	336	4.5	157	4.3	24	4.0
Australia	240	3.2	121	3.4	22	3.7
Bahamas	232	3.1	78	2.1	20	3.3
Italy	220	2.9	102	2.8	18	3.0
Brazil	192	2.5	102	2.8	11	1.8
Venezuela	162	2.1	105	2.9	40	6.7
Colombia	154	2.0	59	1.6	15	2.5
Other Overseas	3,137	41.6	1,419	39.1	299	49.8
Total Overseas	7,537	100.0	3,624	100.0	601	100.0

	1980-1985		1975-1985		1960-1985	
	Volume Change	% Change	Volume Change	% Change	Volume Change	% Change
	(000)	(%)	(000)	(%)	(000)	(%)
Japan					+1,476	+7,274
United Kingdom	−269	−24			+ 766	+ 812
West Germany	−171	−25			+ 473	+1,291
France	+ 16	+ 5	+ 178	+113	+ 311	+1,288
Australia	+ 15	+ 6	+ 118	+ 98	+ 218	+ 989
Bahamas	n.a.	n.a.	+ 154	+199	+ 212	+1,055
Italy	+ 25	+13	+ 118	+115	+ 202	+1,112
Brazil	+ 34	+21	+ 90	+ 88	+ 181	+1,655
Venezuela	−303	−65	+ 57	+ 55	+ 121	+ 303
Colombia	n.a.	n.a.	+ 95	+161	+ 139	+ 917
Other Overseas	n.a.	n.a.	+1,718	+121	+2,838	+ 948
Total Overseas	−378	− 5	+3,913	+108	+6,936	+1,154

Source: U.S. Travel and Tourism Administration.

Table 5
U.S. DESTINATIONS VISITED BY OVERSEAS VISITORS IN 1984

U.S. Destination Visited	Estimated Visitors*	Share of Total Overseas Visitors
	(000)	(%)
New York	2,627	35
California	2,612	35
Florida	1,656	22
Washington, D.C.	888	12
Hawaii	836	11
Nevada	617	8
Illinois	580	8
Massachusetts	550	7
Texas	542	7
Arizona	444	6
Pennsylvania	391	5
New Jersey	376	5
Louisiana	309	4
Washington	263	4
Georgia	233	3
Total United States	**7,528**	**100**

Source: U.S. Travel and Tourism Administration.
*Multiple visits (more than one destination could be visited on a single trip).

Understanding the Consumer

VIRTUALLY EVERY ARTICLE IN THIS BOOK discusses the consumer. Some of the contributing authors confess little knowledge of these elusive creatures; others have invested considerable sums in trying to track them down and understand what makes them tick. The task is neither easy nor necessarily rewarding.

Consumer behavior is at best an inexact science. Many of its principles are drawn from disciplines with scientific underpinnings, such as anthropology, social psychology, and statistics. Others come from politics, philosophy, and economics — none of which have proven themselves in the arena of scientific application. Moreover, because of the complexity of the decision-making process when travel behavior is concerned, a discussion of who this consumer really is often begins to sound like the six blind men trying to explain the same elephant by feeling different parts of his anatomy. To the airlines, the consumer is a very price-sensitive individual. To hotels and resorts, he or she is *value conscious*, an entirely different concept. Social researchers have tried to explain motiva-

tions for travel in such terms of socio-psychological phenomena such as an escape from a perceived mundane environment, or as a form of prestige. To destinations and tour operators, consumers are romantics who fantasize about falling in love on a pink coral beach at sunset or adventurers who want to go flying in hot air balloons.

One recent trend that has risen as travel marketers have developed in sophistication is to segment consumers psychographically, a technique that has been used in the package goods field for some time. An attitudinal segmentation study done for the Bermuda Department of Tourism concluded that there were three groups of vacation travelers that represented potential target markets: A *price/sights* segment, a *sun/surf* segment, and a *quality oriented* segment. The price/sights segment consists of travelers who want vacations that are inexpensive and offer a good deal of sightseeing. They are partial to places of historic interest with interesting museums. Sun/surfers want relaxing holidays with good weather and good beaches.

They are willing to pay more than the first group but want outdoor sports like golf and skiing to be readily available. The third group, quality oriented consumers, want first-class hotels and restaurants, good service, fine shopping, and a variety of nightlife.

This information can be useful because these groups can then be identified demographically and geographically, and a carefully targeted message can be delivered utilizing cable television and direct response mediums.

On the whole, however, the main thing known about consumer behavior is that it is subject to a great many forces from both the marketplace and the environment. The forces at work in the marketplace are for the most part observable and measurable. They result from attitudes and beliefs about products and services that consumers have gathered through experience and personal research. They are affected by salient product features and benefits as well as by emotion. Thus we can find, using a variety of research techniques, what the needs and wants of the market are and how they can be filled. We can discover what users and nonusers think about our services and those of our competitors. And we can analyze usage patterns as well as the geographic origin of present and potential business.

Despite the availability of this information, a major problem that must be overcome is getting usable, actionable data at a reasonable cost. Contributing author Robert Lewis, a professor of marketing and research in the department of hotel, restaurant and travel administration at The University of Massachusetts, Amherst, addresses this in his article. Lewis discusses how the research process works; how to specify information needs, sampling, and data collection; and finally how to interpret and use what you have found.

The answers to all of these questions are subject to environmental forces and sociological factors over which enterprises have no control. The recent boom in adventure travel may be a good illustration. The *Wall Street Journal*, commenting on this phenomenon, speculated that "Adventure travel popularity seems to be an offspring of numerous factors: the search for fulfillment of the '60s, the hiking, camping, and fitness crazes of the '70s and, more recently, airline deregulation, which makes travel more affordable." These trends did not appear overnight. Many tour operators and other travel enterprises saw them coming and positioned their companies accordingly.

What then are the new trends that are surfacing and will spark the successful businesses of tomorrow? Robert Schulman is the President of Yankelovich Clancy Shulman, the leading research firm that measures such trends in the United States. In his article Shulman introduces us to the new consumers of travel and tourism services: the Gourmet Baby, the Strategic Traveler, and the Senior Citizen. He tells us who they are, what they are looking for, and suggests ways their needs can be satisfied.

Chapter 3

Converting Market Research into Added Sales

Robert C. Lewis
Professor, University of Massachusetts/Amherst

Robert C. Lewis is Professor of Marketing and Research in the Department of Hotel, Restaurant & Travel Administration at the University of Massachusetts/Amherst. He received his Ph.D. in Communication Theory and Marketing in 1980, after 25 years in the hospitality industry. He has published more than 50 articles on hospitality marketing and lectured and consulted in Europe, Asia, and the United States. He is the author of Getting the Most from Marketing Research.

The title of this chapter may seem imposing to many, if not downright intimidating. Many professionals and students alike exclaim "ugh" when they hear the word research, never mind getting the most from it. Visions of funny looking equations with Greek letters, statistics that don't look like batting averages, long computer runs, and weighty, uninterpretable reports are conjured up in the minds of many.

Then there are those who take the opposite approach. Research? We do that every day. We keep guest history records so that we know where our customers come from. We have comment cards in the rooms so we know if our customers are satisfied or not. We even talk to our customers when they leave and ask them if everything was all right.

Both of these views are barriers to getting the most from marketing research, yet it is not surprising that many people hold them. Marketing research is a relatively new phenomenon; in the tourism and hospitality industries, it is even newer. Aside from McDonald's, Burger King, and Wendy's, there are few firms in the hospitality industry that have done serious and meaningful marketing research for any period of time. Today, however, companies like Marriott, Holiday Inn, and Westin have full-blown marketing research departments. Ten years from now there will be no major players in the market who are not either doing or commissioning serious research. The first step in this progression is removing the barriers.

Removing the Barriers

Let's begin then with the one minute manager's guide to marketing research, the only managerial activity that Ken Blanchard has not yet compressed into minutiae. I'll take the first two seconds to define what marketing research is: *Knowing your market!* That's all there is to it; getting the most out of it takes a little longer.

Knowing your market means knowing three classes of people: your customer, your potential customer, and your noncustomer. It means knowing who they are, what they do, what they don't do, what they like, what they don't like, why they like it, why they don't like it, why they come to your place, and why they don't. It means knowing not only what is important and salient to the customer, but what is determinant, that is, why they choose or do not choose your place over the competition. If you don't know these things about your market, you are not getting the most from marketing research. It's very interesting to know the average age of your customer, how many are male and how many female, whether they are on business or pleasure, whether they arrived by car or air, and various other details. But, of what use is it if it doesn't tell you why they are or are not a customer, why they will or will not come back, or whether they will or will not tell others to come? After all, that's what marketing is about — getting and keeping a customer. Of what use is marketing research if it doesn't tell you how to get and keep a customer?

Getting the most from marketing research, then, does not mean understanding the Greek alphabet, statistical formulas, or simply knowing where your customers come from. It means knowing what your customers do and why they do it. Procter & Gamble can tell us how many of us wet our toothbrush before putting on the toothpaste, how many wet it afterward, how many do both, and how many don't wet it at all. If they can learn this, certainly we should be able to learn what people do when they visit our city, stay in our rooms, and eat in our restaurants. But how does P & G know for sure? Therein lies the reason for the Greek letters, the statistics, and the fallacy of cursory and non-rigorous data collection.

First, the Greek letters. Those statistics that we all cringe from are nothing more than the manifestation of an old trick called probability theory. Without probability theory we would have no statistics and no research findings in which to have faith. In its simplest form, probability theory tells us that if we flip a standard coin into the air there is a 50 percent probability that we will get a heads, but we can be 100 percent confident that we will get a heads or a tails. If we flip it again the same odds persist. The odds are no better from one flip to the next. But without a single flip, the odds are excellent as to what we would get if we flipped the coin 500 times. We can be 97.5 percent confident that we will get 250 heads and 250 tails with a 5 percent error margin, that is, by knowing what a few (a sample) will do, we can project what many (the population) will do, with a predetermined level of confidence. Statistics are no more than the controlled estimates representative of population parameters. It is as simple as that and if you think of all statistics as based on that simple premise, you will have no problem understanding them. What's more, you can see their value and how they help make research credible.

Statistical analysis uses various forms of esoteric and unintelligible appearing equations and formulas to interpret the data we collect from the market sample. So what? The statisticians and computers do that. What we need to know is how confident we can be that what we learn (for example, what determines the customers' choice of a hotel), is likely to happen the next time, that is, given such and such, what is the probability that the customer will return? When we can provide, with confidence, what it takes to get the customer to come back, then we are getting the most from marketing research. It's like using a rifle instead of a shotgun or betting with the odds overwhelmingly in your favor.

That takes care of the first barrier, intimidation — no one can dread the coin flip when they know how to call it (but note that you are never absolutely positive) — and the Greek letters. The second barrier, treating guest comment cards and their ilk as marketing research, is the flip side of the coin. If our research is unscientific, that is, it cannot be projected to the rest of the market at a known confidence level, then it does not constitute knowing our market and we are not maximizing what we can learn from the data we collect. If we know a customer comes from Altoona, is male, aged 43, and on business, do we know why he comes? More important, do we know if anyone else comes, or would come, for the same reasons? And if we know that the bellman was friendly but the front desk clerk was not, what then? Does it happen .1 percent or 50 percent of the time? Is it representative? Will it happen again? Maybe the customer was in a bad mood. Maybe management is at fault and the desk clerk had no control over it. What this means is that each case is an isolated instance, and isolated instances are very difficult to correct or control or do anything about in a proactive sense.

This kind of research is called non-probability. A statistical level of confidence or known level of probability cannot be determined, that is, your guess is as good as mine if it will happen again. It is highly prone to error and bias. To rely on it is akin to racing to an oasis in the desert — just when you think you've got it, it changes before your eyes. The best you can do is react to it, and you may be reacting incorrectly to unrepresentative problems. Guest comments, talking to customers, and keeping guest histories are useful, and perhaps necessary, but for different reasons. They do not constitute marketing research.

To get the most from marketing research, to really know your market and be able to make solid and profitable research-based decisions means being able to act with a high level of confidence and a low probability of error.

The Research Process

The generally accepted research process is depicted in figure 1. The flow chart is important here not because of the flow but because getting the most from the research is highly dependent on understanding the importance of each stage of the process.

The assumption made here is that the reader is not necessarily the researcher, but one who requires, commissions, buys, reads, and uses the research product. As such, it is the definition of the research, its interpretation, and its ultimate use that are of prime concern. You are the controller of the process. When you buy equipment, you read the specifications before you buy and check them out after you buy. Buying research is different; you are the specifier and you set the specifications. The researcher develops the product, designed and tailored to your specifications.

Far, far too often this responsibility is abdicated by the research buyer, the research ends up in a file drawer, and the buyer proclaims, "That research didn't tell me anything I didn't already know." Poorly executed research, of course, lacks validity and reliability and isn't worth the paper it is written on. Well-executed research, on the other hand, is just as worthless if it doesn't tell you what you want to know. If the specifications haven't been made clear, the findings may be unrevealing. Let's look at the buyer's role as part of the research process depicted in figure 1.

The Research Purpose

Many people seem to have tremendous difficulty defining research purposes and problems. Perhaps one reason for this difficulty is that they seem so obvious and self-evident. In fact, they are usually not, and these stages are among the most critical of the research process in optimizing the outcome.

All important marketing research begins with an exact understanding of the purpose of the research. The purpose of the research is defined as what you will *do* with the findings once you have them. A typical and obvious response to the question, "Why do you want to do this research?" is, "To find out why my occupancy is down," or, "what's wrong with business." These statements are not really very enlightening to the researcher. Given the constraints of time and budgets, not to mention respondents' patience, you just can't research everything you would like to know at one time. So, you have to narrow it down and be very specific about what you hope to do with the findings. Change your advertising? Your product? Your market mix? Your positioning?

These sound simple enough, but actually they are not. Defining the

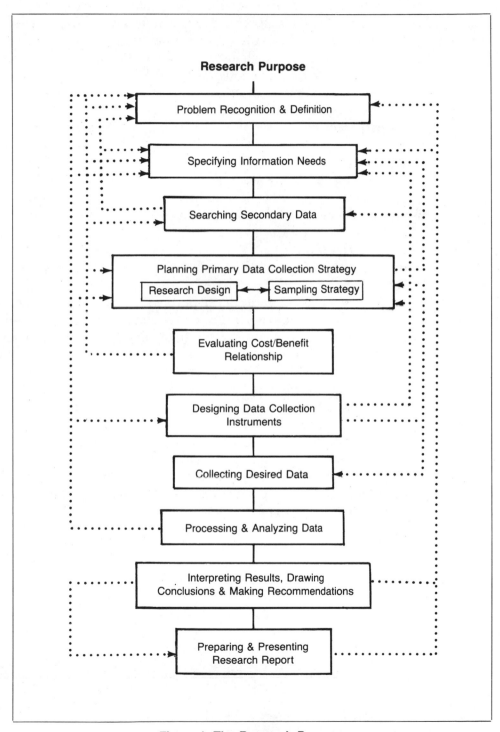

Figure 1. The Research Process

purpose is a joint effort with the researcher and often takes the form of brainstorming. But it is absolutely critical unless you want your report to end up in a filing cabinet. Here is a statement of purpose arrived at, after considerable discussion, for an exclusive French restaurant that was getting rave reviews but wasn't doing enough business to break even:

> To determine what XYZ should be in the marketplace in terms of market demand.

This statement directed the entire research process. The operators' original expressed purpose was this: Is there sufficient market for a good French restaurant in this area? You can see that if all the research were directed in that direction and the answer was no, which it was, that the research would provide no direction as to what to do next. Management, although a little wiser, would be back where it started.

The Research Problem

The research problem obviously follows from the research purpose but the two are not the same. The answer to the research problem should tell us what we have to know to fulfill the purpose. Failure to recognize and define the correct problem(s) is, without a doubt and assuming good research procedures are followed, the most frequent cause of wasted and useless research. The research purpose sets the framework of the research; the research problem drives the research.

The problem is the *research* problem, not the business problem, but it is derived from a full understanding of the marketing problem. For example, low occupancy is not a research problem. What might be is what *causes* low occupancy, that is, the marketing problem. This is not mere nitpicking. It can be shown that the difference between the two is also the difference between the sample selection, the questions asked, and the statistical tests that are used. More important, it is the difference between whether or not usable findings are obtained and the research purpose is satisfied. Real research problems almost always lie much deeper than the questions being asked or the obvious surface issues.

The problem should be stated precisely and clearly and agreed to by all parties before the research is commenced. In the case above where the purpose of the research was stated, the research problem turned out to be,

> What are the needs and wants of the market and how can they be fulfilled?

Often there are subproblems as well. One or two or four at the maximum. If you have more than four, you should break up the research. More likely, however, you are off-target. In the above case, the subproblem was stated as,

> How are the needs and wants of the market currently being fulfilled?

Notice that both these problem definitions directly address the research purpose. Notice that the definitions came only after recognition of the business problem and that, as in all good marketing efforts, both recognition and definition are in terms of the consumer, *not* management. It took a while, in this project, to persuade management that the problem wasn't what they were (they were good at that), but what they should be in terms of what the market needed and wanted.

This business of persuading management warrants more discussion. Not only is problem definition critical to the research, it is also a major element in the client-researcher relationship. It is a two-way street where problems can occur in either direction. It is tempting to say that when hiring researchers, a good test is the ability of the researcher to articulate the problem. Such a statement, however, may have two major failings. The first is that management won't provide enough information to enable the researcher to ascertain the problem. The second is that management may not understand the problem in research terms. This is not merely a criticism, but is based on both possible lack of research experience as well as the old "can't see the forest for the trees" syndrome. The final point is that the two parties must work closely together and understand fully what it is that they are trying to accomplish.

It is not uncommon for initial discussions about a research project to consist of relatively superficial dialogue. From summary background data and statements of objectives, the researcher forms the basis of the research proposal. Additional dialogue concentrates on details rather than the original context. Good researchers need not only detailed and accurate information to define the problem, but also need to recognize the client's subjective, qualitative, and often idiosyncratic beliefs. Because of this need for a solid foundation to the research project, management and researcher need to engage in extensive initial dialogue — the more complex the problem, the more dialogue required. Management's offhand, sometimes cavalier attitude, "that's how I see it, you figure it out" can only be self-defeating.

To get the most from marketing research, management must be open about its problems and recognize that problem definition is not management's prerogative or the researcher's responsibility; it is a joint process. Philip Kotler (1982) comments, on a common view of executives, that marketing research is no more than a fact-finding expedition when he states:

> The marketing researcher is supposed to design a questionnaire, choose a sample, carry out interviews, and report results; often without being given a careful definition of the problem or the decision alternatives before management.[1]

The fault may also lie with the researcher, either for failure to contribute

---

[1] Philip Kotler (1982), *Marketing Management: Analysis, Planning and Control*. New York: Prentice Hall, page 609.

to problem definition or, at the other extreme, for thinking that as the expert he is solely responsible for defining the problem. In the final analysis, mutual, in-depth exploration of the marketing context for a research project must take place. Magic answers simply don't exist.

Specifying Information Needs

This next critically important step in the research process involves setting objectives as to what, specifically, we want to learn and what, specifically, we expect to know when the research is completed. This step leads directly into selection of the sample and design of the questionnaire. *Never* overlook this step because if you do, you will ask yourself two questions after the research is completed: Why didn't we ask that? What good is that information?

Following through on the case discussed earlier, here are some of the specific objectives of what information was expected from the research:

☐ present eating-out habits of the market and why

☐ present awareness and perceptions of users and nonusers

☐ what the marketplace would like to see and would utilize in a new (to disguise the sponsor) restaurant concept

☐ projected demand of the marketplace for an upscale restaurant

Here is what we expected to know when the research was completed:

☐ frequency of dining out

☐ restaurants presently patronized and why

☐ check averages at those restaurants

☐ reasons for going out to dinner

☐ reasons for going to an upscale restaurant

☐ aided and unaided awareness of sponsor restaurant

☐ dining frequency at sponsor restaurant and why

☐ impressions of sponsor restaurant

☐ future intentions to patronize sponsor restaurant

☐ profile of those who like/don't like, use/don't use sponsor restaurant

☐ perceived need for new restaurant concept, what it should be, and intentions to patronize it

Sampling and Data Collection

Other than evaluating the cost/benefits relationship, the remainder of the research process is really up to the researcher. Researchers, however, no matter how good or how expensive, tend to fall down in certain areas that may introduce bias into the results, weaken the validity or reliability of the findings, or fail to capture the richness of the data, that is, greatly decrease the value of the research, make it unusable or worse, if you do use it, lead you down the wrong path. I will make this point by example.

There is a good deal of invalid research in the public and private domains of the hospitality industry caused by poor research design. For example, *Business Travel News* has conducted and published annual surveys to determine which are the best hotel chains in the view of the business travel planner.[2] Hyatt and Marriott have come up the "winners," but the nature of the research design makes such conclusions totally invalid.

First, sampling and data collection are seriously flawed. Questionnaires were enclosed in the paper as well as being mailed to subscribers (I personally received four in the mail). In the 1985 survey there were 462 responses from a possible 200,000 questionnaires distributed. The possibilities for sampling error and nonrepresentative responses are more than obvious when there is no control over the sample distribution or the nature of the respondents.

Even with control of the sample and the respondents, the design introduces serious bias. How many of the respondents had planned business with each of the 66 chains listed on the survey? How many had dealt with all the different properties and how many had dealt with only one? How do you account for different product classes ranging from Motel 6 to L'Ermitage? How do you compare chains with three properties to those with 300 properties? On what basis did respondents make their judgments as to which chains were "best"? Thus, the data collection instrument is also seriously flawed and no analysis or manipulation of the data could possibly salvage it.

All these steps of the research process must be rigorously controlled. While that is certainly the task of the researcher, it behooves management to be knowledgeable enough to ask, both before and after, how will (did) you select the sample, how will (did) you control for bias, as well as spurious relationships and intervening variables.

Spurious relationships and intervening variables, when not controlled by the research and questionnaire design, are two of the greatest causes of invalid and unreliable research data. A relationship between variables is spurious if it is caused by extraneous variables such as the relationship between A and B below, caused by C.

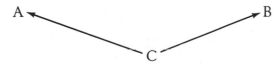

Let us say that A is our evaluation of hotel B and C is the number of times we

[2]*Business Travel News*, November 5, 1984; November 4, 1985.

have been there, so that we are now greeted by name and upgraded when available. The relationship is thus between B and C and the relationship between A and B is spurious because it is dependent on the relationship between A and C.

An intervening variable is conceptually quite different, as shown below.

In this case, variable C intervenes between A and B. Let us say that A and B represent the same variables as above but this time C represents Hyatt advertising. Perhaps I have never been in a Hyatt hotel but Hyatt advertising makes me think they must be fine hotels. Advertising now is an intervening variable if the relationship between A and B is eliminated when the design controls for C.

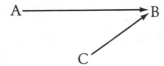

There are two other types of effects of which to be wary. In the first,

we see that C is an independent cause of B. A especially likes hotel B because the manager, C, is a friend and always gives him a suite. This is called an additive effect.

In the next case, there is an interactive effect of variables A and C on B.

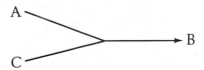

A likes hotel B far more when he is on expense account than when he has to pay the bill himself.

Relationships like these must be controlled to get the most from research. It is the researcher's task to introduce the controls into the design, but he can not necessarily be expected to be aware of all the possibilities and should be given assistance in that respect.

Data Analysis and Interpretation

The final stage of the research process is the data analysis and its interpretation. This is when the researcher's expertise and experience come in, but that does not mean we should not be circumspect and keep him honest. There is a well-known tendency for executives to read only the executive summary and ignore the bulk of the report. This is natural but also leads to lack of verification of procedures followed, failure to sense some interpretations that the researcher may not catch, and possible promiscuity on the part of the researcher. It is wise to at least read the description of the research design and the full discussion, even if not all the findings and statistical analysis. At least, have someone else read them, if not the entire report. If your report does not have these sections in it, be very wary.

What are you looking for? In essence, you are looking for two things: one, has all the richness of the data been captured, that is, is the interpretation maximized? Second, does the data support the conclusions? Are there statistically significant differences or could it have occurred by chance; are the conclusions valid? Validity is the sine qua non of research and in its broad sense is defined as research that actually measures what it is presumed to measure. Some of the critical forms of validity that you should be concerned with are:

> Face validity. Is the instrument measuring everything it is supposed to measure; is the sample representative of the behavior or trait being measured?
>
> Construct validity. Is the construct being measured the one we think we are measuring; that is, if people say bathroom amenities are important are they telling us how they choose a hotel?
>
> Internal validity. Are the findings free from bias? Are they true or are they an artifact of the research design (as discussed above)?
>
> External validity. Can the findings be generalized to other cases?

Although it is common practice, it is usually unwise to have your advertising agency do, or commission, your research because a built-in bias automatically exists. Here is a case in point, although the same problems could have occurred just as easily with any research firm.

The case involved a major hotel chain that commissioned a major advertising campaign in the hundreds of thousands of dollars. The president of the chain, by nature very suspect of the value of advertising, asked the agency, a large well-known international firm, to verify the desired effectiveness of the campaign which was directed at travel agents. The agency researched agents before the campaign began, halfway through the campaign, and a year later. The findings of all three surveys were presented to the hotel chain president as triumphant evidence of the success of the campaign. That is, the report showed that top-of-the-mind awareness of the hotel chain had increased 50 percent in the minds of travel agents since the campaign began.

The president was suspicious and asked us to analyze the data that the agency quickly promised to send on computer tape. The reported findings did indeed look very suspect but we could not verify this statistically without the raw data. Some three months later, after numerous phone calls and promises by the agency, the tape arrived. It was uninterpretable and undecipherable because it was written in special code by the agency's data processor. Experts worked on it to no avail. Numerous phone calls to the data processor, as well as the agency, brought instructions for deciphering. None worked. Rather than expend more cost, after another three months the hotel chain resigned the agency account.

The problem with the data was evident to anyone familiar with research results and statistical procedures even without the full data. No statistical tests were utilized. The "triumphant" findings could all have occurred by chance. There was no control for spurious or intervening variables. There were no cross-validation tests and only a minimum of weak statistical analysis had been applied. In full, it appeared that the advertising campaign was a failure, but of course the agency didn't want the company to know that.

What else is to be learned here is that data paid for by you belong to you. In advance, ask for the computer printouts and the data on tape with instructions as to how it is programmed and can be deciphered, even if you never look at it. To get the most from your marketing research, keep your researcher honest.

Summary

The computer revolution has had a tremendous impact on the use of statistical analysis of data so that we can prove almost anything — and often do. There are three caveats of concern.

The first is that both the unknowledgeable and the highly experienced can manipulate data to prove what they want to prove. Some of the ways to protect against this have already been discussed. Be wary, but don't use it as an excuse not to do research. Do you stop watching television because you don't understand how the picture is transmitted? (And what is more manipulative than television?)

The second caveat is that for all the wonders of statistical analysis, you still have to apply human intuition and common sense in the interpretation. This is where a good researcher's skills really show. Almost anyone can learn to crunch numbers. It is a real talent to be able to question the results and make good sense of them and to be certain that the relationships are accurate and constructive.

A third impediment to research acceptance has been understanding the nature of the different statistical techniques. This is understandable as they are surrounded by jargon and involve complex statistical considerations. In fact, the failure is often with the researcher for presenting results only in statistical format without accompaniment in terms of marketing solutions. Research must be presented as actionable answers to marketing problems if we are going to get the most out of it. We should insist that market research answer specific questions and be translated into a foundation for marketing decisions.

Management's Role

This paper has discussed in some detail the role of research and how to maximize its potential. In conclusion, there is also a burden on management which, after all, is the party that hopes to get the most from the research. The following statements should by now be self-evident.

☐ Take the researcher into your confidence. Make sure he has all the relevant information that he needs to develop optimal research design.

☐ Involve everyone from the start of the project that can benefit from it. Individuals have their own perspective but they also accept results better if they are involved in the planning. The idea is not to pull surprises.

☐ Make a commitment to act on valid findings, whether or not you agree with them.

☐ Don't buy research based on price alone. Like wine, the best is not necessarily the most expensive and the worst is not necessarily the cheapest.

☐ Have faith. Marketing research is a valuable tool, an increasingly necessary tool, and a tool that has a great deal to teach.

The more you put into marketing research, the more you will get out of it.

Chapter 4

Understanding and Influencing Consumer Behavior

Robert S. Shulman
President, Yankelovich,
Skelly & White/Clancy,
Shulman, Inc.

Robert S. Shulman became president and CEO of Yankelovich, Skelly & White/Clancy, Shulman, Inc. in January 1986. Prior to his new position, Shulman had been president of Clancy, Shulman & Associates, Inc. which he founded with Kevin J. Clancy in 1982. Shulman had been vice president of the Laboratory Test Market Division of Yankelovich, Skelly & White, Inc. for six years prior to launching Clancy Shulman.

Most marketers are aware that the American consumer of the 1980s is quite a different entity than the consumer of the 1950s. And those changes are affecting travel and tourism marketing as well as other industries. What I'd like to do is explore how consumers have changed over the past three decades, what that means for travel and tourism marketers today, and what it might mean in the decade to come.

At Yankelovich, we have been studying American consumers exhaustively for years via an annual, in-depth survey called Monitor™. The Yankelovich Monitor gauges consumer behavior through its measurement of American values, providing marketers with an annual data-based reading and interpretation of social change as it affects consumer behavior. By placing the dynamic American consumer in a social context, Monitor guides marketers in developing strategies to fit emerging social trends. Much of what I will say here reflects the insights and forecasts that Monitor has provided us.

Looking Back to a Simpler Time

In the 1950s, when there really was a typical American nuclear family consisting of a mother (who stayed home), a father (who went to work), and 2.2 children, understanding how to market travel and tourism effectively was comparatively simple. At the same time, one reason it was simpler than today is that there weren't as many marketing opportunities then as there are now.

Typically, the 1950s family took an annual two-week vacation. There were no scheduling problems because only one parent worked. Vacations were a time for family togetherness, with the average family piling into a car and driving off to the seashore or mountains for two weeks. Destinations were usually domestic and nearby. Often, mother and the children stayed at the country or shore house from Memorial Day through Labor Day. Father commuted to the house on weekends, and then joined the family for his two-week vacation.

Once Americans came home from World War II, the majority seemed to want to stay here. International travel was not a staple of the ordinary American, but was primarily the preserve of business people and the rich. "An American in Paris" in the 1950s was not likely to be a typical American family.

The Consumer Values Upheaval

In the 1960s and 1970s, Monitor shows us that American society began to undergo considerable change and a major upheaval in consumer values changed the American travel and tourism market forever. Once staunch believers in the Protestant work ethic, many Americans assumed an attitude of "We can have it all, do it all, be it all." They moved away from the traditional commitment to materialism and obligation to others, and made self-knowledge, self-expression, self-fulfillment, hedonism, and the accumulation of experiences their primary goals.

Overall, American consumers began to seek "me products" rather than "we products," to want things that supported an individual's self-fulfillment and self-expression, rather than shared family/household commodities. There was also an emphasis on instant gratification and novelty often displaced conformity, routine, and planned purchasing.

Americans began to subscribe to the *leisure ethic*, viewing leisure as more fulfilling than work. They started feeling that they deserved and needed at least two weeks vacation, and probably should have more. While people still took family vacations, Monitor reveals growing attitudinal support for not taking a family vacation — maybe leaving the kids home. A few even contemplated mom and dad taking *separate vacations*. And some ultimately did.

New Places to Go

These changes in our values caused a change in our attitudes about what constituted the right vacation destination. There was a rise in what Monitor terms "popular elitism," the feeling that "If I have the money to pay for it, I am entitled to go anywhere I want." In other words, that travel abroad wasn't the exclusive preserve of the rich, but everyman's prerogative. Blue collar workers began signing up for package tours to Paris and Lisbon. Retired people started flying down to Mexico, and young couples discovered the Caribbean with a vengeance.

Flower Power Blooms

In the 1960s and '70s, virtually an entire generation of Americans became world travelers: the youth. As never before, American young people strapped on backpacks and hiking shoes and took to the road. They went everywhere — not just Mexico, Spain, France, Germany, but in many cases through Scandinavia, Greece, the Far East, and South America. They didn't travel first class, but they did travel.

Monitor shows that families also caught travel fever, with the rise of an instant gratification culture: mom and dad left the kids at home and made "fly now/pay later" a cliche.

Overall, there was an enormous increase in the 1970s in first-time travelers to destinations outside the United States. Travel was, indeed, the novelty of the 1970s, with people of all walks of life flying off to overseas vacations, seeking peak experiences, and enjoying every place they went, as long as it wasn't home.

A New Realism

As we moved from the late 1970s into the 1980s, the growth of new values came to a halt. Rising inflation, crumbling infrastructures, increasing global competition, and economic recession turned the assumptions of the me decade into a pipe dream. Maybe we couldn't have it all, after all. Maybe life could no longer be lived exclusively in the present tense; now there was serious concern about the future.

The presumed birthright of postwar America — economic security and upward mobility — could no longer be taken for granted. Many individuals found the search for self-fulfillment frustrating and difficult. Penalties of the new life-style began to surface: divorce, a sense of isolation and loneliness, escalating credit bills. Under an attitude Monitor termed *New Realism*, the majority of American consumers struggled to learn how to adapt their expectations and behaviors to a more difficult environment.

What Monitor shows is that many Americans started blending new and traditional values together. They stopped feeling that it was even desirable to have it all; rather, they had to set priorities and become pragmatic. The intensity of the "me" focus lessened and Americans started re-recognizing the need for family ties and allegiances.

This new realism meant corresponding changes in our behavior regarding travel; we weren't traditional, but we had moved beyond the pervasive hedonism of the sixties and seventies.

The Baby Boomers Grow Up

As we move towards the end of the 1980s, we have quite a different population of travel consumers to deal with than before. Different in terms of expectations, experience, attitudes, and wherewithal.

First, basic demographics tell us that the average American family is not the nuclear family of yesteryear. A whopping 53.2 percent of all American women work, including 47.3 percent of all women with children.

The baby boomers, that increasingly influential group of young adults, aged 23-44, are actively engaged in family and household formation. Today, 40 percent of all households are headed by a baby boomer. By 1990, that figure will reach 44 percent. The Census Bureau now divides households into two categories: family and nonfamily. Nonfamily households (householders who live alone or with persons to whom they are not related) are increasing and now represent 28 percent of all U.S. households, compared to 15 percent in 1960.

And, we have a larger mature market than at any time in previous history. Moreover, households headed by people aged 55-64 today have the highest per capita income of any age group.

Let's see what Monitor reveals about each of these major trends as they relate to travel and leisure.

Leisure Is a Given

We've long since moved away from the nose to the grindstone work ethic through the instant gratification or fly now/pay later attitude and now feel we're entitled to leisure time. It has become a given, and even more of a necessity now that baby boomers are out competing in the workplace.

At the same time, compared to the 1960s and early 1970s, young and middle-aged American consumers feel they are under more stress than in prior decades. They work hard and their lives are complicated. With more two-earner households, just scheduling leisure time is more of a problem. There's no one to stay at home doing all the preparation for the long-awaited vacation; rather, there are two people trying to squeeze out time together away from work at the same time.

According to Monitor, this has caused a rise in the number of people who view vacations as a chance to *veg out*, to do absolutely, positively nothing. These consumers are not going to fall prey to the "If it's Tuesday this must be Belgium" syndrome—they are going to demand leisure from their leisure.

At the same time, they want to get good service. They may not get out of a swimsuit the entire time they're on vacation, but they want someone else to bring the frozen daiquiri to the poolside—and it better be well made. And, the person bringing it better act like bringing it is a real pleasure. To some extent, the new American traveler is a nitpicker. We're more educated than any previous generation, and more of us have traveled, to more places, more often, than any other time in history.

We're not a bunch of country bumpkins anymore, willing to settle for bad service because we're away from home. We have greater expectations because we have more travel experience and because we value our leisure more. At the same time, Monitor reveals the emergence of an interesting phenomenon among American travelers: a willingness to defer vacation travel.

The Trade-Off Syndrome

Because Americans today are so much better traveled than prior generations, they are increasingly able to deflect vacations, to trade off two weeks in a foreign country for a down payment on a house or private school for a second child. In effect, there are a lot of things competing with travel and tourism for Americans' dollars. According to Monitor, it's not so much that we're moving back to the traditional values, but that even with the increase in two-earner families, people are finding they can't really have it all — they have to make trade-offs. The two-week vacation may well be on its way to becoming a dinosaur, both because of the need to trade off, and the difficulties of juggling schedules and priorities in today's more complex family structure.

And, because of what we call "the rise of the gourmet baby."

The Gourmet Baby

Young parents today are including children in everything. These new parents don't have the same mental set as parents of the 1950s. They're much more serious and intense about their children. They're more involved with them, and more competitive about them. There seems to be a new version of nothing but the best that is creating gourmet babies. Babies with the "right" stroller, furniture, food, clothing, and toys. Parents are studying to have babies, and have become concerned about educating those babies from birth. In some cases, before birth, through stimuli that are presumed to be sensed while the baby is still in the womb.

Once born, the gourmet baby becomes a portable baby, a baby who is taken everywhere the parents go. This means there is already a growing opportunity for travel marketers to move ahead of their competition by providing extra services for people traveling with infants and small children. More than just special rates for children who stay in the same room as their parents, marketers should be thinking about child-care services, entertainment for children, activities that can include the child, and making appropriate arrangements in dining rooms so that people with infants and small children can eat dinner with them without annoying other guests.

The Harried Traveler

According to Monitor, another factor that travel and tourism marketers need to take into consideration in planning strategies is stress. The new parents and working couples are stretched for time, harried, leading more complex lives. They don't always have the luxury of planning far in advance. Their schedules are at the mercy of two employers and child-care arrangements. Last minute travel will become more common. A destination might increase its business by installing a toll-free 800 telephone number that would-be travelers could call to find out what accommodations are available at the last minute. This telephone service would not only appeal to consumers because of the stress in their lives, but also, Monitor says, because they are generally seeking more control of their lives. They want information and they want to be able to get it themselves.

The stress in their lives also means that people are more likely to take mini-vacations, escaping from the pressures for shorter periods of time, possibly more frequently. This trend is liable to continue and even increase.

The Strategic Traveler

When it comes to the cost of vacations, American consumers could best be described as strategic in their thinking. Despite the trend toward last-minute travel, they are, in the larger sense, planning their purchases more and prioritizing their purchases. This means on the one hand that they are willing to put off certain expenditures in favor of others—perhaps postpone an overseas vacation in order to save money for a down payment on a house. But, it also means they are willing to pay good dollars to indulge their travel impulses. They're not as determined to find a bargain as they once were. Finding a vacation option that fits into one's schedule and that relieves one's stress is as valuable as getting the best price.

Rather than searching strictly for the lowest price, today's (and probably tomorrow's) strategic traveler is looking for the best value. This is as true for the affluent as it is for the less affluent. An expensive vacation can be marketed if it is perceived as being worth the price because of what it offers.

If a strategic consumer feels a strong need to get away and only finds out at the last minute that the time is available, he or she will be more willing to accept a nondiscounted airfare than if the vacation is one planned far in advance. At the same time, consumers have become broadly aware that airfares keep changing, and anyone who has some advance warning about a vacation date—or who can choose when to take a trip—will wait until the fare for that particular destination is on special because consumers feel that sooner or later nearly every fare will be discounted.

The strategic traveler might, on the other hand, be willing to pay more for an air ticket that included the price of a helicopter ride from central city out to the airport — trading an additional expenditure for the ease and comfort this service would provide.

Monitor shows that strategic travelers are also more information-oriented consumers. They want information, more access to information. This means that travel agents have an unprecedented challenge in front of them. The travel agent system as it currently exists does not provide what consumers want. Travel agents cannot instantly summon information from a computer data bank, and they're drowning under a sea of printed literature that most do not have the time to read. In what is fast becoming the technological age, they are operating, for the most part, in old-fashioned ways. Many Americans do not even realize that most travel agents do not charge customers for their services but rather receive their reimbursement from airlines and other travel suppliers.

The danger for agents is that many consumers are becoming computer comfortable and once data banks are created that provide detailed travel information, consumers may bypass the agent and make all their travel arrangements themselves. While many agents are not interested in encouraging individual customers but would rather concentrate on groups and corporate travel, the danger of being bypassed by computer data access capability is, if anything, greater in the corporate travel area because initial costs for hooking into the data bank might be too high for the average individual.

There's little question, however, that down the road it's highly possible that all people with computer access will be able to do their own travel booking, and agents should move now to establish their value as information sources and economic service-providers if they want to maintain and build their business.

The Search for Allegiance

Monitor also shows that consumers today are starting to look for anchors, something larger than themselves to be part of. This is reflected in an increased interest in establishing a family, in a rising emphasis on the home, and increased appreciation for regional products — from cuisine to crafts to wines. They don't necessarily want to buy American but they are more receptive to appeals to heritage and ceremony. What this means for travel marketers is that brand heritage may start to be a more powerful selling tool than it was during the 1960s and 1970s. Destinations might think about recontacting former customers and "inviting them to come home." Regional attractions have an opportunity to increase their appeal to travelers, and domestic travel in general should increase in popularity as Americans seek to fill their hunger for commitment, for allegiance.

In addition, many young parents have already been to exotic, faraway places, and especially with young children as part of their lives, will find it no hardship to stick closer to home.

The Senior Market

One of the major changes in the American travel marketplace that we haven't spoken about is the rise of a burgeoning senior market that's unlike any previous senior-citizen population. Seniors today are not like seniors of former decades. They're strong, vital, active, and have more discretionary income and leisure time than other segments of the population. And their numbers proportionate to the total population will continue to increase.

But, make no mistake, you cannot market to them on the basis of their being seniors. Don't talk to them as if they're older — they'll resent it. Smart marketers put together vacation and leisure offerings that provide the amenities and services that seniors want, without labeling their offerings as targeted to seniors.

Of all segments of the population, seniors are most receptive to bargains and discounts, not so much because they are poor, but rather because they have no time restrictions to contend with. This means that marketers who want to build off-peak business would be well-advised to direct their off-peak bargain promotion at the senior niche, both groups and individuals, rather than the general population.

As seniors are becoming more health conscious, they are likely to move away from the traditional straight sight-seeing tours towards those requiring more active participation. Since many of them did not travel overseas as their children did in the 1960s and 1970s, they should prove a fertile ground for promoting overseas vacation travel.

And, Monitor reveals that like their offspring, seniors are becoming more information-oriented. They want more information and they want it from reliable authorities. A smart destination should make sure its promotional literature included information likely to be of particular interest to seniors, whether it's chauffeured tour service or a doctor on staff.

In addition, the booming senior market offers particular opportunities to tour operators and group travel specialists, since many either live in retirement communities, and/or are members of various clubs and organizations.

The Business Traveler

As competition has intensified, corporate America has trimmed down and become more strategic in its thinking, too. Looking briefly at what Monitor projects about the business travel market, we see a couple of interesting new trends that are likely to continue.

First, even though more and more businesses are competing globally, companies are trying to be more effective and efficient in the spending of corporate travel dollars. They're sending one person on a trip where they formerly sent two. They're encouraging people to make day trips rather than stay overnight, thus increasing demand for early morning and late afternoon flights. They're imposing limitations on how people fly and where they can stay when they reach their destination. The unlimited expense account is becoming an exception rather than a rule.

Some companies are asking their employees to turn in their frequent flyer bonus points or insisting that all business trips be booked through the corporate travel department.

Second, while more businesses may be competing globally and operating in more than one country, business travel may not increase as fast as one would have expected because of the impact of technology. High-speed data and voice transmission link distant points together in seconds. As people become more used to communicating via technology, the need for face-to-face meetings may decrease. There will probably always be a need for some face-to-face interaction, and although video-teleconferencing is not growing at anywhere near the rate once predicted, it is on the increase. A population comfortable with the dex, word processor, zap mail, videoplayer, and television may well ultimately be comfortable with more electronic get-togethers and fewer in-the-flesh get-togethers.

Monitor clearly shows that *service* is going to be a key word in marketing travel to the business community. Providing information as well as an economic product is going to become extremely important. Already business travelers (and it will probably soon be as true with vacation travelers) take for granted the ability to check out without stopping at the front desk. Many expect to be able to do this electronically. They expect cable TV and movies to be available in their hotel rooms. They expect health facilities to be available.

A hotel chain wishing to attract and keep business travelers should make a concerted effort to providing the services that businesspeople need. One enterprising chain is considering installing an "on-the-road" office in each of its locations, containing a word processor, duplicating machine, telex, dex, and information on where to obtain secretarial, messenger, and other services a businessperson might need.

A special note needs to be made about another major change Monitor points out in the business travel universe: the increase of women on the road. As more and more women work, more and more are traveling on business, and smart marketers are looking to see what they can do to make the whole experience more pleasant.

This doesn't mean providing frilly rooms, but it does mean providing skirt hangers, good security, hairdryers in bathrooms, better lighting in bathrooms, and well-lit parking lots as well as training maitre d's to treat single diners as welcomed guests.

For both businessmen and businesswomen, hotels would do well to set up some type of 24-hour room service. Businesspeople frequently arrive in their hotels after the dining rooms have stopped serving food.

Looking Ahead

As travel and tourism marketers seek to attract the American consumer of the 1980s and beyond, as we've discovered through our Monitor studies, they must take a new look at their overall business strategies and make a commitment to marketing rather than selling. Selling is "getting rid of what you've got"; marketing is having what people want.

Service-based companies in general are placing a new emphasis on the strategic marketing planning process. Many see growth as the key not only to increased profitability, but to survival. They are making expanded use of advanced telecommunications and information technologies to reach niches in the marketplace. The travel and tourism industry must do the same. Above all, it must recognize that the traveler of today and the future is a far different one from previous decades, and to attract and hold this consumer successfully, they will have to become marketers of perceived value rather than sellers of bargain package deals.

Transportation Marketing

IT IS NOT EASY TO DECIDE HOW TO AP-proach the role of transportation marketing when looking at it as a part of the entire travel and tourism industry. For instance, where in the Four Ps of marketing does transportation fall? For purposes of discussion, it is treated as a product like hotels and rental cars, but on another level transportation represents the distribution system of the entire industry since its role is to distribute the ultimate consumer to the point of consumption of goods and services. The deregulation of the entire transportation system in the United States has been proceeding at a brisk pace in the last decade. We have deregulated the motor coach business, the rail system, and most recently the airlines. While the latter receives the most attention in the media because of its public ownership and the extent of use by large segments of the population, it would be a mistake not to acknowledge that as this system of moving people reorganizes itself, new opportunities in resorts and lodging, in restaurants, and in destination marketing are continually surfacing. That is because the entire travel and tourism business is somewhat availability elastic, that is, as destinations become more accessible and more cost efficient to visit, they become more desirable economically as places to develop facilities and services that cater to travelers.

The following four articles take a close look at two important segments of the transportation industry: the airlines and the rail system. Since motor coach transportation is generally sold as part of a complete tour it is discussed later in the section devoted to the marketing of tours and cruises. Airline and rail transportation, on the other hand, are usually purchased independently of other travel components.

There are many similarities between the marketing approaches of airlines and trains, as will become obvious to the careful reader. For both, the structure of the marketplace has changed dramatically; however, the railways have had the advantage of a federal subsidy in coping with the new world of travel. Lacking that, the airline industry has reacted with mergers, acquisitions, and failures. Of the more than 100 airlines formed since deregulation in 1978, only 40 were still operating by 1986; 36 had ended up in bankruptcy proceedings and 26 had been bought by others or agreed to be purchased. The trend is almost certain to continue. Major airlines today have $15.5 billion of debt versus $7 billion in 1978, a direct cost of the end of the era of protectionism. The concentration in the industry is unmistakable. It is now estimated that America's six largest airlines carry between 75% and 85% of all passengers.

As a result of all of these upheavals, airlines have had to become marketing oriented for the first time in their experience. They have had to learn how to use service, fares, routes, and schedules not only as sales tools but as marketing tools, which has meant making some hard choices between short-term tactics and long-term strategies. The choices have not always been the right ones which becomes clear by studying the untimely demise of carriers like People Express, Air Florida, and Braniff. Others, such as Piedmont, quickly grasped concepts like market segmentation and ran with them. As John Pincavage, an airline analyst for Paine Webber said in an interview with *Advertising Age*, "It's marketing 101 for airlines."

New strategies in the war for market share include frequent flyer plans, the establishment of new hubs, computerized reservation systems, and a fresh look at the means of distributing tickets. Next to equipment and fuel commissions paid to travel agents are the third largest expense for most airlines. That, combined with the new power many agents have gained to direct business, has put the airline industry in an uncomfortable position, one from which it may well feel the necessity to extradite itself.

All of these subjects are dealt with at length by contributing authors Richard Ferris, John Eichner, and Whitley Hawkins in articles 5, 6 and 7. Ferris is the former Chairman of Allegis Inc., the parent company of United Airlines. Eichner is the president of a respected airline consulting group. Hawkins is the Senior Vice-President of Marketing at Delta, an airline that appears to have mastered the art of surviving and prospering in the new environment. You will want to read the section discussing tour marketing as well as that in which Edward Rudner, President of Certified Tours, discusses the marketing of Delta's Dream Vacations and also the section on travel agencies that explores the love-hate relationship that exists between agencies and airlines and suggests the course the future might take.

Robert Gall, Vice-President of Sales and Advertising for AMTRAK, then tells about the company's marketing strategy in article 8. Like the airlines, AMTRAK divides its customers into business and nonbusiness travelers and uses different pricing strategies in dealing with both. He points out the importance of the leisure travel segment to AMTRAK in contrast to the emphasis put on business travelers by airlines. Gall also identifies a subgroup of nonbusiness travelers — those traveling to visit friends and relatives — who seem to be especially good prospects for rail travel and discusses about how AMTRAK pursues them.

Because all other parts of travel and tourism depend on the availability of travelers and the cooperation of the transportation industry, an understanding of the problems and opportunities facing these enterprises is essential in strategic market planning.

Chapter 5

What Lies Ahead in World Aviation

Richard J. Ferris
*Former Chairman and
CEO, United Airlines*

*Richard J. Ferris is former chairman and chief executive officer of
United Airlines and its parent company. His business career began in
1962 after he graduated from Cornell University and joined Westin
Hotels & Resorts. United Airlines chose him to head its food services
division in 1971; only three years later he was elected president. An
advocate of airline deregulation, Ferris led United through the early
phases of deregulation and expanded it from a primarily domestic
carrier into a leading international airline.*

The airline industry is so visible in the public eye that a reporter once told me he writes four stories about aviation for every one story he writes on trucking, shipping, or railroading. Hardly a day passes that most Americans don't read or hear about an aviation development. It might be United Airlines placing a $3 billion order for aircraft, another salvo fired in the great airfare war, the design of quieter, more efficient jet engines, or one airline buying another airline. What's more, people take a great interest in aviation. Maybe it's because the airlines are in the mass-transportation business, because the majority of Americans have flown in commercial aircraft, because flying still is associated with glamour and excitement, or because there is something deep within the human psyche that responds powerfully to the idea of flight. Absent news of commercial aviation, stories of hang gliding, ballooning, and aircraft with gossamer wings fill the gap.

Airlines have come a long way since the days of the Wright brothers, but a new kind of evolution has taken place since 1978. It has taken airlines out of the hand of the regulators and placed them into the heart of the marketplace. It permanently altered the industry. Because the airline industry has changed so rapidly since deregulation, I call the phenomenon *instant evolution*, even though that's an oxymoron comparable to jumbo shrimp, postal service, and military intelligence.

Before considering where this change is taking us, consider briefly where commercial aviation has been. It had been regulated since 1938. The Civil Aeronautics Board had the virtually impossible mandate of regulating the airlines while encouraging competition. The mandate often produced classic, if not confusing, results. For example, a bureau counsel's brief in a CAB rate case involving live animals and birds read: "For purposes of this investigation, chinchillas, guinea pigs, hamsters, mice, rabbits and rats are classified as large birds. Fox and mink are classifed as small dogs."

Of more serious consequence was the long-term effect of CAB regulation. By the 1970s, it was clear regulation, whatever its merits in the early days, was hobbling an entire industry. The system was burdened with costly, unnecessary restrictions. Long-haul service subsidized short-haul service. Earnings were dismal. Airlines were bloated and inefficient. What little competition there was existed solely at the service, not at the price, level.

Beginning with the Ford administration, economists, consumerists, and politicians acknowledged that the suffering and stagnant industry could be more innovative and profitable if it were free of government shackles. Congress acted. President Carter signed the Airline Deregulation Act of 1978. On New Year's Eve of 1984, the CAB went out of business to the sound of a bugler playing taps. And certain CAB functions — too many in my opinion — transferred to the Department of Transportation.

What happened next?

Some new airlines took flight and some existing ones got their wings clipped. Airlines left old markets and entered new markets, raised and lowered prices, expanded and contracted, became efficient and remained inefficient, gained turf and lost ground. Just like any other business.

The isometrical struggle continues today to the benefit of consumers who have a wider choice of airlines, routes, and fares, and to the benefit of airlines that defined their missions and developed their strategies to fit this new era in aviation.

A 1986 Brookings study on the economic effects of airline deregulation supports the view that consumers as well as airlines have benefited. For example, the study pointed out:

☐ The total annual benefit of deregulation to travelers is $5.7 billion.

☐ The savings benefit is the result of lower fares, added frequency, and an increase in single-carrier service, which travelers find convenient.

☐ Business travelers benefit the most from deregulation, but pleasure travelers have gained as well — mostly from reduced fares.

☐ Deregulation has not contributed to a net loss of service to people in small communities.

Those are just a few of the important facts the Brookings study uncovered. Here are some of the conclusions:

☐ Airline deregulation has served the public interest much more effectively than regulation would have.

☐ Once carriers have aligned their fleets with their deregulated route structures and markets, benefits will be even greater.

☐ Neither public policies nor practices by carriers should be allowed to interfere with the competitive process and undermine those benefits.

☐ The industry shakeout will not cause any harm to travelers' welfare.

The authors of the Brookings study referred to the industry shakeout. Others call it restructuring or consolidation. Headline writers call it merger mania in the sky. Whatever it's called — shakeout, restructuring, consolidation or merger mania — it's an inevitable process that really is no different and no more astounding than the merger wave that has been washing over American industry. Like the boss said to his secretary in a *Forbes* cartoon: "What a marvelous fiscal year — mergers, acquisitions, divestitures, deregulation, restructuring, maximized shareholder values! Refresh my memory — what business are we in?"

The airline industry is the object of more attention than other industries. Airline activity in 1986 proves consolidation is in full swing. One early story credited United Airlines with starting it all by agreeing to buy Pan Am's Pacific operations. That was one of the most exciting events in recent aviation history because it turned United into a major international carrier virtually overnight. But other industry activity better fits consolidation criteria.

A few examples of this phenomenon are: Carl Icahn took over Trans World Airlines, then TWA acquired Ozark. Texas Air, the parent company of New York Air, Rocky Mountain Airways, and born-again Continental, took over Eastern, Frontier, and People Express. Republic merged with Northwest. Delta acquired Western. Is all this consolidation good or bad? For consumers? For the airlines? The answer is not yet clear-cut.

From the consumer standpoint, the effect on competition in the market must be considered. If an airline merger still gives a traveler enroute from Allentown to San Francisco a choice of carriers, routes, and fares, competition has been maintained. If a merger gives one airline 75 percent control at one city, it must be determined if the local market continues to be well served.

From the airlines' standpoint, the possible gains must be considered. Consolidation can help airlines enlarge route networks, strengthen hub operations, provide resources to introduce major marketing programs, and improve cost control. If the airlines, as a result of consolidation, improve their balance sheets, they will have the resources to buy new planes, order new equipment, and capture the passengers that continued growth of the travel segment of the economy will produce. In some cases consolidation can even help a carrier survive. However, United and the other airlines that developed sound strategies have survived and grown in the years since deregulation.

What of the future?

Airline industry consolidation will continue because the industry is in transition. The instant evolution isn't over.

True: Since 1978, airlines have been freed from route and price constraints.

True: Passengers and shippers vote with their dollars for lower prices, better schedules, and service innovations.

True: The free market is proving it offers more benefits than any system of economic regulation.

Regardless of its merits and its benefits, however, deregulation will be debated not only in the United States, but in other countries, for years to come.

Deregulation has gone beyond U.S. shores, rippled across both oceans, and skipped over the border to the north. The same foreign governments that looked down on deregulation of the U.S. airlines are exploring deregulation. It has become a global issue.

In Canada, the government has proposed reform, following the principle that the Canadian airline industry needs less regulation and interference and more reliance on the forces of competition and a free market. Although Canadian air transportation regulations have been liberalized, they have a way to go. Still, the guidelines require carriers only to meet fit, willing, and able standards, comply with safety requirements, and submit proof of adequate insurance coverage. The Canadian government plans to resort to subsidies only in cases of urgent necessity.

In Australia, a highly regulated domestic air system limits major routes to two airlines, one government owned and one privately owned. Both supporting and opposing forces of deregulation in Australia cite the U.S. experience in their arguments. It appears, however, that Australia is headed toward some gradual deregulation of its airlines, rather than the all-or-nothing approach the United States adopted.

The same is true of European countries, where the political environment is quite different from the United States and caution is the watchword. In 1985, the Parliamentary Assembly of the Council of Europe adopted a resolution urging the European Civil Aviation Conference to promote a more competitive and consumer-oriented system. In this regard, British Airways is leading the way. Only four years ago, the government-owned airline was on the ropes and few thought it would survive. Colin Marshall, head of British Airways, thought otherwise. With Chairman Lord King, Marshall developed a plan to make the airline profitable and popular. Today, British Airways is thriving because it is a market-driven, rather than an operationally driven, airline. The British government is expected to sell the airline to the general public through the stock exchange.

There are those who say deregulation of air travel is inevitable for Europe and other free-world countries. Certainly the signs point in that direction, but inevitable is a strong word.

Consumers have welcomed the benefits of deregulation, as have most carriers. Nevertheless, there is some public concern about air safety. Some critics believe there is no economic incentive for an airline to fly a plane safely to its destinaiton. I disagree. Safety is critical to a viable product; operating safely can help in the marketplace; and an outstanding program of preventive maintenance keeps costly planes in the air where they can make money, not on the ground where they can't. Other critics charged that deregulation forced airlines to cut costs at the expense of safety. Not true. The safety record of the major U.S. carriers since deregulation is excellent. It also outdistances the safety record of carriers in other countries where the air transport system still is government regulated.

At United, customer and employee safety is the number-one priority. It is fundamental to everything we do. It is upheld without compromise. The other major U.S. carriers have that same unwavering commitment.

In addition, safety has not been deregulated. In the United States, the Federal Aviation Administration still ensures and enforces the safety of the nation's air-transportation system.

If the airlines were still caught in regulatory cobwebs, they would have no incentive to compete and to grow. If the airlines were still caught in regulatory cobwebs, it would have been impossible for United to purchase the assets of Pan Am's Pacific division and for other carriers to merge. If the airlines were still caught in regulatory cobwebs, they couldn't provide travelers with low fares, frequent service, mileage programs, and other benefits people have become so accustomed to in the past few years.

The free market has no substitute; the free market works; the free market will see the airline industry of the 1990s realizing its full potential. And the real beneficiaries of this free-market system in the 1990s and beyond will be 600 million U.S. travelers who depend on the airlines to get them where they want to go — quickly, conveniently, and, above all, safely.

Chapter 6

Using Fares and Schedules as Airline Marketing Tools

L. John Eichner
President, Simat,
Helliesen & Eichner,
Inc.

L. John Eichner is President of Simat, Helliesen & Eichner, Inc. (SH&E), an economic research firm with offices in New York and Waltham, Massachusetts specializing in airlines and transportation. Since joining the firm in 1966, Mr. Eichner has directed more than 500 consulting assignments in every area of air transportation. With an extensive background in aviation marketing, planning, and litigation, he has advised governments, airline companies, manufacturers, insurance companies, financial institutions, and law firms.

Fares and schedules have been important marketing tools for airlines since the industry's birth. The deregulation of the airlines in 1978 reinforced the lesson that scheduling and pricing are two keys to profitability.

Since the early 1970s, but especially since the Airline Deregulation Act of 1978, a massive rationalization of airline routes and schedules has occurred. With only a few surviving exceptions, jet carriers have come to deploy their equipment in similar arrangements. Typically, two- and three-engined jets feed into central locations, termed *hubs* (although arrangements around their centers are not generally symmetrical). Passengers interchange between connecting flights, with groups from smaller aircraft aggregating onto longer-distance connecting flights with larger aircraft. Under regulation, there were only four major hubs—Atlanta, Dallas/Ft. Worth, Chicago, and Denver. Under deregulation, even smaller cities such as Nashville, Dayton, and Salt Lake City are viable hubs.

The increase in competition permitted by deregulation also has produced broader and more sophisticated marketing efforts involving schedules adjustments and fare initiatives. The development of Computerized Reservation Systems (CRS) by the largest carriers has facilitated the distribution and dissemination of carrier fare and schedule. In particular, it has speeded the market's ability to become aware of schedule and fare changes. The development of automated systems and the dynamism of a deregulated industry, however, have also produced a rapid rise in distribution costs.

The Reasons for Hub and Spoke Route Systems

Hubs have become a particularly important marketing tool for a number of reasons. Most significantly, hubs empower carriers to offer more frequent departures and more numerous routings at a lower cost than possible with so-called linear systems. Prior to deregulation, frequency levels were often inflated beyond competitive requirements because of strict government control over market entry. With deregulation, carriers could rationalize their routes into hub and spoke route systems. These new route systems create density by laminating more traffic flows. More segment traffic permits more frequency, often with larger, more efficient equipment and with higher load factors. Consequently, a hubbing airline's costs per revenue passenger mile fall so that it can profitably reduce fares below those of its non-hubbing competitors.

Figure 1 illustrates the extent of hub development as of mid-1986. It is unlikely that many of these hubs will disappear from this map in the future, although some of the recent mergers may ultimately reduce the significance of certain hubs or lead to the elimination of those that would needlessly compete with one another. In short, airlines have established their turf and have built a powerful marketing presence in their hub cities. Hubbing creates franchises that, in effect, have replaced the government-granted franchises that existed with regulation.

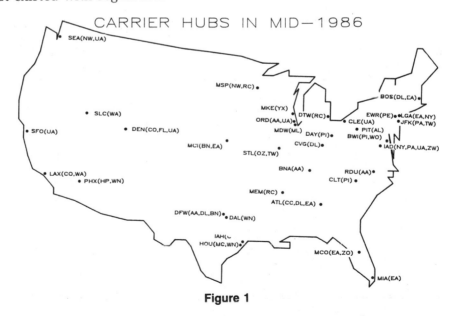

CARRIER HUBS IN MID—1986

Figure 1

It is thus unlikely that any airline will create a hub at Chicago's O'Hare Airport to compete with the giant United Airlines and American Airlines hubs there. United serves 90 nonstop points from O'Hare. This system, for example, permits travelers from small cities such as Providence, Rhode Island to conveniently fly to cities as small as Lincoln, Nebraska with only a single connection at O'Hare (United has two daily round-trip connections between these two cities). The tremendous array of possible connections available through each and all of the major hubs has been amplified further by marketing agreements and purchases of commuter airlines, permitting easy connections in even smaller markets.

The marketing power of these giant hubs also poses a retaliatory potential, discouraging head-to-head entry by competing carriers. Nevertheless, hubs also empower smaller carriers to offer their own broader arrays of schedules and so remain, through their own lesser hubs, competitive with giant carriers. Thus, Western's Salt Lake City operation serves 55 nonstop points. Theoretically, a hub with 55 spokes can create approximately 1,500 connecting city-pairs. Through its hub, Western, like many former regional airlines, has extended its coverage nationwide. With each additional spoke, a carrier gains new local traffic and feeds traffic to its numerous other spokes. Figure 2 demonstrates graphically how broadly the number of markets can proliferate through building and expanding hubs. In view of this relationship it should not be surprising that some of the smallest specialized carriers filling specific market niches have been impelled to expand their hubs toward a nationwide scale.

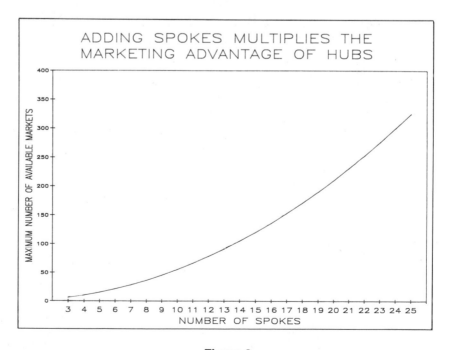

Figure 2

Scheduling as a Marketing Tool

Hubs and connecting complexes have become the primary scheduling mandates, versus the schedule times of multi-stop flights under airline regulation. In addition to the efficiencies they impart to travelers, hubs allow more economic utilization of airline resources, permitting lower costs and in turn, lower fares. The large concentrations of connecting traffic afforded by hubs produce higher load factors and enable more efficient use of aircraft.

Scheduling is an important consideration for the planning and marketing of hubs. Schedules for connecting complexes must be tightly coordinated to facilitate connections and maximize passenger convenience.

The prime thrust of carrier marketing efforts, however, has increasingly been toward gaining the loyalty of high-fare and mobile business travelers flying important high-density routes. A principal tool for reaching this objective is the frequent-traveler program.

High-Density Markets

High-frequency scheduling remains a vital marketing aid in such high-density, business-oriented markets as Boston-New York, Dallas-Houston, Los Angeles-San Francisco, and New York-Washington.

A survey conducted by the U.S. Travel Data Center and *Travel Weekly* confirms the importance of schedules for business travelers selecting an airline. For 70 percent of surveyed business travelers, schedules were the most important factor for carrier selection. Fares—the next most important factor—were cited by 54 percent of the survey's respondents.

Experience has demonstrated that successful participation in the most important business travel markets requires hourly or half-hourly frequencies. For example, the New York-Washington market is the nation's second largest travel route, with more than 3.2 million passengers during 1985. Trans World Airlines operates only a single daily round trip in the market at $39 one-way (versus $75 for its shuttle competitors). Despite the low fare and free drinks offered on these flights, TWA's DCA-LGA load factors range from as low as 11 percent to a high of only 34 percent, with a mean of only 20 percent. (It should be noted, however, that TWA seldom promotes this service and that its unpopularity is therefore not exclusively due to scheduling.)

Although the number of such high-density markets is limited, their importance to airlines participating in them is astonishing. In 1986, for example, Pan American was so eager to enter the Boston-New York (LGA)-Washington (DCA) market that it agreed to pay Texas Air Corporation $65 million for the 64 landing or departure slots and three gates it required to set up its own hourly shuttle service for those routes.

Airlines axiomatically covet the high-yield business passenger. That desire translates into schedules that are most convenient for business travel, with high frequency, an emphasis on early morning and late afternoon departures, as well as an emphasis on nonstops rather than flights involving stops or connections.

Orders and deliveries of small twin-engined aircraft and a noticeable lack of current wide-body orders suggest a future with diminished reliance on hubbing and more point-to-point schedules attuned to the high-fare business flyer.

International Markets

Scheduling is also an important marketing tool for long-distance trips and for international trips in particular. Faster schedules for transcontinental and transoceanic travel depend upon advances in technology as well as routing decisions. These advances have been promoted aggressively. For example, the Boeing 747-SP long-range wide-body enabled Pan American to fly the first nonstops between New York City and Tokyo in the late 1970s. The SP shaved more than six hours off of what had been a 20 hour one-stop flight on the B747-100. (Similarly, the supersonic Concorde enhanced the reputations of Air France and British Airways, even though these aircraft account for only a small share of these carriers' outputs and have generally operated at sizeable financial losses.)

The earlier advantage of the SP vanished with production of more advanced versions of the B747 that could fly long distances at substantially lower costs per seat-mile than the SP (the SP has less than 250 seats). The next development was twin-engined widebodies, such as the B767 and A310, that can operate over the Atlantic. With the smaller size and superior operating cost of these aircraft, we may expect more frequent schedules on long-distance legs using the new hubs developed since deregulation (for example, St. Louis) as the source of business.

The Role of Airfares

The role of fares in airline marketing has grown appreciably in recent years. Prior to deregulation, its use as a marketing tool was severely constrained by government regulation. Consequently, airlines focused on aspects of their product that could be more easily varied, such as schedules and service. With increasing competition from new entrants and expanding incumbents after deregulation, fares became a means of product differentiation. Excess wide-body capacity and two severe economic recessions further encouraged fare cutting.

A staggering diversity of fare innovations has followed airline deregulation. New entrants, such as America West and People Express, were generally the initiators of fare cuts. As upstarts intruded upon the turf of the major carriers, the larger carriers retaliated with apparently similar low fares. Unlike the upstarts' fares, however, the low-fare offerings of industry giants generally are encumbered with advance-purchase requirements as well as sharp restrictions on the number of available low-fare seats. Other innovations include peak/off-peak fares, senior-citizen fares, and corporate or government discounts.

Distribution Changes

Rapid schedule changes, frequent fare changes and heavily restricted, capacity-controlled fares are only possible because of computerized reservations systems. These systems have now been placed in approximately 90 percent of the retail travel agencies in the United States. CRSs give travel agents on-line access to flight and fare information. Automated bookings increase agent productivity and in turn provide carriers with ready information about bookings.

The Apollo and Sabre CRS Systems of United and American dominate the travel industry. Their systems account for 70 percent of the domestic revenues booked by U.S. travel agents. Although the verdict is not yet in on whether CRS owners are extracting excess profits from the systems, it is clear that system owners, in particular American and United, currently receive more bookings merely because of their affiliations with their systems. This is termed the *halo effect*.

CRS systems are maintained by the largest carriers, which coincidentally tend to have the highest fare structures. Smaller, low-fare carriers are typically disadvantaged because they lack these systems and so make increasing efforts to share more equitably in the existing systems or develop their own. Thus, Texas Air's acquisition of Eastern enables Continental and New York Air to gain control of Eastern's SODA CRS.

CRS owners can obtain more bookings from their systems than they otherwise would have, either because of display priority, last seat availability, or simply because of their affiliation with their respective systems. The long-term result is apparent in the trend toward increased concentration in the air transport industry.

The next frontier in airline marketing is the direct distribution of tickets. The role of travel agents in the distribution process has grown dramatically in recent years because of increasing travel as well as an enlarged complexity of airline fare structures. Between 1976 and 1986 the number of agents has increased in the United States by 125 percent, from 12,000 to 27,000. Airlines have become increasingly concerned with the increased commission payments that have accompanied the proliferation of retail ticket outlets. Figure 3 shows the percentage of sales that commission expense represents for U.S. Major and National Carriers.

Carriers thus far have principally combatted commission expenses in three ways: on-board ticketing, automated ticketing, and improved telephone reservations capabilities.

On-board ticketing, such as with the Eastern Air Shuttle and People's Express, has proven to be one workable approach toward minimizing commission expenses for some airlines and in some markets. An on-board ticketing policy helped People Express control its commission expenses (see Figure 3).

Automated ticketing has proven convenient for passengers, besides imparting airline cost savings from reduced reservations and ground personnel wages and benefits, as well as reduced travel agent commission expense. Its use, however, has been limited to a few high-density markets.

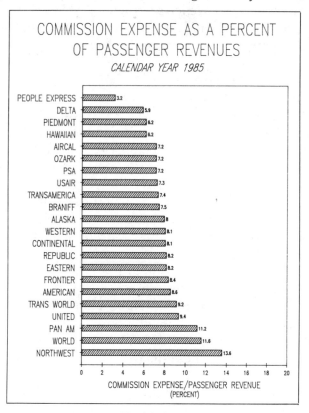

Figure 3

Improved telephone reservations capabilities also enable carriers to curtail their commission expenses. Improved telecommunications technologies and more economic pricing by suppliers have permitted new efficiencies in telephone reservations. Calls are now frequently cycled to different reservations centers, minimizing revenues lost from busy signals and waiting. Furthermore, carriers can achieve considerable savings in labor expenses by locating reservation centers in low-wage areas.

The greatest cost advantage may yet be realized with systems that combine telecommunications technologies with computer applications. One approach is a reservations system that enables travelers to book flights by keying in appropriate responses on push-button telephones. It is doubtful, however, whether such a system could successfully be applied to the complex fare structures that airline marketing increasingly demands.

A technology that circumvents this problem is direct on-line ticketing through travelers' microcomputers. ABC International, the Official Airline Guide and other such networks give computer users access to the complete spectrum of service and fare options.

Automated Marketing Programs

An outgrowth of CRS systems is the frequent flyer program, the first of which was American's "Advantage" program. Frequent flyer programs essentially are motivated by a desire to develop brand loyalty in an industry with little product differentiation and a large number of purchasers. Another motivation is the airline industry's preference for business passengers, who generally are also frequent travelers (business flyers average 6.5 trips per year versus 1.5 annual trips for pleasure travelers, according to a Gallup Poll).

In terms of business fares, frequent flyer programs affect the allure of a discount to the flyer, while his or her firm pays a typically undiscounted or less-sharply-discounted fare. Frequent flyer programs therefore effectively provide business flyers a rationale to fly at higher fares.

While CRS systems are not required to conduct frequent flyer programs, the systems do reduce some of the administrative costs of such programs. Not surprisingly, CRS systems owners are large airlines that fly to many destinations, making their own frequent flyer programs particularly attractive to potential participants.

The future in fares as a marketing tool appears to reside solidly in sophisticated computer technology that facilitates the aggressive pursuit of high-fare business traffic while accommodating low-fare pleasure travelers. This technology has already successfully been applied in numerous instances and doubtless will increasingly influence airline marketing. Thus far it has been most evident in such areas as computerized reservation systems (CRS), frequent flyer programs, and yield management/capacity control systems.

Deregulation and easy entry into the airline industry imply a continual threat of low-fare competition. Yield management and capacity control techniques address this prospect. Yield management is the airline discipline of optimizing revenues while offering a broad array of competitive fares. Capacity control is in turn a yield management technique for minimizing the use of low fares.

Yield management/capacity control has been particularly successful in combatting low-fare assaults on major carriers' turf. These techniques enabled American Airlines in early 1985 to offer its "Ultimate Super Saver" promotion, which cut ticket prices by up to 70 percent. These fares were subject to capacity controls and required 30-day advance purchases, among other restrictions. This promotion helped to reverse the start-up carriers' profitability, without any significant damage to American's own yields.

Such sophisticated pricing systems combined with frequent flyer programs and CRS systems will continue to pose problems for start-up carriers as well as comprise a substantial barrier to entry for future new entrants.

Conclusion

In the future, the key to airline profitability clearly lies in the advancement of distribution systems. Schedules and fares will continue to occupy an important place as tools for airline marketing. The survivors in the airline marketplace will likely be those carriers who most effectively and most innovatively apply computer technology toward improving revenues.

Chapter 7

What Makes Delta Successful — An Inside Look

W. Whitley Hawkins
Senior Vice President, Marketing, Delta Air Lines

W. Whitley Hawkins is Senior Vice President/Marketing for Delta Air Lines. Mr. Hawkins joined Delta in 1955 and has served as a Transportation Agent; a Marketing Representative; Assistant to the Manager, and later Manager, of Military & Government Transportation; and Regional Sales Manager. He became director of Advertising in January 1973, was named General Manager/Passenger Sales in November 1975, and was elevated to Director/Sales in July 1978. He was elected to Assistant Vice President/Marketing in 1979, to Vice President/ Marketing in 1984, and to his present position in May 1985.

Airline marketing as it exists today came into being in October 1978. That date marks President Carter's signing into law the Airline Deregulation Act. Overnight, the industry was released from 40 years of government regulation into a freewheeling, competitive marketplace.

As the industry wrestled with the many opportunities and accompanying problems related to deregulation, specific strategies began to emerge from the chaos. What became immediately evident was the need for the airlines' primary focus to change from what was mainly an operation oriented industry to a full-fledged marketing industry.

For the first time, decision making regarding route modifications, pricing, scheduling, and operations was possible without regulatory restrictions. Deciding which routes to add, drop, or maintain and how much to charge — all questions very basic to other industries — were essentially being addressed for the first time. In answering these questions it became apparent that airline marketing organizations would have to become first string players on any team that wanted to compete successfully in this game.

Although the airline industry anticipated many of the changes that were forthcoming, it was not entirely ready to absorb the sheer quantity and frequency of these changes. Today, it is ready, though still learning.

Very valuable lessons have been learned since 1978, some the hard way.

However, fundamental strategies have evolved which will undoubtedly have a bearing on who will be the successful, and perhaps surviving, air carriers in the years to come.

Positioning the Product in the Market

In determining our place in the market, it was necessary to define just what the airline product actually is. Very simply, airlines sell space on board an aircraft traveling from point A to point B. There is a potential market for this space for both passengers and cargo.

The market for the airline product is composed of various segments, each occupied by carriers providing similar service, yet an entirely different product. What then differentiates these products from one another? Primarily price and service. The product mix ranges from the low cost, no frills airlines to the full-service carriers having a generally higher fare structure and a full range of passenger amenities. Identifying the position of the product is the first step in implementing a successful marketing program. This appears basic, but once again, it's a relatively new concept in the airline industry.

An airline seat is said to be the most perishable commodity in the world. A seat on a given flight between two cities on a particular day can only be sold once. When the flight takes off, the unsold seat is lost, worthless, and can never be sold again. This makes the selling of that seat vital in the successful operation of any airline. In order to sell this seat, it must be properly packaged and priced to attract a potential buyer. The same concept also applies for effectively marketing air cargo.

Identifying and Reaching the Potential Buyer

Essentially, there are two types of buyers in the airline market, those that are time sensitive and those that are price sensitive.

The time-sensitive buyer is the business traveler. He or she is not critically concerned with cost, but requires a product that is convenient, reliable, and comfortable. Although a total accounting is not possible, business-related travel is the primary source of revenue for major carriers. The number of people traveling each and every day to attend a company meeting, convention, or for sales purposes is staggering.

Many airlines have various incentive programs that reward the regular, volume user of air transportation. These programs, started as a means to reward these travelers, have evolved into excellent vehicles for building brand loyalty. With the reward of free and reduced rate travel, passengers travel with the airline on which they have accumulated the most mileage. This has created an extremely positive situation because not only are the airlines developing brand loyalty, but they are also receiving the added benefit of incremental revenue that was possibly diverted from a competitor.

Frequent flyer programs have been very effective. Marketing to this group requires that a carrier establish and maintain a nationwide network of flights and be financially fit to provide an attractive frequency of service on these routes.

Essentially, any travel not related to business can be considered leisure, or price sensitive. These travelers make their travel plans months in advance and usually have a significant amount of flexibility in these plans. Their primary concern is cost savings, and they are often willing to travel on an unusual routing or at off-peak days and times to obtain these savings.

Even though the time-sensitive buyer produces the larger revenue, a significant leisure market does exist. In fact, a great deal of an airline's marketing efforts and advertising dollars are used to attract these leisure travelers.

The leisure product is extremely diversified. Air/Sea,Fly/Drive, and the all-inclusive package are all programs marketed directly to the price-sensitive traveler. Consider the number of people who have utilized one of these programs and then include air travel simply to visit friends and relatives and the potential revenue becomes extremely significant.

The Hub Concept and How It Affects Marketing

A successful way to provide this nationwide route structure is through an effective hub and spoke system. Although the hub and spoke concept is not new (it was, in fact, first utilized by Delta at its Atlanta hub in late 1950), its popularity among carriers is rapidly increasing. A quick look at the major airlines route systems shows an obvious pattern of structuring around at least one major hub. Two or three secondary hubs are not uncommon.

The hub concept provides many marketing advantages to an airline operation. The spokes can be viewed as marketing arms reaching out to gather passengers to the hub. Larger aircraft and longer flights may be operated from this gathering point and departures scheduled to coincide with the arrival of many spoke routes. Smaller aircraft are used on the spoke routes allowing for a greater frequency of service and a more cost-effective operation.

As mentioned, Delta's hub operation in Atlanta is a good example of this theory in action. Although there is a significant market for international travel from Atlanta, local boarding passengers cannot support a wide-body aircraft on a daily basis. Accordingly, many flights are scheduled to arrive from the 86 spoke cities to connect with the international flights. In this fashion, Delta is able to actively market its international service from many cities in addition to Atlanta, some as far away as the west coast.

Although most passengers have grown to accept connecting flights, competition demands that a carrier provide a direct line of flight and prevent circuitous routings. This is where the need for secondary hubs becomes evident. Major carriers have been establishing these secondary hubs, as regional gathering points, and are often being marketed to directional passengers. It is now possible for a passenger to originate in a particular city with the possibility of utilizing two or three hubs, from the same carrier, depending on the final destination.

An exception to the above principle has come into existence with carriers utilizing a single directional hub and actually marketing back haul routings. Why would a traveler accept this type of routing? Very simple, the marketing is to price-sensitive passengers who are flexible with their time. It offers considerable savings for this routing.

There are also many marketing advantages possible for a carrier with a multiple hub route system. Consider, for example, Delta's ability to market the Philadelphia to Dallas/Ft. Worth city pair. Obviously, the first seats sold will be the discount seats on our nonstop flight. Discount seats may be limited on this flight since history shows a strong demand by the time-sensitive, higher-fare passenger. In order to accommodate the price-sensitive passenger, discount seats may be increased on flights to the hub complex in Atlanta or Cincinnati. We then offer the price-sensitive passenger connecting service to Dallas/Ft. Worth at a reduced fare. It is not unusual for a price-sensitive passenger to use a combination of these routings on one particular trip.

The flexibility of multiple hubs provides an opportunity to market to both consumer groups while still maximizing revenue.

Pricing

The relaxation of pricing controls coupled with the expansion by regional carriers and the start-up of low-cost entrants in the early 1980s has created an airline marketplace in the United States that is very price sensitive. According to a recent report from First Boston Research, 85 percent of all air travel has been at some type of discount fare. Anyone who has flown recently probably feels that there is total confusion concerning airline fares and pricing. However, there is in fact a method to the madness.

The airline industry averages more than 60,000 pricing or pricing related changes every day. To remain competitive, these changes must be monitored and the ability to take action and react to these changes must be in place.

The primary objective is to price the product to remain competitive while realizing a modest profit. Pricing profitability can be an elusive goal, since there are few industries where there are so many internal and external variables that can affect the ultimate price of the product. There are also few industries where the price of the same or very similar product can vary as much as airfares do. These variances can be a source of customer dissatisfaction primarily because the average air traveler does not understand the complexity of airline pricing.

Most carriers attempt to maintain fares on a basic mileage formula, yet all that goes out the window when competitive adjustments are required. In such competitive situations, fare adjustments are made on a market-by-market basis. It is poor economics for an airline to reduce fares in one market pair simply because they discounted fares in another.

Because of the variety of considerations that are weighed in establishing an airfare, most airlines cannot price each unit on a cost-plus basis as most industries do. Instead, they rely on a pricing regime that maximizes the revenue each seat or cargo space produces. With the emphasis shifting to a revenue or yield per seat mile basis, it has become necessary for management to introduce a relatively new element to the day-to-day operation of an airline. At Delta, we call it *Yield Management*. While the functions of Yield Management (setting the level and availability of discount seats) has been around for many years, the technical expertise and size of the department have increased dramatically over the past few years.

Basically the Yield Management system allows us to predict with a great deal of accuracy how many full-fare and discount seats are needed in inventory on a market-by-market, flight-by-flight, and day-of-week basis. These inventories are based on historic demand curves and booking trends with the uniqueness of each market taken into consideration. This comparison process begins 60 days prior to departure. If the actual curve is too slow out of the blocks, then additional discount seats are added to the inventory. Conversely, when a flight books up too fast, discount seats are removed from inventory. The primary objective of this program is not to sell a seat to a low-fare passenger when the same seat can, and statistically will, be sold later to a higher-fare passenger.

Marketing Alignments with Commuter Carriers

With the onset of deregulation, many experts predicted that the commercial air routes in the United States would eventually develop into a two-tier system. The major carriers would connect large hub cities and serve the long-haul markets with their large capacity, wide-body aircraft. The national (smaller than major) carriers would then feed traffic to the major carriers at these traffic-gathering hubs. This is not the way things developed. Instead, many national carriers have utilized the opportunity of expanding their own routes to develop their own hub and spoke systems successfully. Instead of feeding the major carriers, they are now carrying many passengers on their own aircraft from origin to destination and bypassing the major city hubs completely.

Losing considerable feed traffic at major hub complexes has led the major carriers to develop alternate plans for filling aircraft operating from larger cities. Many carriers have successfully aligned themselves with various regional/commuter carriers to fill this void.

Currently, there are more than 50 regional airlines that have dedicated alignments with major carriers. These regional airlines participate in a code-sharing agreement with their aligned major carrier that allows them to be listed in the OAG, timetables, and computer reservations systems, as on-line service. Passengers traveling on these aligned regionals are able to take advantage of pricing equivalent to one-airline service and are able to participate in the major carriers' incentive programs used to attract and reward the frequent traveler.

This program has been advantageous to all concerned, the major carrier, the regional airlines, and the smaller communities needing access to a nationwide transportation system. Although only a small percentage of regional carriers participate in these partnerships, they represent more than 60 percent of the passengers carried by all regional carriers.

The Expanding Role of the Airline Marketing Representative

Much of what has been previously discussed can be considered management's packaging of the product. The key to success is the ability to effectively sell the product in the marketplace. Advertising and sales promotion programs help, but the ultimate responsibility rests with the field marketing representative. Today's marketing representative is required to be a technician, advisor, salesman, and skilled negotiator in such complex areas as tariffs, promotions, consumer relations, and competitive analysis, not to mention being computer salesmen.

The marketing representative has been transformed from a service rep to a sales rep. He or she has been given a product line to sell and negotiating tools to accomplish these sales. Emphasis has shifted from creating an image to selling a product. Creativity and flexibility are traits that have become essential. Today's airline marketing requires a person who is capable of dealing with a fast-paced, ever-changing environment and, in order to be effective, he or she must have the dedication and innate drive to succeed.

Conclusion

Although the air travel industry has certainly experienced some rather tumultuous years, the future holds some exciting possibilities, with tremendous growth potential. Economists predict that a growing market of self-expressive, inner-directed consumers, many in their 30s and 40s, and most with college educations and high earning power will have significant impact on the travel industry during the next twenty years. In 1962, only 33 percent of U.S. adults had ever flown on a commercial airplane. Only 30 percent of adult women had ever flown, and only 57 percent of people in professional occupations had flown. By 1990, it is predicted that 75 percent of the adult population will be regular users of air travel, 71 percent of adult women will fly, and 85 percent of those in professional occupations will fly. This represents a significant increase in the acceptance of air travel as a major mode of transportation in this country. As many as two billion travelers will make tourism the world's largest industry by the year 2000, according to some travel analysts.

It will be our job to reach these people and sell them our product. It has become apparent that the airline that can reach its customers in the most efficient and visible way will be the ultimate winner. High technology has had its impact on the travel distribution system. Airlines are presently communicating with travel agents through computer reservation systems. Travel agents have the ability to electronically communicate with their accounts and actually deliver the product directly to them with Satellite Ticket Printers (STP). Automated Ticketing Machines (ATM) can deliver the product directly to the consumer. One thing is certain, the conventional method for the distribution of the airline product is changing and automation will be a major factor in the ultimate direction of this change.

The airline that cannot adjust to these changes cannot ultimately survive in the future environment. In order to do more than merely survive, the successful airlines of the future will have to produce, package, market, and distribute their product better than ever before.

Chapter 8
The Amtrak Story

Robert E. Gall
Vice President, Sales
and Marketing, Amtrak

Robert E. Gall has served as Amtrak's Vice President of Sales and Advertising since 1985. He is responsible for all related sales functions including travel agencies, mail and Express, and international sales. He is also responsible for all of Amtrak's advertising and sales promotion, among other duties. Previous to this position, he served as Vice President, Transportation Marketing, and as Assistant Vice President for Market Planning and Analysis for Amtrak. He has a B.B.A. and M.B.A. from Loyola University in New Orleans, Louisiana.

Providing all of the regularly scheduled service in the United States, Amtrak represents the newest chapter in a long history of rail passenger service in America. Created in 1971, the National Railroad Passenger Corporation, as it is officially known, was essentially a vehicle for relieving the existing railroads of passenger operations that had become unprofitable. The business that Amtrak began operating had been neglected in virtually every aspect for many years. The product itself had deteriorated significantly and knowledge of the market was nonexistent. There was more than a little concern about the actual market viability of the product.

The Amtrak that operates today has gone through several phases of development, or redevelopment, if you consider that today's rail passenger service is the modern outgrowth of the historic service. Amtrak's interpretation of its job is to provide quality, competitively-comparable transportation service for the amount of federal subsidy provided. In quantitative terms, Amtrak's most important goal is to produce continual improvement in the proportion of costs that are covered by revenues. From its low point, in 1976, Amtrak's revenue-to-cost ratio has increased from 42 percent to 58 percent in 1985, an improvement of 38 percent. While improvements were made in cost control, the real force in this result was revenue growth, which more than tripled in that nine-year period. This fact would seem to indicate overwhelmingly that the market is a viable one. Amtrak's knowledge and ability to market the service has also increased greatly, and I can only assume that what we know and what we have done has played a role in that success. In what follows I will share some of Amtrak's knowledge and market approach.

The Basic Product

In 1971, Amtrak was given a mandate to operate certain services and certain routes. While the new company had a great deal of flexibility in how it could structure and market the product, it had limited flexibility in terms of some items, most notably route and city pairs. The situation was not too dissimilar from a company takeover. In such situations, certain product basics are given and it falls to the new operations to work with the fundamental elements of the product.

Geographically, the route network was spread from coast to coast, serving most major U.S. cities and many smaller intermediate towns (nearly 500). The majority of these cities, in the network, were served by daily trains traveling routes of approximately 700 to 1,000 miles in the East to more than 2,000 miles in the West. Some shorter distance city pairs were served by multiple frequency operators. The most notable of these was the Boston-Washington corridor, which includes the high-density New York-Washington operation with more than 20 trains per day.

The speeds of the trains were also relatively fixed, since one of the principal determinants of speed is track structure, and substantial improvement in the track itself is a relatively long-term item. Speed varied a great deal from route to route, with the New York-Washington service operating at speeds in excess of 100 miles per hour and the majority of other trains operating in the 50 to 80 miles-per-hour range.

The passenger cars that Amtrak inherited posed very real problems as far as their condition was concerned, but the problems were rectifiable and so the equipment did not present long-run limitations. And the problems were largely addressed within the first five to eight years.

With the remainder of the classical market variables, Amtrak had a great degree of freedom. In fact there was one major plus. Amtrak, unlike other common carriers in 1971, was granted unregulated pricing. Given these initial conditions, we can begin to understand the market for rail passenger services. While there have been substantial changes in some product elements, the fundamentals, route network, and schedule speeds haven't changed very much. And in general, the characteristics of the market have also remained constant, with some shifts in the size of certain segments.

The Market

Similar to other carriers, the market for rail services falls into two general categories: business and nonbusiness. The term nonbusiness is preferable, since there are categories of nonbusiness trips that are certainly not leisure trips (for example, visiting family, attending family or social events). The critical part of the marketing process is matching or creating services that satisfy a market need.

In general, Amtrak travelers are relatively close to the average U.S. traveler. Business travel accounts for slightly less than 20 percent of the total market, compared with approximately 26 percent of total trips. (Data on total travel market [non-Amtrak] are taken from U.S. Travel Data Center publications). Demographically, about half of Amtrak travelers fall into the 25-44 age group, while 49 percent of the total travelers are in the same bracket. In terms of income, the Amtrak traveler is somewhat more upscale. From an overall perspective, the Amtrak market is relatively broad, cutting across nearly all segments of the travel market. There are both benefits and costs associated with this situation. From a strategic position, this means that Amtrak is not heavily reliant on any one segment; however, structuring marketing communications to such a diverse group presents some clear challenges. Beneath this general umbrella are several distinct segments.

Business Travelers

As the name indicates, trip purpose is the chief consideration in marketing to this traveler. And, of all the product features possible, speed is the dominant consideration. Consequently, Amtrak's business travel market is determined by the city pairs that can be served with a trip time competitive with the fastest available alternative (usually air, but sometimes private auto). In Amtrak's experience, a competitive trip time does not necessarily mean equal to the competition. It is possible to offer the traveler the possibility to trade off trip time for service or station location (most of Amtrak's stations are downtown). Obviously there are practical limits to the amount of trip-time trade-offs that the business traveler is willing to make and that a carrier can offer economically.

In the case of Amtrak's route structure and trip times, the business travel market is concentrated in city pairs of no greater than 400 miles distance and sufficient population size. Due to the extent of the route network, there are a number of good business travel markets. Those which are already of significant size and growing include New York-Washington, New York-Boston, New York-Albany, Los Angeles-San Diego, Chicago-Detroit, Chicago-Milwaukee, and Chicago-St. Louis. There are others developing and showing promise that are easily identified by applying the general criteria mentioned above to a map of the Amtrak route network.

Of all the business markets, the New York-Washington corridor is worthy of unique mention. The New York-Washington city pair represents substantial potential, but the route between these cities also passes through Baltimore, Wilmington, Philadelphia, Trenton, and Newark. Combine all of the trip possibilities available from this matrix of cities, and it's easy to understand why this route encompasses Amtrak's highest density service. Indeed the population density of this route is among the greatest anywhere.

Nonbusiness Travelers

This group represents the largest share of rail travel business, in excess of 80 percent. But the group is not nearly as homogeneous as the business travel segment. In fact, the largest trip purpose is to visit friends and relatives, which is true of all trips and Amtrak trips. More than one-third of Amtrak trips are for this purpose. The size of the group makes it a very interesting target. Of all the travel segments, this group is probably the most price elastic. Like the vacation traveler, they are not traveling on business, so cost is not reimbursed. But because the main purpose of the trip is not recreation, they are more likely to look for ways of cutting cost corners.

Vacation Travelers

While similar to the nonbusiness travelers in that they are susceptible to value-oriented packaging, whether alone or with family, their purpose for a vacation is self-gratification. For these travelers money spent on services and experiences that are compatible with their vacation desires is well spent. This is not to say that they are not cost conscious, but rather that they are more flexible in their purchase decisions because of their basic purchase motives. More than one-fifth of Amtrak travelers are taking vacation or recreation trips.

Other Travel Categories

This includes trips made to or from school, trips made to attend to personal or family business, and other purposes. These segments are relatively small and diverse. With the possible exception of school travel, they are difficult targets to market too efficiently.

Product Specifics

Assuming that our understanding of the various markets is accurate, the different Amtrak services have been structured to fit the needs of the market. This should not be interpreted to mean that there are great differences in the service from market to market; but rather that adjustments that are sensitive to the market have been made in order to provide some product distinctiveness in the marketplace.

Metroliner Service

Perhaps the best example of the way in which Amtrak services are differentiated is in Metroliner Service. There are 28 Washington-New York departures per weekday (with some minor variations during the course of the year). About one-half of those are Metroliner Service trains. The additional features that distinguish Metroliner Service are:

☐   30 minutes faster schedule (approximately)

- ☐ On-the-hour departures from both New York and Washington
- ☐ Widely spaced leg-rest seats with special interior decor
- ☐ Menu items unique to the service and dining area
- ☐ Will-call ticketing for those passengers wishing to purchase tickets at the station
- ☐ On-board telephones
- ☐ Premium price (roughly $12 premium, no discounts applicable)

The Metroliner Service is Amtrak's principal business-oriented product. The service package also reflects the fact that this is a very upscale market with more than half the passengers having household incomes in excess of $50,000 per year and one-third having some post-graduate study. The service is designed to support a selling proposition that allows Amtrak to offer a reliable extra-attention product that won't add to the stress of a business trip, but, on the contrary, gives the customer a relaxing environment while traveling. While there is an emphasis on speed and reliability (Amtrak's internal minimum standard for Metroliner Service on-time performance is 90 percent), the selling emphasis is on comfort and relaxation.

Other Business-Related Products

The remainder of Amtrak's business-concentrated markets aren't developed to the point that they could economically support a service as fully differentiated as Metroliner Service. In these instances, Amtrak's approach is close to the traditional class-structured method. Either a full-service, first-class coach is included in the train or a more modest custom-class coach.

Finally, there is a small segment of business travel that occurs on long-distance trains primarily because certain city pairs have very sparse alternative service. These markets are generally too small for any sort of a targeted marketing approach.

Long Distance Services

These are the trains that provide Amtrak with the largest share of its revenue, a little more than one-half. Since the basic market for these services is diverse and not well focused (mainly vacation, recreation, and visits to family and friends), the approach has to compromise diverted needs to suit all market segments. The general approach is to make the trip as much a part of a vacation as possible while preserving the ability to be cost competitive. Certain amenities and services are available to all—dining car services, lounge service, and sight-seeing cars (in some areas). Food and beverage services are on a purchase basis, allowing passengers to spend as little or as much as possible. Menus are planned to offer a variety of items that will fit a variety of travel budgets (from steaks to sandwiches).

Sleeping accommodations are available on all long-distance trains and these (with a few exceptions) are positioned as an upscale service. Passengers receive complimentary wine and cheese baskets, coffee and juice in the morning with a newspaper, and recently, meal charges were bundled into the ticket price.

The trains themselves are from two different styles of cars. In the East (basically east of the Mississippi River), trains use the more familiar single level cars. On the Western routes, where the scenery is generally regarded as much more spectacular, the trains use *Superliners*, that is, cars with two levels. Seating and sleeping accommodations are mostly on the upper level, affording passengers an unmatched view of the country through which they're traveling.

The Superliners also have a variation in sleeping accommodations. They carry both first-class rooms (with complete toilet and shower facilities) and economy rooms (with common toilet facilities). This feature permits marketing to a wider range of people and provides a better product mix.

Auto Train

Of special note is the Auto Train product. This is the one long-distance service that has a highly defined target market permitting a focused product approach. The Auto Train permits a passenger to travel on the same train with his or her car in a special set of auto-carrying cars behind the passenger cars. The service operates from suburban Washington D.C. to a town about 14 miles from Orlando. The dominant trip purpose is vacation and recreation. Demographically these travelers are upscale, mostly retirees, who vacation for extended periods (two weeks or more) in Florida. Many own or have access to Florida residences and live in Florida during the winter months. Some of these part-year residents return to their northern homes during the course of their winter stay, mostly for the winter family-oriented holidays (Christmas, Thanksgiving, etc.).

Accordingly, the product is decidedly more luxury oriented than standard long-distance trains. The ticket price includes meals for all passengers (coach and sleeper), complimentary snack foods served in the lounge car, and movies shown after dinner. The product is positioned as a value that is worth the price and not as an alternative to a discount airfare. The real alternative is the drive between the northeast and Florida, and the advertising and promotion focus on this point.

Strategies

Having made as many adjustments as is economically feasible in the product, it falls to the other marketing tools to help craft a package that is acceptable and successful in the marketplace. The market for rail service is diverse, and the essence of Amtrak's marketing challenge is to create a package that meets the needs of the different market segments in a way that is economical and presents a unified image. It is a relatively simple task to arrive at a pricing scheme that appeals to each segment and local situation and then to create an effective promotional plan to communicate that message; however, the costs of executing such a localized approach are prohibitive. Further, programs that only sell products of highly local appeal do not contribute to position Amtrak as a nationwide carrier, a position Amtrak needs to attain if it is to compete effectively over its entire route structure. Consequently, in all of its sales and marketing, Amtrak has sought to create programs that can both maintain a national positioning and address opportunities and concerns in local markets.

Pricing

Pricing passenger services has become an extraordinarily challenging sport since price deregulation. The challenge rests in not only reading the competition, but in constructing a program that works with a product's distinctive features. This latter point is extremely important to Amtrak's strategy. In competing for the nonbusiness travelers, it is clear that low airfare is a key competitor. However, simply setting prices based on prevailing airfare discounts is a game stacked against rail service. It is virtually impossible to set prices that equalize the disadvantage in speed for most long-distance trips. To be successful, Amtrak must lead the consumer to consider the benefits of the product in his or her decision.

To accomplish this purpose, Amtrak's principal promotional pricing program, for several years now, has been its All Aboard America Fare. This is a modified form of travel-pass, which Amtrak has used in the past and still offers for sale abroad. The current version allows a customer to take a round-trip between any two cities in one of three zones (roughly; east of the Mississippi River, the Mississippi River to the Rocky Mountains, and the Rockies to the West Coast) for a single price, go and return over different routes, and stopoff at one additional city on the outbound and return trips. Tickets that include two zones and the entire United States are also available. While the plan is competitively priced, it should also be apparent that this scheme plays upon the advantages of rail travel. A traveler can experience the unmatched view of America that only the train affords as well as schedule side trips into a trip itinerary.

While the All Aboard America Fare has been successful, one of its problems is that with only three zones, some markets, chiefly in the shorter-distance ranges, are left with competition situations that are not adequately addressed. A number of approaches have been tried, but the solution that has fit best is a "one-way plus" construction. Simply, for any trip over a specified mileage (most recently 50 miles), a round-trip ticket can be purchased for the price of a one-way, plus a constant amount (most recently $7.00). This plan is much more of a direct price-off program; however, for these types of trips it is much more difficult to interest prospective travelers in travel enhancements. So, the tactic is to take the price issue on in a more direct way. The one-way plus construction allows a very strong promotional positioning, while at the same time producing a common plan that can be sold on a local or national basis.

Advertising and Sales Promotion

At this point it should be apparent that Amtrak's underlying strategy is to position itself as a national carrier with many common components, but with the flexibility to appeal to specific market segments and local situations. To work well, support of this strategy must be central to the use of any of the traditional marketing tools. Because they present the selling offer to the consumer, nowhere is a marketing strategy more apparent than in advertising and sales promotion.

For some time Amtrak's commercial messages have operated on two levels. First, media delivering the most important benefits of the train are used in the majority of Amtrak's most important revenue markets. This is done generally in broad-reaching media such as television and national magazines. Second, on a local basis messages are delivered to close the sale with news of a special offer or promotion, usually in local newspapers. More recently, tests have been conducted to determine the effectiveness of combining selling offers with more product benefit oriented TV ads. Regardless of the approach, the main objective is to communicate the benefits of train travel and close the sale with a value-oriented offer.

Distribution

Without adequate distribution the best marketing plan would never realize its full potential. In the travel industry, the travel agent provides a critical role in the distribution system. Amtrak realized this fact long ago. Amtrak also realized that the airlines had devised the most efficient tools to facilitate the flow of business through the travel agency community. With the help of the travel agent community, the airlines established the Area Settlement Plan, to handle the common needs of the carriers and the travel agents to handle the ticket selling process. The major airlines created the automated reservation and ticketing systems for travel agents that have become a dominant force in the industry.

Selling vacation and recreation travel is a task highly suited to a one-on-one selling situation. Because Amtrak relies heavily on the nonbusiness traveler, it must have a core of educated sales professionals to sell the product. To realize the full potential of the travel agent system, Amtrak had to gain access to the Area Settlement Plan and the major automated systems. Happily, in September 1985, Amtrak became a member of the Airlines Report Corporation (which administers the Area Settlement Plan). And, as of this date, Amtrak is participating in the three largest airlines automated systems: PARS, SABRE, and APOLLO. Amtrak is on the edge of what should be a period of accelerated growth in travel agent sales.

Destination Marketing

My experience as Director of Tourism for Bermuda along with work I have done for other destinations has convinced me that destination marketing has a higher degree of complexity and more variables than any other segment of the business.

Start with the variety of accommodations in any destination. There is usually a broad range, from luxury resorts to budget bed-and-breakfast facilities. Each of these has a different positioning and a different target audience. Some are after large conventions that require exhibit space. Others want small group meetings. Some want golfers, others are after fitness devotees. There are commercial and airport properties, places for swinging singles, recluses, families, and senior citizens.

Attractions and restaurants also cater to highly segmented audiences. There are museums and theaters for culture seekers, water slides and killer whale shows for families, fast-food outlets for children, and romantic bistros for honeymooners.

The job of marketing a destination encompasses helping all of these different enterprises attract visitors, to say nothing of the airlines, tour operators, and cruise ships that have identified different target audiences of their own.

There are political and sociological implications as well. Cities and states need revenue from visitors to provide basic services to their own residents. Tourism creates badly needed jobs everywhere. But, while too few visitors can affect an economy adversely, too many can pollute the environment and endanger, if not destroy, the entire industry. A delicate balance must be maintained.

In the next section, five contributing authors discuss these issues. The first article, by Preston Robert Tisch, talks about "The Big Apple" and how it has succeeded in marketing itself as an urban destination. Bob Tisch emphasizes that the secret of New York's success was pure and simple cooperation and the wholehearted involvement of the entire community. Another key factor, Tisch explains, is that politics have been kept out of the picture.

Sidney Levin, former Secretary of Commerce of Florida and widely credited with successfully reorganizing the state's tourist industry, also comments on the need for destinations to resist politics as well as pressures from individual interests. Levin's formula also includes involving those who have the most at stake and getting rid of bureaucrats who do not understand the nature of sales and marketing. The bottom line in Florida according to Levin is to get everyone behind achieving measurable objectives with agreed on target dates.

The next two articles are case studies written by independent observers on Bermuda and Cancun. The Bermuda case was written by Professors Robert Lewis and Thomas Beggs; the Cancun case by a perceptive travel agent, Virginia Bessert. The two articles, side by side, make an interesting pair. One problem in Bermuda in 1982 that is common to many destinations which depend on tourists for their economic viability is that members of the travel and hospitality industry and local government officials do not share the same goals. Conflicts concerning what kinds of promotional activities are appropriate occur frequently. Politics interfere with sound marketing decisions and elected officials who have no business being involved may try to influence matters such as airline service and hotel development. The situation this article discusses is Bermuda's promotion of its off-season business. The government has a long-standing policy of promoting "Rendezvous Time." This is not a market-driven promotion. It stems, as Lewis and Beggs point out, from the union, taxi drivers, and even the airlines who have threatened to curtail their service to the island if tourism is not promoted in the off-season. As a result of these pressures, Rendez-

vous Time has been extended so that it now begins November 15th and ends March 31st—a full 30 days more than when this article was first written. Expenditures too have been increased. The results, however, remain somewhat disappointing.

There are at least two reasons for this lackluster performance. First, as the authors point out, while the hoteliers and others support this promotion in principle, in practice they do not. Some of Bermuda's most charming cottage colonies shut down entirely. Many hotels curtail their evening entertainment and use the winter season to do extensive remodeling projects. Some shops and restaurants close. While the Bermuda Festival strives to bring first-class cultural entertainment to the island during this season, often times few seats are available to visitors.

Secondly, while it is much nicer in Bermuda in January and February than it is in New York, the market that used to head for the island at that time of year has shifted to Florida and the Caribbean. Even though this is their prime season, competition has forced down airfares and hotel rates so they are competitive with Bermuda's off season rates.

Nevertheless, the government cannot allow large segments of the population to be underemployed for five months. This political reality could cost them an election. Since Bermuda has not yet successfully developed other industries to take up the slack, the problem of Rendezvous Time will not go away. Other Caribbean islands and even destinations like Alaska face similar challenges. What is needed is a willingness to experiment with new and unfamiliar concepts and an ability to put aside differences for the common good. Most recently the People's Republic of China has shown a remarkable flexibility in adopting new government policies to attract and accommodate foreign visitors.

The Cancun case study is also dated but it has been included here because it shows what can be done when a careful plan is developed and then implemented by Presidential decrees and appropriate laws. At this writing the Cancun success is being duplicated by the Mexican government in Huatulco. Cancun today remains one of the most successful destinations of its kind in the world. But the difference between it and Bermuda is that the government decided what needed to be done and who needed to do it and only players who would abide by their rules were allowed in the game.

The last article in this series is by Tom Elrod, Vice-President of Marketing for Walt Disney World. Imagine a continuum of packaged and controlled environments. New York City is at one end an entirely uncontrollable destination. Florida, Bermuda, and Cancun are in between, holding progressively tighter to the reins. For the ultimate in control there is the Magic Kingdom, where not only the facilities are controlled and carefully coordinated but even the guests are told where to go, what to do, and when to do it.

If we accept that having the right product is the first and most important key to successful marketing, then these five articles taken together show the pitfalls and practicalities of accomplishing this goal.

Chapter 9

Why Millions Pick The Big Apple

Preston Robert Tisch
Postmaster General of
the United States
Former Chairman,
New York Convention
& Visitors Bureau

Preston Robert Tisch, Former Chairman of the New York Convention & Visitors Bureau, was president and chief operating officer of Loews Corporation, which includes Loews Hotels, the Lorillard Division, CNA Financial Corporation, and the Bulova Watch Company. Mr. Tisch was a member of the executive committee of the Association for a Better New York, and has been the recipient of numerous civic awards, including the "Distinguished New Yorker Award" of The City Club of New York, and the first "Outstanding New Yorker Award" from the New York Society of Association Executives.

Mighty Manhattan. Glittering Gotham. City of Dreams! Whenever New York is mentioned, superlatives get a workout. The words used to describe this world capital, its people, and its goings on are as towering as its skyscrapers and as vivid as its nightlights.

"Each man reads his own meaning into New York," wrote Meyer Berger. And so they have. O. Henry called it "Baghdad-on-the-Subway," and to Walt Whitman it was a "city of spires and masts." To Rodgers and Hart, back in the 1920s, it was "an isle of joy," and in 1906, when the little old town was just hitting its stride, B.R. Newton wrote that "New York, thy name's Delirium." New York City told Helen Keller "that mankind is real," and Spanish artist Joan Miró cried, "This city is a tonic!" To Anaïs Nin it had "animal vitality"; to Henry Miller it possessed "a trip-hammer vitality"; and to Truman Capote it was "the only real city-city."

Even New York mistakes register high on the Richter Scale. A Broadway show never fizzles, it bombs. New York politicians never simply lose, they lose by a landslide. Local ballplayers who have an off day are never pictured as lax or lazy, they're putrid and pathetic, if not downright lousy.

Here we have this magnificent, often mysterious, city that everyone talks about, but few truly understand. For those of us who live in New York and know the city well, this is often difficult to understand. Of course we realize that the city is large and complex (that's part of its fascination), but we find it anything but intimidating. For us it is Our Town: a conglomerate of hundreds of distinct neighborhoods, often foreign in flavor but familiar and inviting—all part of the New York pattern. Yes, this city scintillates and stimulates, but it also soothes and satisfies. Ask any of us true New Yorkers where else we could live and we're completely stumped. We may gripe about our city constantly and chronically; that's our birthright, but we can't imagine living anywhere else.

Perhaps it takes an out-of-towner to explain us to other out-of-towners. After all, one of the best books about this country, *Democracy in America*, was written by a Frenchman, Alexis de Tocqueville. And it's true that some of the best writing ever done about New York City was done by such transplants as Englishman V.S. Pritchett and Upstate New Yorker E.B. White, who became a New Englander.[1] It was E.B. White, by the way, who wrote what is perhaps the single truest statement ever made about this city: "No one should come to New York to live unless he is willing to be lucky."

The last thing White meant was that you should sit back and trust everything to fate. He knew, as all successful New Yorkers know, that you make your own luck. If you want to succeed in New York, you must believe in yourself and your ability to succeed, and you must be prepared for a struggle, perhaps a long one. There is no such thing as an "overnight success," and even winners of the lottery will soon find out that money may guarantee security but not necessarily success.

No one knows better than the New York Convention & Visitors Bureau (of which I proudly served as chairman for more than 18 years) how difficult it is to achieve and maintain success. This statement will undoubtedly surprise most readers. As we have already established, New York is a great city—a world capital, if not *the* world capital. It dazzles everyone, even its detractors. Surely it is an automatic best seller. How can attracting visitors and conventions to The Big Apple be a challenge, much less a difficult challenge?

My answer should be instructive to everyone in the visitor industry. Never, ever, take anything for granted. Never, not for a moment, think that any product or any place will survive strictly on its own merits. Competition in tourism has always been keen (remember, the whole world is involved in the visitor industry) and today it is keener than ever. In the United States alone, more than 100 cities and areas are beckoning to the same customers. If these potential visitors aren't persuaded to come to New York, if all their questions about accommodations, attractions, convenience, and comfort are not answered efficiently and satisfactorily, they will go elsewhere. It's that simple. Travel is a buyer's market.

How then does New York City go about meeting the competition? How have we built tourism into The Big Apple's fastest-growing industry, one that

---

[1]V.S. Pritchett wrote *New York Proclaimed;* E.B. White wrote that small classic, *Here Is New York*.

employs more than 400,000 workers? How have we achieved the success that attracts more than 17 million people and more than 2.4 billion dollars each year?

First of all, any city or area must develop a *philosophy of success:* a long-range program upon which to build all other promotions or marketing campaigns. In other words, your city or area, your product, must have an image, and it goes without saying that it must be an attractive one.

In our case, that philosophy of success, that bright and shining image is embodied in a magical phrase, "The Big Apple," and here's how it all began.

New York City is now such a sought after destination that it is almost impossible to believe that it once had a terrible image. Back in 1970, people all over the world believed that everything bad happened in New York. We were, they thought, the dirtiest, rudest, noisiest, most crowded city on earth. We were the cynosure for all crime. "Fear City," "Sin City," "Stink City," were just a few of our (printable) appellations. Johnny Carson, whose "Tonight Show" was then based in New York, was on the air every night with jokes about mugging, rape, murder, and mayhem. There were endless digs about every aspect of the city's life, and even the term "Fun City" was twisted into a sarcastic slur. Now, there is nothing wrong with humor. We love it. In fact, New York is famous for its unique, biting sense of the absurd. The problem was that everyone *outside* of New York who heard these jokes took them to be the truth. People said to themselves, "Well, we certainly do not want to go there!"

To top off an already deplorable situation, the city government was in a severe economic crisis. So bad was the city's reputation at that time that sympathy for our plight was in short supply. Even the national government seemed to be against us. When outside aid, especially federal aid, became necessary to ward off bankruptcy, a now-famous, front-page headline of the *New York Daily News* read: "FORD TO CITY: DROP DEAD!" No one, not even the President of the United States at that point, could believe that New York truly needed, or deserved, help.

Obviously, our backs were up against the wall. Something had to be done.

Those of us who lived in New York, those of us knew and loved the city, realized what a great city we had. We simply had to convince the rest of the nation and the world. Furthermore, we had to remind people elsewhere that saving New York City was not a selfish concern. No city stands alone, no city is an island, to paraphrase John Donne. All cities are interdependent. When one city is in trouble, especially one as big and important as New York, other cities will, sooner or later, feel the damaging effects. This is just as true of Atlanta, Boston, Chicago, Detroit, Houston, Philadelphia, and Los Angeles as it is of New York.

Our problem was complex; the solution was not easy, but we found it. Our mayor, joined by some of the nation's finest financial minds, finally persuaded Washington to get off our case and on our side and the immediate economic crisis was eased.

Then came the less crucial, but in the long run more important, problem of improving the city's image. We already knew why the city's image was so poor. People everywhere thought that New York had a monopoly on problems that are common everywhere simply because this city has the best press coverage in the world. Everything that happens in New York is covered thoroughly by all media. We live constantly in the spotlight. Serial murders, crime waves, and colossal disasters can occur from Timbuktu to Tierra del Fuego, from Canberra to Calcutta, provoking perhaps a paragraph or two, but if a celebrity trips on a pothole in New York City, the news flashes around the globe. In truth, New York has never been number one in any of the problems that are found in all urban centers today. According to FBI statistics and other independent sources, we have never led the nation in the crime rate tables. (For example, in 1972, surveys conducted by the U.S. Census Bureau for the Law Enforcement Assistance Administration revealed that New York was the safest of 13 major American cities.)

Thus, the problem was identified, and that's always the first step toward solution. We had to find a way to restore faith in our city. We had to make our potential friends and customers outside of New York believe in New York as much as we did. To do this, we had to start with a most important first step. We had to begin with the New Yorkers themselves — all 8 million of them. We who loved and understood the city knew instinctively that you cannot stage any successful improvement program anywhere if the people concerned, the people who represent that program, do not believe in it and support it completely.

The situation was challenging, to say the least. New Yorkers have always prided themselves on their rather blasé attitudes toward their city. They love to take it for granted and make fun of it. Gallows humor is a New York trademark. In a way, this is a healthy attitude; people should never take themselves too seriously; however, under our circumstances back in the early 1970s, we couldn't afford the luxury of this outlook on life. We had to stick together to boost our city, not tear it down. And we had to have a program to rally behind.

That's when our famous Big Apple campaign was born. At the New York Convention & Visitors Bureau, Charles Gillett (the Bureau's president) and I realized that the positive aspects of the city were being neglected. We knew we had the world's greatest museums (more than 100), the world's finest and most active theatre (40 Broadway houses and more than 300 off- and off-off-Broadway), 25,000 restaurants representing every known cuisine,

100,000 hotel rooms in more than 100 hotels, thousands of stores and shops, and incomparable sightseeing attractions like the Statue of Liberty, World Trade Center, Empire State Building, Rockefeller Center, South Street Seaport, and the United Nations to name just a few. Yet the negative aspects of New York were being stressed.

With no desire to sweep problems under the rug (as pointed out earlier, all urban centers have problems these days), we had to remind prospective visitors and conventioneers that New York City is a perfect destination for both vacations and meetings. In the words of the old song, we had to "accentuate the positive," and thereby restore and polish a badly tarnished image.

When we selected "The Big Apple" as the theme of our major marketing campaign in 1971, we picked a symbol that has always carried pleasant, positive connotations—one that stands for the ultimate in achievement, vitality, diversity, and excitement. Before 1971, and dating back to the 1920s and 1930s, The Big Apple was a term used by jazz musicians, sports figures, and entertainers as a synonym for The Big Time. In other words, there may be many apples on the tree, but when you pick New York City you have picked the big one. You have played The Main Stem; you have made it in The Big Town—The Big Apple. But even though The Big Apple was not a new term, it was not until the New York Convention & Visitors Bureau created and launched its Big Apple campaign that the term became known outside an esoteric circle.

As soon as the Bureau's Big Apple campaign was launched, the city's tourism industries began to grow steadily. In spite of trends that have seriously affected the travel industry throughout the world, including recession, inflation, and the fuel crisis, New York's tourism continues to thrive.

The success of The Big Apple campaign has been phenomenal. Building steadily in stature and importance since 1971, it has become the most successful city tourism marketing campaign ever created. In 1983, when The Big Apple won The National Travel Marketing Award of The Travel Industry Association of America, the campaign was described as:

> Widely recognized as a classic in urban destination marketing. It was dramatically effective in changing the image of a product. It converted decline to success, and it helped revitalize a city.

Today, New York City is known throughout the world as The Big Apple. The symbol, which our Visitors Bureau placed on all literature, stationery, visitor, and convention materials, is also the world's most famous lapel pin. Because the Bureau made no effort to copyright the campaign (to the contrary, we encouraged its use), The Big Apple has also appeared on T-shirts, ties, jewelry, scarves, glasses, breakfast mugs, plates, posters, and objets d'art. Needless to say, it has appeared in headlines the world over and even when

TV or radio announcers shorten it to "The Apple," everyone knows what they're talking about.

Here's a cautionary word, especially to those who think that tourism success is simply the matter of selecting a catchy slogan. When we say that New York City's visitor industry boom is directly attributable to The Big Apple campaign, we do not mean that a slogan alone changed the image of our city. Behind all of the success was the credibility of the campaign, backed up by the diligent, day-to-day efforts of the Bureau's highly professional staff. The Big Apple simply gave everyone a goal and a cause to rally behind; its supreme strength was in motivating millions of people and hundreds of organizations to support the city's best interests. As a result of all their efforts, orchestrated by the leadership of the New York Convention & Visitors Bureau, people really do believe in New York once again. In fact, nobody dares to knock The Big Apple these days without risking a heated argument!

Cooperative effort, the interrelationship of various elements, is the true secret of any business success, but it is absolutely mandatory in the visitor industry. Tourism is composed of so many diverse elements (hotels, restaurants, stores and shops, sightseeing attractions and services, entertainment facilities, and transportation in all of its numerous forms) that pulling together is essential. Of course, hotels have sales staff, but they should work in close concert with the Convention Bureau's sales staff for maximum effectiveness. The same holds true with the promotion, publicity, and sales staffs of restaurants, stores, theatres, attractions, and services. Such individual members of the visitor industry must realize that the Convention & Visitors Bureau exists to help and support their efforts, not to compete with them. This is true whether you live in Atlanta or San Francisco, Albuquerque or Virginia Beach. Cooperative effort should also extend to other tourism organizations. It is a firm policy of the New York Convention & Visitors Bureau never to take unfair advantage of another city's or another area's unfortunate situations, whether they be strikes, economic crises, natural disasters, personal tragedies, political upheavals, or anything else. Yes, competition is bred in the American bone, but so is fair play.

Our Bureau president, Charles Gillett, and I were members of all leading tourism organizations, and Charles is a past president of the International Association of Convention & Visitor Bureaus and current board member of the Travel Industry Association, where cooperative effort is a guiding philosophy. Charles and I both were members of the board of the Travel and Tourism Government Affairs Council.

In the late 1970s, The Big Apple campaign was enhanced by the "I Love New York" campaign of the New York State Department of Commerce. Although this prize-winning campaign serves to promote the entire state, while we concentrate solely on the city, the New York Convention & Visitors

Bureau worked closely with the state program from the beginning, and we have joined it in numerous cooperative programs.

The benefits of such cooperation are well documented; all of us in the business have learned from long experience that whatever is good for tourism in general is good for the industry in particular. Unfortunately, the reverse is also true. Look at the damaging effects caused by recent incidents of terrorism, nuclear accidents, and economic restrictions. Naturally, certain areas of the world suffered directly from these adverse situations, but they also dampened the public's enthusiasm for travel everywhere.

Several years ago I had the honor to address a hotel industry conference whose theme was "Teamwork in Tourism." Among my remarks was the following observation:

> As a businessman (I am also president of Loews Corporation), I am often asked: what do you look for in making investments? What is it about an area that makes it attractive to both investors and customers? The first thing I look for is strong evidence of teamwork and cooperation, because for any one person, or any one business, to succeed, all must pull together. This is certainly true of my own corporation, and it is true of any other successful operation I have ever observed.

In New York City, as I have already pointed out, we are fortunate to have a great product. It would be easy, I realize, for outsiders to say, "Of course you have been able to achieve great success in tourism, look what you have to start with." This is not only an easy response, it is the wrong one. I cannot think of a place in the world, even the South Pole, that does not have something to attract visitors. It simply remains for someone to uncover it and market it successfully. Look at Williamsburg, Virginia, a sleepy southern town, forgotten and bypassed by the world until John D. Rockefeller, Jr. revealed its history, its beauty, and its charm.

Once the product has been identified, a philosophy of success established, and a favorable image created, the rules for maintaining and building an area's visitor industry remain remarkably the same, whether you are talking about a large city or a small hamlet, a well-known and well-developed area or an emerging tourist attraction.

Over the years I have developed a check list of these rules. I call them *The Ten Golden Rules for Success in Travel and Tourism Marketing*:

1. **Professionalism.** Everyone loves the travel industry, everyone thinks it is a snap, but in this business there is no room for amateurs; we must have professionals. This is why a Convention and Visitors Bureau, which leads and ties together all elements of tourism, is so vital. In turn, a bureau must be directed by tourism professionals, and it must have the support of a board of directors and an executive committee com-

posed of top executives in banking, retailing, real estate, entertainment, and the hotel and restaurant industries — in short, every phase of the visitor industry.

2. **Independence.** It is important for a Visitors Bureau to be free to exercise its professionalism, unencumbered by economic restraints and political control. This means proper funding and a minimum of interference by pressure groups and other political sources.

3. **Service.** Whenever the public is asked to evaluate a tourism organization, everything hangs on service. Is it complete, competent, and courteous?

4. **Hard Work.** Attractive as it is, tourism is no picnic. Diligence, concentration, patience, stamina, and energy — all of these traits, combined with the realization that there are no short cuts — are essential.

5. **Attitude.** If you do not love the area you represent, you will never make anyone else love it or want to visit it. Enthusiasm is probably the most contagious of all emotions.

6. **Control.** Eternal vigilance, keeping on top of things, is a basic requirement of an industry whose elements and trends change so rapidly.

7. **Imagination.** All places, products, and people have qualities that can be enhanced in order to make them more attractive. Imagination is the key.

8. **Flexibility.** Rigid behavior or rigid attitudes are anathema to the visitor industry. Compromise is as important to tourism as it is to diplomacy.

9. **Availability.** Next to service, the public always brings up availability in rating any tourism operation. Travel is a 24-hour, 365-day activity and those who work in tourism should realize this.

10. **Cooperation.** It cannot be stressed too strongly. Not only cooperation between all elements of tourism, but cooperation between all employees in the visitor industry. For example, if the maids, bellhops, waiters, desk personnel, and elevator operators of a given hotel do not realize the importance of serving the public with speed, efficiency, kindness, and consideration, it will not matter how expert the overall management may be. The front line of service is every bit as indispensable as the front office. In short, this is an industry for team players.

When I was asked to contribute to this textbook Editor Andrew Vladimir passed along suggestions for topics to be covered. In discussing the overall philosophy of the book, Mr. Vladimir said that he was more interested in the subject of marketing, which he defined as "thinking of what people want," rather than selling, which, he thought, too often means "getting rid of what you have." I have been intrigued by this idea, because I think it contains the essence of what I have been trying to say about the visitor industry. In other words, I feel that if you constantly think of what people want and need — and if you provide same — then that is the finest possible example of selling.

Chapter 10

Selling Florida to the Masses

Sidney Levin
Partner, Beber
Silverstein & Partners

Sidney Levin is a partner of Beber Silverstein & Partners, a prominent Miami advertising agency. His responsibilities include internal management, long-term strategic planning, and marketing for the agency and its many clients. Levin earlier served as Florida Secretary of Commerce by appointment of Governor Graham (1979 to 1981). Under his administration, the Department of Commerce was restructured into an aggressive sales and marketing organization.

My father told me that a camel was a horse designed by a committee, but he never worked in government. Obviously, whatever the issue, you can't give everybody everything they want. If you did, precious resources of people and money would be stretched to the point where they would be useless, and the goals — the main thrusts — would be at best left unborn, or at worst ripped to ineffectiveness by the gaggling demands of parochial demanders. The trick in government, most especially government that finds itself in the promotional and advertising business, is a clear line of communications to area, political, and industry leaders who have been consulted at regular intervals, leaders who have seen small parts of their best interests become important parts of an overall plan. If more than most of those who want to be involved are involved periodically, they will accept a degree of responsibility and to that extent pull hard for the overall plan. In other words, they will have bought in to the program, and as "owners," want to see it win. So, if you want a successful tourist campaign by a city or region or state, you must first determine who has the most at stake and go out and listen to him or her. That's where the foundation begins, but by no means where it ends.

Regardless of what state or region or area you are concerned with, it won't be helped much with an underfunded, inadequate series of mini-campaigns no matter how good their individual leadership. But there is always a group, in some places dozens, that lacks the understanding that the appeal of a destination can assist its property, even without specific mention in the main campaign. Those kind of traps are the potential destruct mechanisms that can destroy creativity or force it to expand to an unrecognizable mass (perhaps "mess" would be better). You cannot then, in my opinion, begin the process in any other way than to spend quality time listening.

I believe if you can get a consensus of those who really believe you know their problem and further believe that you genuinely want to find a solution, they will give you that most wonderful of assets in building an outstanding visitor program — time to accomplish it. But trust me, they are watching their clocks and they are apt to ask, like the kids in the car on their way to Florida, "are we there yet?" or state, "I don't feel any improvement," at terribly short intervals.

The second most important asset is the people who work with you to deliver the successful goal. Frankly, I entered my short-term government assignment with some real fear, having heard many bureaucrat stories. To help solve the problem, with Governor Bob Graham's assistance, we lobbied the legislature to remove all regulatory authority from our department.

We met the existing staff and told them that we were now, plain and simple, a sales and marketing organization. We told them where we intended to go and how. We explained that this was to be a new effort and the old ways were all to be tested and reimplemented, modified, or cut. We know that not everyone, in or out of government, can accommodate him- or herself to hard-driving sales and marketing at the cutting edge, or on the home support team, or in the supply lines. We worked hard with those who couldn't handle it. They certainly were not to be penalized or embarrassed. They were better off doing other things that they could do better, and with the help of Governor Graham and Lieutenant Governor Mixon, we were able to find lateral moves for many of them in other departments of government.

The ones that remained taught me well and thoroughly that all those jokes about government work and bureaucrat's skill are hogwash. I found some of the most talented, experienced people I had ever worked with. Later, some would admit that they were unsure of whether it was worth oiling their wheels if government rules and regulations were only going to freeze them shut again.

In the case of Florida, we were able to gather a great deal of support from within, so while the political forces were gathering outside, newly excited and motivated employees were being challenged to provide objectives that would thrust toward our goals, and in addition, specific strategies to get there. Those strategies were then assigned a cost.

If a leader (in my case, I was the secretary of the department that had responsibility for economic development on one side and tourism on the other) is to be responsible for the gathering of outside opinion and the setting of a path that the industry believes it wants to follow, then there must be another leader, equally skilled in carrying out programs and needs. I was able to entice Ed Gilbert, who had small city and large city tourist/government experience plus an enthusiasm for making things happen. He was willing to come aboard, and he was not afraid of failing.

Ed took the title of Director of the Division of Tourism within the larger Department of Commerce. He began to meld what had been done with what we were hearing and being told from the outside. He selected his own staff, some from outside, but surprisingly many from existing personnel that were capable of promotion to higher levels. A goal was not enough, nor were objectives and strategies, unless we could show what would be accomplished, how that result could be measured, and how much it would cost.

When we went back to the state legislature the second time, we were there with the programs that their constituents back home had been asking for, programs that could be accepted or rejected in order to meet a specific budget figure. It was no longer "Tourism's all right this year," or "I guess everything else is going up 10 percent . . . so . . ." It was a long list of things to do, each with the cost in dollars and staff time attached. "Don't cut dollars," we asked, "cut programs, they all have price tags attached." That was the year the Tourism Division budget went from $4.2 million to $9.6 million. No magic, just hard work by a lot of talented and dedicated people.

We found that if a person representing an outlying corner of the state said, "This looks good, but it's not going to help me," there was still work to be done. Any program needs time in the kettle to cook. The fledgling plan now needed a loving defense, a continuing communication, with promises of revision.

Building a consensus and genuinely prospecting for new ideas are essential, but are useless without an internal mechanism that will craft that incoming information into programs that will address the problems and concerns brought to the planners.

To accomplish our objectives, we shifted some responsibilities within work groups or bureaus, and we added a new one, as well as several new sections or sub-bureaus.

To get away from governmentese, we named groups what they would be called in private business. This reinforced the concept that we were a sales and marketing arm within the government, but not wholly government-structured or driven.

We used six separate groups to address the six areas of concern that we believe we needed to address. Research was the first. It was not a full bureau, but reported directly to the division director's office. It was a small, talented group that became more and more valuable as decisions were being made in all areas. Not only did this research group "count noses" of the Florida visitors by air, by car, by bus, and other forms of transportation, but it provided a qualitative look at people, from those that were regular visitors to those who would never come to Florida. Research helped identify new markets for us and taught us how to adjust our routine sales effort to different areas and countries of the world.

The advertising campaign was the second major element that we decided not to operate as a bureau. Instead, we selected an advertising agency in a formal search. Bob Graham was the first governor in recent Florida history who allowed an open review. Previous governors merely selected the agency that handled the successful gubernatorial campaign. Our new agency worked with all of our groups but particularly with the research section and the division director.

Sales and Promotion became a full bureau headed by a bureau chief or general sales manager, and that bureau was subdivided into sections with responsibilities for domestic tourism, international tourism, and meetings and conventions, each with its own sales manager.

The Publicity Bureau was, as you might expect, divided into a section of writers, one of photographers, and one responsible for the creation and production of audiovisual presentations.

The Visitors' Bureau was responsible for all hospitality programs including the welcome stations studded across Florida's northern border to welcome automobile travelers with friendly information, a glass of cold Florida orange juice, and a pleasant break from the long drive. This least known of the bureaus became even more successful as we learned to answer mail and greet visitors with not only a friendly hello but with exciting information about "what's going on" around the state during their stay. Properly approached, that greeting could add one to three days to a visitor's time in Florida. We told the staff endlessly that they were in the sales and marketing business, and it was their responsibility to attract visitors to the state, help make their stay pleasant, inspire them to see more sights, and have them choose to return — soon.

Even the fiscal and administrative area, our sixth division, found ways to make an important and successful contribution to the overall goals.

All this time we kept our eyes focused on four publics: the Travel Industry, the Florida Legislature, the professional who directly benefits from consumer bookings, and the consumers themselves.

It would take more space than I have been given to discuss the programs used to court the travel professional, and in turn to help him or her court the general public, or the programs designed to reach out to the consumer directly. We followed many tried and true steps but even there our people worked hard to give them a special flair or uniqueness that allowed us to sell better per dollar invested. A few examples follow:

☐ Every destination hosts a *Fam Tour*. This trip allows successful travel agents and wholesalers to be familiar with your area so they can sell it more effectively. Our folks solicited a few sports celebrities and created *Florida Sunsports* in which travel agents competed in games for fun and prizes in a part of the state that specialized in the sport they were participating in, and more. They went home smiling and writing about not only what they saw, but what they did.

- ☐ Fam Tours for travel writers and photographers were also a must, but no one had ever met them with cars clearly marked "For The Florida Road Rally" as well as rally jackets, maps, and a compass. This virtually forced our talented friends to see Florida as we wanted them to see it, to stop (rally style) at resorts and inns, attractions, and hotels that showed them the best of Florida, to write about their experiences, and to take the pictures we wanted to appear in travel publications.

- ☐ We organized themed exhibit areas at various trade and travel shows. We provided directories for meeting planners and directories for tour operators. We operated shows for each area of interest where Florida hoteliers and domestic or international meeting planners or wholesalers could sit eye to eye and do business that would take much more time for each of them alone, and without the positive energy that is generated at the "Buy Florida Shows."

- ☐ We built a library of 250,000 photo transparencies of Florida, fully cataloged and available to any professional travel writer or publication.

- ☐ We opened Florida Tourism promotion offices in Toronto, London, and Miami (for Latin American promotion). Miami was selected on the advice of the Division of Economic Development, which is Tourism's sister division within the Department of Commerce. Part of the effort involved convincing companies with Latin American headquarters in Latin America that they could communicate faster and at less cost from Miami to any country in Latin America, than from any Latin country to another.

Our industry partners within the State gave us the time to succeed because they had an opportunity to speak out, because they had a chance to have someone listen, and because they believed we were genuinely going to try. And that anticipation was communicated clearly to legislators who had not heard much from the tourist folks back home before. The legislature in turn offered help and cooperation, and funding that it had withheld in the past.

Everywhere we went we found new friends and new believers. In cases where it didn't work, we searched hard with the help of the industry to find out why, and committed ourselves to trying again, even harder.

Our marketing plan for Florida was in excess of 600 pages. It described goals, objectives, and strategies. It showed how to measure success in each strategy statistically, and it left room in every part for a timely entry of what was achieved. Our staff warmed to it after a while, because if you really pushed it, their objectives were there in black and white — not a bloodless employee annual review on Form XYZ, but the basis for a real review of the person and his or her performance as well as the strategy itself.

We found that legislators were far more able to relate to these plans. What was not achieved, and what it will take to make it right, is more convincing than any request, no matter how sincere, to "do something for tourism this year."

I accepted the Secretary of Commerce's role in Florida after Governor Graham said he wanted nongovernmental people to lead key departments of government, even if they could only do so for a few years. I agreed to two; I stayed three. It was enough, except to say that no matter who you are, if the real boss does not want you to succeed, you're going to lose. In my case, the match of Governor Bob Graham and Lt. Governor Wayne Mixon not only wanted it to happen, they demanded that it should. With that encouragement and a staff including the Division of Tourism Director, Ed Gilbert, who never stopped innovating and driving; and Dean Gaiser, the Assistant Director, who provided the perfect balance as "Mr. Inside"; and the rest of the wonderful and talented people who were encouraged to try to help make it work, it was hard to fail.

Florida does have beauty and weather — God given — but in the competitive travel world you've got to add a lot of hard selling and marketing if you want to keep the leadership pace, and then strain to reach even farther. Somebody once told me the best way to learn something is to teach it. That certainly describes my time in state government. It sure taught me a lot.

Chapter 11

Selling Bermuda in the Off-Season

Robert C. Lewis
Professor, University of Massachusetts/Amherst

Robert C. Lewis is Professor of Marketing and Research in the Department of Hotel, Restaurant & Travel Administration at the University of Massachusetts/Amherst. He received his Ph.D. in Communication Theory and Marketing in 1980, after 25 years in the hospitality industry. He has published more than 50 articles on hospitality marketing and lectured and consulted in Europe, Asia, and the United States. He is the author of Getting the Most from Marketing Research.

Thomas J. Beggs

Mr. Beggs is co-director of a new consulting and development organization that is in its formative stage. The organization, headquartered in Amherst, Massachusetts, will specialize in the rehabilitation of properties and products. His background is in marketing and consumer behavior. He was formerly on Faculty at the University of Massachusetts and is former Director of Marketing for Mount Snow, Vermont.

This chapter is reprinted with the permission of the Journal of Travel Research.

The relationship between a national department of tourism and the tourism industry of a country is an important one. In Bermuda it is an especially vital link necessary to perpetuate the viability of both entities. The Bermuda Department of Tourism reports that tourism dollars supply 43 percent of Bermuda's gross domestic product and 71 percent of its foreign exchange earnings. There is literally no other significant industry on the island.

The economy of Bermuda is not only almost totally dependent upon tourism but is also totally dependent on the island as its own attraction. Enterprises such as cruise line facilities, taxis, shops, and hotels do not in themselves bring the tourist to Bermuda; the uniqueness of the island is what brings them. This characteristic is somewhat peculiar to Bermuda; a tourist may go to many Caribbean countries without great regard for an island itself or without any plan to partake of the amenities of the island outside of a particular hotel. Most Caribbean hotels sell the sun, sand, stars, and sea, before the island; the island just happens to be there. In Bermuda the island's features largely are sold first, and then the features of the hotel — which just happens to be there.

After its friendly people, the openness of the entire island, the things to do, and its other natural resources, the main attraction of Bermuda is its proximity to the United States. Minimized travel time has been found to be of utmost importance in selection of foreign destinations. Bermuda is cheaper and quicker to get to from the eastern United States than all of the Caribbean and Florida, and over half of the island's visitors come from this area. Bermuda has limited conference facilities (only one hotel has the space and facilities for a large convention) and the hotels are comparable to those at alternative destinations. It is the island and its location that keep Bermuda's nearly 5,000 hotel and guest house rooms above 90 percent occupancy in high season from March 15 to December 1. This article examines the efforts of the Department of Tourism, and its interaction with the hotel industry, to fulfill the need to maintain the tourist flow during the off-season of December 1 to March 15.

The Department of Tourism

The Bermuda Department of Tourism has become a sophisticated and professional organization since the government first declared tourism to be the national industry. A continuous random sampling of departing tourists at the Bermuda Airport Terminal is used to tabulate complaints, compliments, and constructive criticism, and these comments are acted upon as quickly as possible. The market is well-defined demographically: tourists earn over $40,000 a year in income and are primarily middle-aged couples and families. Media such as *Business Week, Time, Gourmet, National Geographic* and Sunday supplements are used by the Tourism Board to promote Bermuda as a total destination area, and the Department of Tourism prints hundreds of thousands of brochures, maps, and travel tips for distribution both on and off the island.

Promotional efforts by the Department are not limited to advertising and collecting questionnaire responses. In January 1981 (prior to the introduction of direct flights from Atlanta to Bermuda by Delta Air Lines) the Honorable C. V. Woolridge, Minister of Tourism, led a contingent of 34 Bermudians on a four-day whirlwind tour of Dallas, Houston and New Orleans, cities which have air links with Atlanta. Seven hundred and fifty travel agents were feted and given presentations on the virtues of Bermuda by tourism, hotel and other officials. In January and February 1981, in what is a near-annual event, over 900 U.S. travel agents were brought to Bermuda to be wined, dined and shown the hotels and attractions of the islands, in four separate four-day stints. In April 1981 another Bermudian contingent visited West Germany in anticipation of Air Florida's proposed flight from Miami to Europe through Bermuda. Some Bermuda hotels, of course, do their own advertising. But it is the marketing and promotional expertise, energy and funds of the Department of Tourism that have established Bermuda as a unique tourist destination area that maintain the markets and develop new ones. These efforts led to a record breaking 609,556 visitors in 1980. Every year, for 8½ months, they bring the hotel occupancies to a level that would please any resort destination area. Added to this is a 42 percent repeat business ratio.

What then, are Bermuda's tourism problems? "Maintaining our quality image and value," says Francis Purvey, Manager of Promotional Services of the Department of Tourism. Minister of Tourism Woolridge has submitted that "Bermuda's tourism industry cannot expand indefinitely, and is probably close to reaching saturation point." A capacity study was instituted in 1981 to see just how many visitors the tourist superstructure could tolerate. "We are cognizant of the fact that we would be endangering the uniqueness of our product if we outstrip our ability to provide our services," said Mr. Woolridge.

An 8½-month season with this high an influx of tourists would make most destination-area warm weather islands content for the entire year. Bermuda, unfortunately, cannot afford to ignore the off-season. A militant and demanding union seeks year-round income for its members. Taxi drivers, shop owners, boat crews and others find meager employment during this time. Many services on the island come to a near standstill, and without off-season business airline service would virtually cease. All parties in Bermuda agree that Bermuda must develop its off-season business. The Department of Tourism was given that responsibility.

Rendezvous Time

The Bermuda off-season, December 1 to March 15, was officially designated as Rendezvous Time in 1960. The Department of Tourism initiated a marketing campaign to establish this period of the year as the time to "come back to Bermuda." Tangentially, of course, it was hoped that many others would come to Bermuda for the first time and become part of the later "rendezvous."

Why should the tourist come to Bermuda during Rendezvous Time? Although the mean temperatures are in the 60s, occasionally dipping into the 50s, these temperatures are moderate compared to 10 degrees in the northeast United States. Hotel rates are lower; stores, restaurants, streets, highways, golf courses, and tennis courts are uncrowded; and service is better because people have more time. In fact, the whole island is more relaxed, casual and friendly; the unhurried, uncrowded, low-key atmosphere has been found to be important to significant segments of international travelers.

Rendezvous Time is unique for other reasons. The Department of Tourism spends $25,000 just to provide featured events every day of the week (Monday, a guided tour of historic St. George's, Tuesday, Market Day Exhibition with Bermudian artisans and free English draught beer; and so forth). The Bermuda Festival of the Peforming Arts, initiated in 1975, presents five weeks of classical entertainment by featured artists during January and February. Considerable effort is made in these ways and others to make Rendezvous Time an attractive alternative to the summer edition of Bermuda.

Rendezvous Time has been heavily promoted by the Department of Tourism, and has led to repeat business during the off-season. In fact, Rendezvous Time has more repeat customers than the rest of the year; however, it should be noted that these visitors are older and less affluent than those who come during the summer.

Although Rendezvous Time is considered a success, the program has changed over the years, and this change hasn't gone unnoticed by visitors. Occupancy rates on the island have failed to hold up, as shown in Table 1. One smaller operator reports that he *must* achieve 95 percent occupancy during the in-season to offset his $50,000 to $60,000 a-month losses in the off-season. There is a scramble for small group business, and special promotions aim at filling more of the rooms. Most seriously, there appears to be a sense of resignation. Special events, promoted diligently by the Department of Tourism, seem largely cosmetic and are performed with less than enthusiasm by the participants. Hotel staffs now seem lethargic and lackadasical; the feeling that "it's the slow season, what can we do?" is expressed both verbally and kinesthetically. "After all," say some, "we couldn't sell all our rooms anyhow; this is the time of year we have to renovate."

TABLE 1
RENDEZVOUS SEASON HOTEL OCCUPANCY RATES, 1976-1981

Month	1976	1977	1978	1979	1980	1981	1982
January	29.4%	29.0%	13.9%[a]	25.0%	25.6%	27.2%	17.1%
February	59.8	54.2	44.1	43.9	51.2	40.8	30.0
December	38.1	24.6	27.9	32.7	34.2	24.4	

[a]*January, 1978 was affected by a union walkout.*
Source: Bermuda Hotel Association

Renovation Time

Rendezvous Time today could well be subtitled Renovation Time. "Closed for renovation" signs proliferate, although in some cases, there is not renovation going on; establishment owners simply feel that it doesn't pay to stay open. The tourist who has been lured to the island with the promise of the "whole" Bermuda at lower rates finds that Rendezvous Time is full of many unfulfilled promises, including some made even after arrival.

Unfulfilled promises, which occur when reality does not meet expectations, lead to dissatisfaction and have a deleterious effect on the sale of any product. When actual outcomes of a vacation in Bermuda are judged by a buyer to be at least equal to those expected, the buyer will be satisfied. Satisfaction results when, as Howard and Sheth (1969) have pointed out, "actual consequences are greater than or equal to expected consequences. If, on the other hand, he adjudges the actual outcomes to be less than what is expected, the buyer will feel dissatisfied; that is, actual consequences are less than expected consequences. If the brand [Bermuda] proves more satisfactory than he expected, the buyer has a tendency to enhance the attractiveness of the brand. If it proves less satisfactory than he expected, he is likely to diminish its attractiveness."

The diminished attractiveness will most probably result in a diminished likelihood of the visitor returning to Bermuda, or referring it to a friend.

What is happening in Bermuda, then, is a familiar problem. The hotels say they cannot afford to maintain full facilities because there are not enough tourists, but no one tells this to the tourists, who come full of expectations. When expectations are unfulfilled the tourists not only do not come back, they also tell friends back home of their unsatisfactory experience. The Department of Tourism promotes Rendezvous Time for the benefit of all, especially the hotels, but the tourism industry is not cooperating to maximize the effect of the program. Hotels frequently fail to give their guests the information on special events that have been carefully arranged by the Department, and they continue to advertise features that are not actually offered at this time of year.[1]

What *does* the tourist get for his money during Rendezvous Time? At one time hotel lounges featured a different native act every night. For those who wanted it there were dine-around privileges at other hotels; lunch and drinks were served at the beach, in fact, all restaurants, boats and other facilities on the island were open and available.

Today much less activity is available. One of the largest and most expensive hotels serves as an example of what is happening all over the island. This hotel advertises, "Have lunch at our Beach Club on a spacious terrace overlooking the sea." When one arrives at the Beach Club there is a well-worn sign announcing "closed for renovations," but there is no sign of anything being renovated. Similarly the tourist is invited to "enjoy a late snack in the coffee shop," which is, according to the cocktail waitress, the lobby porter,

---

[1]It should be noted that this problem is not unique to Bermuda. Palm Springs, California advertises to attract summer visitors but is by-and-large closed down when they get there. Vermont winter resort areas promote summer traffic but many attractions are in operation only sporadically. Many hotels around the world spend hundreds of thousands of dollars to develop slow periods but also are renovating their public facilities during those times. The problem is worldwide and industrywide. Bermuda is only a single example.

the front desk and the sign on the door, open until 1:30 a.m. However, at the coffee shop door at 1:00 a.m. one is told "we always close at 12:30 in the winter." The new Wine Cellar — billed as "a uniquely designed lounge built in and around one of the world's largest hotel wine cellars" is closed. "Top name local entertainment and international stars" are advertised for the Empire Room; the Empire Room is closed. Even the lobby restrooms are "closed for renovations."

Around the island itself, widely advertised island cruises do not operate. At least one golf course (uncrowded) charges $54.00 for two with cart. The native Calypso music, advertised year-round on the full front page in *Bermuda Weekly*, is not available. These features and more are promoted regularly in the monthly *Bermudian*, the weekly *This Week in Bermuda* and *Bermuda Weekly*, and the seasonal *Bermuda Today* publications, as well as in brochures and mainland hotel advertising. In fact, the monthly *Bermudian* proclaims that "Bermuda Rendezvous is bigger and better than ever." It is obvious, however, that Bermuda Rendezvous is dying, and one suspects that the Bermuda tourist industry is killing it.

Reappraisal Time

Image development is a major factor in tourism development. In Bermuda, the off-season image currently seems to be one of a destination which is always under renovation and full of inconveniences and unavailable pleasures. Even more critically, this negative rendezvous image may overflow into the main season and affect the image of Bermuda for the balance of the year.

Bennett and Kassarjian point out that "other things being equal, things near each other tend to be perceived as belonging together." Rendezvous Time in Bermuda would likely be perceived by many to be proximate to other Bermuda vacation times in a perceptual mapping. The concept of generalization in learning theory further supports the probability that Rendezvous Time may overflow its boundaries. This concept invokes the notion that consumers tend to respond to a new situation (another Rendezvous Time or another vacation time of the year) the way they did to similar past situations (a previous Rendezvous Time vacation in Bermuda). As Mayo contends, "Whether or not an image is, in fact, a true representation of what any given region has to offer the tourist, what is important is the image that exists in the mind of the vacationer."

Katona theorizes that market behavior is largely a reaction to the actions taken by industry management, and industry management's actions are largely in response to their perception of what the market behavior will be at a given point in time. In the Bermuda case, management's perception is that business will be slow and normal service levels will be unnecessary, thus facilitating closings and renovation. Customers who patronize the property/ island in the off-season then experience dissatisfaction and cognitive dissonance. They leave; many do not return and, worse, advise their friends of the problems they experienced. Perceptions and subsequent actions thus cause the perceptions to become reality. Support for this theory is provided by the figures previously presented in Table 1.

The Tourists' Viewpoint and Advice to the Industry

Why should the tourist come to Bermuda for Rendezvous Time? One of the greatest incentives to visit a resort destination area in off-season is, of course, lower rates. How much lower are hotel rates in Bermuda at this time? About 10 percent, according to the Department of Tourism (smaller hotels lower rates by about 20 percent). Other rates — golf fees, tennis courts, drinks, cover charges — remain unchanged from the summer.

So, for a 10-20 percent reduction in room rates and somewhat lower air fare, the Rendezvous Time tourist gets 60-degree weather and half an island that is relaxed, casual and friendly. For many this is satisfactory and they come back year after year. But to concentrate on this small market segment is to ignore the vast potential of another market that wants to see Bermuda at its best — as it is promoted. Hotels which operate as they now do and expect to fill their rooms at the same time ignore the basic marketing concept: the needs and wants of the consumer must be fulfilled. Worse, failure to meet expectations is the poorest marketing practice of all in an industry so dependent on word-of-mouth promotion. Selling travel agents is a tactic, not a strategic maneuver.

The tourist industry in Bermuda should work hand-in-hand with the Department of Tourism rather than looking at it as an administrative function. Joint marketing, joint promotion, joint advertising and a guarantee that one will carry out the promises of the other are basic to the systems concepts of marketing. Given a geographic setting of only 22 square miles, it is hard to imagine groups of convergent interest not working hand-in-hand; furthermore, Bermuda law, unlike that in the United States, permits industry collaboration.

If a hotel needs a major renovation that will disturb the entire patronage it should close down. Without the interference of guests and staff, this work can be concentrated in a shorter time period and be finished sooner, and without alienating anyone. Minor renovations can be restricted to closed-off areas where guests will be unaware of them. If public rooms have to close because of renovation or minimal patronage, guests should be so advised and alternatives should be offered. *All* employees should be made aware of any curtailment of facilities so they can pass this information on to guests.

Hotels can take turns offering the features a guest expects. One of the beauties of Bermuda is the ease of getting around the island. One or more hotels at a time can provide features the island advertising promises and the hotels can alternately share in this patronage. Advertising should be truthful and current, both on and off the island; it should be changed to show what the island really offers at each time of year. Rendezvous Time should be promoted for what it is — a different Bermuda.

Since curtailed services mean the guest gets less, the guest should also pay less. Consumers want what they pay for, and they want to know what they are paying for. Lower prices can provide great vacation incentives and encourage the vacationers to overlook other failings in today's economy.

Hotels and restaurants should cooperate and collaborate not only with each other but also with the Department of Tourism. They should remember that the product is an entire island, not just a hotel or restaurant, and if the island as a whole doesn't deliver then all businesses suffer. Some facilities may need to operate temporarily at a loss until tourists discover, once again, that Bermuda *is* a bargain at Rendezvous Time.

Chapter 12

Cancun: A Study of Planned Resort Development

Virginia K. Bessert, CTC *Former Researcher,*
Institute of Certified Travel Agents

Tourists murdered in a racially tense Caribbean; the loveliest beaches of Spain turned to "concrete jungles"; ancient revered tribal rites now performed daily for tourists for pay; sewage dumped in waters off Italy thought to be origin of cholera epidemic; charter planeloads of people turned back from Waikiki as a result of overbooking: troubles in the world of tourism. Increase in travel's popularity leads to conditions that diminish its attractiveness.

Tourism means contact with people from other places; such contact usually means change, and not always for the better. Tourism can be a spoiler of the environment, of quiet solitude, of cultural and social patterns, of people, of relations between races or between nations. Land values inflate; prices are pushed up by the presence of tourists. Internal conflicts are spotlighted.

At its best, however, tourism is a source of great enjoyment for the traveler, an opportunity to see other cultures and life-styles and perhaps to understand them better. The tourist has the chance to be an ambassador of goodwill.

In addition, money from tourism can raise the standard of living for poor people in underdeveloped areas by providing jobs and injecting outside money into their economy. Tourism uses lands not truly necessary for supporting the life of the local population, such as seashores and mountain trails. As tourism brings improved economic conditions, the local population will live a better life with more comforts.

Planning Resorts

How to avoid tourism's pitfalls and take advantage of the benefits is the question. The answer is planning.

Planned resort development, which is new to the world of tourism, represents its best hope for the future. The idea is to observe past failures and foresee future problems and then to avoid both, thus creating a truly quality product.

Steps[1] in planning a resort are to:

1. Determine the target market.

2. Discover the vacation desires of that market.

3. Inventory available attractions, natural setting, facilities, distance from target market, accessibility.

4. Consider the needs of the country and its people (are there economically depressed areas into which tourism could bring a better life?).

5. Identify problems and include solutions (example: tourists will not come if they fear sickness — water purification and sewage systems are the answers).

6. Make a master plan for development.

The master plan should prepare the region for tourists before they arrive. Such a plan should:

1. Estimate tourist traffic.

2. Design infrastructure sufficient to support the expected traffic.

3. Set standards for style and structure, number, and spacing of hotels.

4. Define, maintain, and stress the area's unique features: food, art, ancient monuments, dance, costume.

5. Maintain control of publicity/marketing campaign.

6. Arrange sale of land and oversee construction on it.

7. Provide regular periodic quality examinations.

8. Make credit available to private investors and offer inducements to interest investors.

[1]Robert W. McIntosh, *Tourism Principles, Practices and Philosophies* (Cleveland: Grid, Inc., 1972) and Study and Reading Guide: "International Travel and Tourism" (East Lansing, Mich.: 1972).

Either a government or a single owner should control resort development. They alone possess sufficient authority to demand compliance with a master plan. (An example of a single-owner-directed project is Walt Disney World.)

The government should build and pay for the basic infrastructure of roads, airport, and utilities needed for the hotels. Then, it will be easier to encourage private investors to build the superstructure of hotels.

Cancun

Mexico today is in the forefront of planned development. The star of the show is Project Cancun on the Mexican Caribbean.

A tiny island off the tip of the Yucatan, Cancun is in the state of Quintana Roo. In 1967, when Mexico began the search for a resort site, Quintana Roo was still a territory, administered from the Federal District. It was a poor region with only a little agriculture and fishing. Resorts existed on Isla Mujeres and Cozumel, but nothing on the mainland. The gateway airport at Merida was more than four hours away by car. The mainland population around Cancun was 117. The island itself was uninhabited.

Today, Cancun has a $10 million jetport, a bridge to the mainland, a new highway to Chichen Itza and Merida, ultra-modern hotels, and tap water that is safe to drink. The permanent population of Cancun City on the mainland is expected to reach 70,000 with one million tourists a year.

How was this transformation achieved?

In 1967, recognizing tourism as the most important source of foreign exchange and a potential employer in economically underdeveloped areas, Mexico began a two-year study to select sites for resort development. The search included market studies and on-the-spot examination of the country's entire coastline.

When all the data had been analyzed by the computer, the name Cancun was printed out as the chosen spot. Surprised researchers had to consult the map to see where it was!

Though previously unknown, Cancun indeed seemed ideal. Closer to the United States than any Caribbean area except the Bahamas, it had pure white sand beaches, mean temperature of 82°, and over 240 days of sunshine a year.[2] Since sun and sand were resort features tourists said they wanted, Cancun should have great appeal.

Quintana Roo would benefit economically from the presence of the resort since Cancun would provide many jobs in construction and later in the tourist industry.

Site selection was followed by three other important government actions: the Presidential Resolution of April 30, 1970; the Tourist Industry

[2]Cancun Information Bureau, "Cancun" (New York: 1973, 1974, 1975, 1976).

Development Law; and the establishment of FONATUR.[3]

The objective of the Presidential Resolution of April 30, 1970, was promotion of tourism and industrial development in coastal and border areas. It granted foreigners the right to use and derive the benefit from such land without owning it. Mexican Trust Institutions would purchase property and hold it in trust for up to thirty years with foreign investors as beneficiaries. The investors would have the right to live on the land, build on it, rent it, take any profits from it. After thirty years, the land would be sold to another trust or to a Mexican national. This was the first time coastal lands had been available to foreigners.

The January 1974 Tourist Industry Development Law affirmed the Federal Government's intention to unify authority for planning tourism development and to coordinate actions of various government agencies then involved with tourism. To implement this law, the government on April 16, 1974, created FONATUR, The National Fund for Tourism Development, consolidating several previous agencies into this one superagency. FONATUR's assignment was to encourage private investment in tourist projects and to develop new tourist centers. It was responsible for creating and implementing a master plan for Cancun.

Cancun's construction was planned in three stages. The first stage covered completion of the basic infrastructure (airport, highways, streets) and about 2,000 hotel rooms, plus the support town of Cancun City. Phase Two comes after about seven years of operation at Cancun and adds another 2,000 rooms. After fifteen to twenty years, Phase Three will begin, designed to bring the hotel room count to a total of 10,000.

FONATUR's master plan prescribed safeguards for the ecology and the Mayan heritage. It created a bird sanctuary on the island and carefully preserved any temples or other artifacts unearthed during construction.

With help from the Inter American Development Bank, the government paid for the entire basic infrastructure. This was built with an eye to the future so it would continue to sustain the growing resort.

Cancun City was built for the permanent population. At first, only construction workers lived there, and they did not make a permanent move to Cancun. However, it was expected that more people would move to Cancun City once the resort was in operation. Houses, schools, a clinic, and a market were built.

The resort was promoted through the Cancun Information Bureau in New York. Almost overnight, Cancun moved from obscurity to being a household word in the travel industry. The campaign was very thorough, but alas, too soon.

The resort was still a construction camp when the first tourists arrived.

[3]*Ibid.*

They found elevators that failed to function, staff untrained, room service unavailable, the beach road still unpaved, and noise and dust in abundance. In spite of these problems, hotels were charging $40 to $60 per day for a room — too much money for the value received. At last, Mexico advised the travel industry to wait a while before sending clients to Cancun.

Meantime, language classes and training courses were being conducted for service personnel of the hotels. Agricultural experts taught Yucatecans to grow products needed by the resort. Pest control eliminated the mosquitoes. All land was sold, and buyers had to begin construction at once. This provision was to keep out land speculators.

The island was zoned into hotel, residential, and commercial districts. In most early construction, the government was a partner, but later projects were financed almost entirely by private capital. Government approval was required on all projects for style and structure (for example, no signs were permitted). Use of Mexican technicians and local materials was encouraged.

This careful approach will make Cancun a resort planned by Mexicans to benefit Mexico and its people, even as it provides great pleasure for its visitors, Mexican and foreign.

A Visit to Cancun

In October 1974, I went to see Cancun. It was a tremendously exciting experience. One hotel was completely open, another partially; the rest of the island was under construction. The airport was of sufficient size to accommodate a 747, but the "terminal" was a thatched roof hut!

I had a feeling of being on the moon, so isolated was Cancun; there was not even any phone service. It was pitch dark by 6:00 P.M. Endless green jungle-like growth stretched away to the west, the blue Caribbean to the east. Constant wind rattled the palms, and mosquitoes came in if the balcony door was left open.

What a place! I gasped at the courage of such an undertaking: to start from absolute zero and build an entire resort. I had never seen so much construction, so many bulldozers. Sewer pipes and pieces of pre-fab dwellings were piled high. Men worked twenty-four hours a day, working under lights during the night. It was said there was not a sack of cement or a construction worker to be found in Merida — all were at Cancun. Wages on the project were much higher than anywhere else in the Yucatan.

The beaches were gorgeous and empty. Mayan children played on Chac Mool Beach, their profiles just like those of the temple carvings, as the tour brochures had promised.

The dirt road along the island had the biggest ruts I had ever seen. The station wagon jounced and bounced as we went from one hotel site to the next. It was the first time I had done a hotel inspection in a hard hat!

A representative of the Aristos hotel chain spoke of conventions and charter movements while a tanned workman pushed a wheelbarrow through a nonexistent "wall." Cancun was full of such contrasts. At Camino Real, we clambered over boards and nails along barren hallways only to open the door of a totally finished and furnished bedroom with pictures on the walls and spreads on the beds: a display bedroom. Later, when I saw the pictures of this room in promotional literature, I laughed to think of the piles of metal rods outside its door and the workmen hammering in the next room.

So much to do yet, but the view from the glassless windows was of the brilliant blue sea, cloudless sky, pure white sand, and glorious sunshine. Who could doubt Cancun's success when in such surroundings? Who could fault the promoters for their enthusiasm, premature as it was?

Statistics rolled easily off the tongues of construction foremen, hotel managers, tour company reps: "5,000 workers on an island 14 miles long and only ¼ mile wide"; "Two years ago there was nothing here"; "117 people here in the area"; "$100 million has been committed to the project"; "Two more hotels opening next month—already full!" The excitement was contagious.

To see Cancun at its birth was to be filled with hope: for Cancun, for the travel industry, for other tourist areas that might benefit from this striking example.

Other Planned Tourist Destinations

Can other areas follow Cancun's example? Many have taken steps in that direction. October 1973 saw the First International Conference on the Relationship between Tourism and the Environment of the Baja California Peninsula make recommendations to the Mexican Government. Conference participants stressed the importance of a comprehensive plan for development of Baja under which unplanned construction would be prohibited and respect for prevailing architectural styles required. The conference said that a system of ecological preserves along the coast would give pleasure to both tourists and local residents. Concern for the ecology and for archeological and historical sites increased after the completion of the Transpeninsular Highway. An education campaign was suggested to impress tourists with the need to safeguard the Baja's fragile environment.[4]

Representatives from South Pacific nations meeting early in 1976 for a conference on "The Social and Economic Impact of Tourism on Pacific Communities" expressed the opinion that tourism can hurt the very people

[4]Proceedings from the First International Conference on the Relationship Between Tourism and the Environment of the Baja California Peninsula," Sea Grant Program, University of Southern California, 1973.

it is supposedly helping.[5] They sought to place responsibility for this situation and then to ask those people responsible to help correct the situation. All representatives felt that governments should do more to build sound economies and reverse the dependency on tourism. Outsiders have done most of the developing in the Pacific and have taken their profits out. Zoning, restrictions on building height and size, protection for cultural sites — these and other measures will help make tourism fit the people's needs instead of the people's having to adjust to tourism's needs.

Also in the Pacific, PATA has authorized a study of Moen in Micronesia to determine tourism's value to the island, which would have to import so many products in order to sustain the industry.[6] Such questioning of tourism's worth is new.

Governments in other tourist regions are taking steps to stop the proliferation of hotels by requiring building permits. Hotel building must now conform to government specifications in Bali, Jamaica, and Cayman. The Cayman Islands issue building permits only when a definite need for more rooms has been demonstrated. The Tourist Office stresses that bigger is not always better.

Hawaii's state government has placed a moratorium on development in Waikiki and has restrictions on building height on the outer islands. Developers complain that investment in a four-story hotel is not economically justifiable; that only an eight-story one will do. At present, the state of Hawaii is standing firm. Its publication "Growth Policies Plan: 1974-1984"[7] discusses many alternatives for the future. There are no easy answers to the many thought-provoking questions. Hawaii would like to lessen its dependence on tourism as a source of revenue, pointing out that this position leaves the state vulnerable to economic downturns in countries such as Japan, which sends many tourists to Hawaii. Also, the hope is for better distribuiton of jobs and people throughout the islands instead of such a heavy proportion on Oahu. For Hawaii today, controlled growth means slowed growth, and there is much opposition to the government rulings. Money talks so loudly that it is hard to resist. "More jobs," argue the developers. "Better income, increased sources of government tax revenues — let us continue to build." The state hopes that its course will lead in the long run to the maintenance of the status of sought-after tourist destination, its unique beauty and culture preserved.

[5]S.R. Wilson, "Tourism in Pacific Hurts the People It Helps," *Travel Agent* (March 22, 1976) pp. 90-93.
[6]"PATA to Study Economic Impact of Tourism at Moen," *Travel Agent* (February 23, 1976) p. 84.
[7]"State of Hawaii Growth Policies Plan: 1974-1984," Hawaii Department of Planning and Economic Development, Honolulu, 1974.

Conclusion

Planned resort development will not be easy. However, starting it now may be simpler than trying to correct out-of-control situations in the future.

In such efforts, Cancun can serve as a model for other developers. It represents enthusiasm and effort at all levels: government, local people, private investors, construction companies, hotel chains, airlines, and the travel industry in general. The important feature of its development is that this effort was channeled in the desired direction by the government's master plan so that all participants worked for the same goal. Tourists, Mexicans, and the travel industry will continue to benefit from this resort in the future because it was planned today.

Chapter 13
Marketing the Magic Kingdom

Thomas R. Elrod
Vice President,
Marketing,
Walt Disney World

As Vice President of Marketing for Walt Disney World, Thomas Elrod is responsible for all Marketing Division functions including advertising, promotion, publicity, public relations, special events, and an in-house creative team. Prior to joining Walt Disney World, he was Public Relations Director for the Amateur Athletic Union (A.A.U.) of the United States. He is also a former television newscaster from WKBN-TV, Youngstown, Ohio, and WLWI-TV, Indianapolis.

In 1923, an ambitious, energetic young man from Marceline, Missouri began entertaining people for a living by showing them humorous cartoon strips of his newly developed character, Mortimer Mouse. Little did he realize the enormous ramifications he and his animated friend would have on entertaining people the world over, and little did he know what far-reaching vision and insight he would also have on the world of marketing.

The gentleman's name was Walt Disney. His Mortimer Mouse was renamed Mickey, and together they embarked on a dream that took them from simply drawn cartoon strips to technological achievements in entertainment that perhaps they didn't even visualize (though I doubt it). They created an organization, The Walt Disney Company, that has become a remarkable form of marketing synergy and has emerged as a tremendously successful and highly emulated organization.

To understand this marketing synergy is to document Disney's corporate history. For through it all, the underlying concept Walt seemed to have was an organization not only as diverse and unique in the entertainment business as his mind would uncover, but one that also relied on its individual components to form the spokes of a wheel that could take it down the road on the path to success.

Walt traveled this plan starting with cartoon strips then moving to talking cartoons (the world's first in 1927). From there he moved on to full-length animated feature films (*Snow White and the Seven Dwarfs* in 1937). Once characters could be made to actually move and talk and sing, why not take them to a place where they could live and breathe in their own happy environment? Disneyland. As long as people could be happy in a clean, wholesome environment for an enjoyable day, why not provide an environment, where they could spend their entire vacation, of a size that could contain the space needed to travel to every dream they ever had? Enter Walt Disney World.

Along the way, not coincidentally, would come other forms of entertainment that from the same germ of an idea (craftily concealed as a mouse) begot businesses of their own — books, records, and toys to name just a few. Ideas that formed concepts that today have become essential ingredients in Disney and many other companies' marketing formulas also arose: licensing, corporate sponsors, training, and quality assurance among others.

And, within time, forms of communication emerged that opened up exciting new vehicles not only to entertain but to market as well: television, cable, video cassettes, and satellites.

This corporate evolution has formed the basis for Disney's marketing philosophy, which has become one of the most successful in the world. The synergy with which Disney is able to sell its own components makes the marketing task both easier to understand and more readily accepted by the consumer. Television shows promote the parks; the parks promote the characters; the characters promote merchandise; all three promote the Disney name which, in turn, promotes them all. It is this tactic, coupled with the resolute conviction to offer a unique menu of quality shows, high employee motivation, and marketing that have made its theme parks — Disneyland, Walt Disney World, Tokyo Disneyland, and (soon) a European Disneyland — the most popular vacation destinations in the world.

The offshoot approach that Disney has to marketing Walt Disney World is to adhere to the corporate philosophy of providing "the finest in family entertainment" by doing so in a vast setting of 27,400 acres of beautiful land in sunny central Florida. Here an environment has been created that provides for all facets of a family vacation — hotels, campgrounds, lakes, swimming pools, shopping villages, golf courses, tennis courts, boating, biking, nature trails, and fishing. All are adornments of the crown jewels, the Magic Kingdom and Epcot Center.

It is within this carefully planned environment that Disney guests (not customers) are entertained, communicated with, and even controlled with the intent of providing them with the finest and most unique vacation experience possible, all at a good value.

Interestingly enough, the setting works so well, is so operationally efficient that it has become a model for cities, planned communities, world's fairs, and the like to emulate.

The prestigious Urban Land Institute has given Walt Disney World its award of excellence. Architects, planners, and the like are singular in their praise. Network television commentator David Brinkley perhaps summed it up best, though, when he remarked to viewers across the country after his first visit, "When you look around at this new town they have built here in central Florida . . . it's the most imaginative and most effective piece of urban planning in America. We all remember seeing, years ago, those slick futuristic drawings saying what the future of the American city was going to be . . . well, this is the future and none of it has happened. Nobody has done it but Disney."

It is this kind of public praise and the company's adherence to strong convictions for the quality of its product that have given Disney such an incredible reputation in the marketplace. It is accepted, respected, first-class, and as American as apple pie. It's no Mickey Mouse operation. It's Disney.

Vacationers come to Disney from near and far. Though the primary originations are from states east of the Mississippi River, guests visit from every state in the Union and dozens of foreign countries to enjoy the unique form of Disney entertainment that appeals to young and old. Disney appeals to oldsters? Quite right. Adults outnumber kids by a hefty four to one ratio. And whether they're three or ninety-three, there are activities and programs and amenities available that make a stay at Walt Disney World a unique vacation experience, not just a day's visit to a kiddie park, as doubters might think.

Why they come has less to do with the warm Florida sunshine and vacation amenities than the wonderful components of our two theme parks. Without question, Florida's sunny weather and beaches make for an outstanding home base that itself draws millions of tourists each year, but Disney in itself is a destination and as a result its competitors are geographic — the Caribbean Islands, vacations in the West, Europe, and the like.

A visit to Walt Disney World seems to have all-American appeal for all Americans, too. At this writing, more than 230 million visits have been made since the opening in October 1971 at, amazingly enough, virtually the same percentage penetration in each market across the country. Both the Magic Kingdom and Epcot Center provide the ultimate in entertainment experiences that aren't duplicated anywhere else in the world.

The quality of the showmanship in each and every ride, attraction, and film is inherent in the Disney tradition of outstanding performances. Whether your personal favorite is the exciting Space Mountain Ride in Tomorrowland or risking the tumultuous waters of the Jungle Cruise in Adventureland or whether it is watching the extraordinary 360° film in Epcot's China Pavilion or taking a ride through history on Spaceship Earth in Future World, guests are entertained and (horrors!) subconsciously educated in a way totally inherent to Disney.

This entertainment occurs in an environment that is probably as far removed from guests' normal confines as any place they've ever been. Not coincidentally, the two reasons for this are also the primary comments guests make when commenting on their visits: the place was clean, exceptionally so, and the people were helpful and friendly — characteristics hardly indigenous to most hometowns.

The park's cleanliness is no by-product. It is a conscientious effort that all employees take pride in participating in. Streets and sidewalks are squeaky clean, hosed down every night. If they see a scrap of discarded paper, they pick it up. Attractions are rehabbed, cleaned, and painted on a regular basis. Flower gardens are meticulously groomed. It becomes a different world. The employees are as well groomed as the gardens. No long hair or mustaches are allowed. No excessive makeup or jewelry. Employees both look and act the part of friendly, helpful members of the cast, each of whom continually attends the Disney University for stimulating and inspirational programs designed to educate and motivate them into better understanding the company's philosophy of doing business and giving them a sense of their importance in it.

We're in show business and you're all a part of the show. Our cast is on stage and performing in front of thousands of guests each day. We are portraying the true Disney image and that's what makes our performance the best around.

It may seem a bit odd that a marketer would spend this much time touting the quality of the product and its employees instead of his or her own programs and strategies. It's difficult to overemphasize the importance we place on the quality product we have to offer. The Disney people and the quality show that is put on every day are the reasons guests visit. As marketers, we capitalize on the outstanding opportunities a company with such a wonderful worldwide reputation has. It is this attention to quality and unique product that people appreciate and talk about to their friends, neighbors, and relatives.

It's tough to admit, but word of mouth is perhaps our most important marketing tool. Word of mouth extends not just to the quality of the product but to price/value relationships as well. The public will pay for quality. It's as simple as that. This isn't to say that Disney can overprice its product, that there is an unlimited elasticity in pricing for a rather captive market once it's arrived. We constantly examine this issue through regular price/value guest surveying, which confirms (as do our attendance figures) that though we are more expensive than other parks, people are willing to pay for the outstanding value they receive from their visits.

The Disney philosophy manifests itself in the marketing arena. We pride ourselves in creating programs that are done right or not done at all — campaigns consistent with the Disney image and efforts that rely on the synergistic approach. Both capitalize on and utilize the respected Disney name.

The Walt Disney World marketing program is accomplished by an all in-house effort that has as its continuing objective three goals: attendance,

attendance, and attendance (not necessarily in that order!). With more than 23 million visits made a year and increasingly ambitious annual attendance goals, Walt Disney World is a high volume business that relies on marketing activities that can generate large numbers of guests, literally thousands with each.

We recognize that the appeal of a Disney vacation is primarily focused on the two theme parks; so, while our responsibility covers the marketing of all of the property (hotels, restaurants, shops, and the like), we concentrate our programs to emphasize the parks, highlighting the fact that we are a total vacation destination.

Two primary markets exist: tourists and residents of Florida. Roughly three-fourths of our business comes from the tourist market; thus, that portion of time and budget is allocated to tourists. Still, a good deal of emphasis is placed on the state of Florida through a myriad of special events and programs that Floridians are offered.

Within the tourist and resident market evolve two categories: the family market and the nonfamily market (that is, those that don't visit with children). Each of these categories is subdivided to determine the time of the year they visit, which differs significantly from fall to winter to spring break to summer.

Of primary importance is when vacation decisions are being contemplated. As a result, a good deal of research is done to determine this and then consequently to position our marketing programs around these time periods. An exact science this isn't. Even the past few years have seen a considerable lessening of the time people take between when they're thinking about taking a vacation and when they actually do. Nevertheless, we must concern ourselves with this timing issue because it is of paramount importance to be in the marketplace when prospective customers are ready for us to be.

The most important criteria we feel we must contend with in generating attendance, ironically, are the uncontrollables, those elements that make or break consumer decisions concerning disposable income: general economic conditions, the price of fuel and airfare, the weather, the relative value of the U.S. dollar against foreign currencies, and international political situations.

Certain of these uncontrollables are unique to tourism and certain others are inherent in any business; regardless, they are factors we must contend with regularly. Their positive or negative aspects can drastically alter the course of a business like tourism that so depends on a positive environment to be successful.

The Walt Disney World marketing division is an in-house team of some 200 talented individuals who departmentalize into specific marketing functions that contribute to the overall success of a campaign or program. Five line departments are advertising, promotions, publicity, public relations, and group services. Each is assisted by an in-house creative team.

Advertising, Promotions, and Publicity

This department has the responsibility of planning, budgeting, placing, and creating media designed to both motivate and communicate to either prospective or potential guests at their point of origin, en route, or even while on our property. They perform this with the able assistance of an agency, Young and Rubicam, which helps plan and buy our national media.

Advertising is perhaps the most recently changed department in marketing in that we have only been a utilizer of paid media on a national basis for the past three years. Prior to that, we had no national media budget. In fact, in 1971, Walt Disney World originally opened (and was extremely successful) and in 1982 Epcot Center opened with no advertising! Disney relied on various publicity, promotional, and third-party efforts as its mainstay marketing efforts. What other product can you name with such sizeable investment that had no ad budget? We recently determined that despite our success without it, paid media advertising programs can be efficient and effective in generating incremental attendance above and beyond what our other programs did and can do.

The advertising area encompasses three unique categories. First, the paid national media we use is usually in the spot television category where a brand development index is determined for each of our top 100 attendance markets. This index gives us a formula to determine where to best spend our money. This index combines attendance history from a market, cost of media, proximity, and economic conditions to determine markets with the greatest attendance potential. Utilizing such creative handles as "Together at Disney" and "The World's Greatest Resort" and "This Is the Year to See the World," television spots are aimed separately at the family and nonfamily markets within flighted campaigns in specific markets during peak vacation decision-making times of the year.

Secondly, the ad area takes advantage of both the Disney name and our position as a primary geographic destination by offering other tourist-oriented advertisers (hotels, airlines, car rental agencies, and tourism bureaus) an opportunity to join us by buying ads in cooperative advertising programs, usually in newspapers and magazine sections. This multimillion dollar program affords us the right to be the dominant theme of highly visible multi-page ad vehicles that highlight many aspects of a Disney/Central Florida vacation that give us most of the exposure at a fraction of the total cost.

Advertising's responsibilities don't cease once the guests arrive at Walt Disney World. On any given day, the number of people staying and playing at all the various locales throughout the property can number 20,000 or more. People are hungry for information: where to go, what to see and do, what time, and how much it will cost. As a result, a sophisticated network of communication modules are employed to try to answer all these questions and, at the same time, motivate guests into experiencing as much as they can. These efforts can have an enormous impact on our individual businesses.

Two closed circuit television channels are used that creatively beam information into hotel room television sets. A low power radio station transmits information to drivers as they enter the property each day. A bimonthly newspaper is distributed. And literally hundreds of brochures, pamphlets, and the like are distributed to keep everybody in what is in effect a small city's population (that changes every week or so) abreast of what there is to see and do. Imagine a typical consumer goods marketer having the opportunity to communicate to purchasers in similar fashions throughout grocery or retail stores. A marketer's heaven!

As advertising's responsibility lies in the creation and placement of paid media, it is the promotions department's responsibility to achieve similar kinds of results on a free basis, something any marketer can relate to.

The media at large can be a tremendously effective source of exposure on a promotional basis because of the highly competitive nature of the business; everybody trying to outdo the other by stealing away readers, viewers, or listeners in order to win ratings games, which then dictate what advertisers will pay for their communication services. This ratings requirement and the opportunity to a television or radio station, local newspaper, or magazine to enhance its image by tying in with the Disney name enables us to conduct various forms of contests and sweepstakes for outlets to offer that feature all-expense-paid vacations to Walt Disney World in exchange for our receiving a required minimum amount of overall media exposure promoting the activity.

Hundreds of programs are developed where media outlets assist us and themselves (and their ratings) by taking part in these contests. Thousands of entries are generated. Consumers are excited at the possibility of winning. And Walt Disney World receives hundreds of thousands of dollars worth of media exposure.

Many times these promotions are expanded into target markets where the objective of intensively dominating a specified marketplace is enacted. In conjunction with the contest giveaway, a venerable Disney attack is launched; the Disney characters fly into towns (via our own corporate plane, the "Mickey Mouse," which many times alone garners media attention when it arrives) to visit local television talk shows, shopping malls, hospitals, and orphanages both to spread good will and, at the same time, gain attention in the local news.

Local retailers often tie in to the activity by becoming points of entry for the contest, and theming their stores as outlets for "Walt Disney World Days" at all their stores. In-store activities such as Disney character visits, Disney themed merchandise areas, cooking and sports demonstrations, Disney fashion shows, employee Disney themed costuming are all supported by advertising describing the events. At times, even special free concerts are offered that feature entire Disney entertainment troupes who come to town to perform. In all, what is created is uniquely ours — a marketplace that sees, reads, hears, and witnesses the magic of Disney.

Capitalizing on these media promotional opportunities doesn't just exist within the marketplace either. The appeal of the Disney product extends to our property as well. Most radio and television stations we work with remote broadcast from Walt Disney World, utilizing our own satellite uplink facility. Local disc jockeys, morning, noon, and evening newscasts, talk and variety shows are featured at sites throughout Walt Disney World, giving them a fantastic stage from which to broadcast as well as enticing their viewers to visit.

As the media world embraces the world of Disney, the corporate world does so as well.

The appeal of the name Disney can perhaps be no better demonstrated than by learning of the prestigious companies who pay for the rights to utilize it in their own marketing programs. General Motors, American Express, Coca-Cola, Exxon, Delta Airlines, Kraft, Kodak, AT&T, and dozens of others recognize the opportunities an association with Disney can mean for the success of their products. They sponsor attractions in the parks, become official purveyors for us, and develop various marketing programs of their own that highlight their Disney involvement.

What a tribute to the genius of Walt Disney; to have him recognize the opportunities available to a company like Disney whose high standards and reputation enable it to enact a unique program that motivates this country's most prestigious companies to pay for the right to utilize its name and then pay again to advertise the fact! It is a program that has been emulated by not only the theme park industry, but sports organizations, world's fairs, and the national media as well.

Broadcast media organizations distinctly separate themselves between the programming and news areas as print organizations divide themselves into coverage categories. As a result, the Disney publicity department separates itself from the promotions area, but has a similar objective: positive, free coverage of our product. Consequently, a team of publicists continually scours the Disney property and the world attempting to develop story angles for both us and outside journalists to capitalize on.

This is practiced in three ways. First, by hosting and accommodating the thousands of press representatives who annually visit Walt Disney World, on their personal vacations or on assignment; secondly, by visiting markets in an attempt to generate coverage and develop and renew media contacts; and finally, by creating our own stories.

Hosting and accommodating involves the obvious: giving press reps the time, attention, materials, and suggestions they need to produce a story on us, placing pre-prepared press kits, stories, pictures, and audio and video tapes at their disposal.

Traveling to marketplaces and generating coverage are, of course, different and more difficult tasks. Countless stories and pictures are unfolded by the publicity team that are then sent to organizations as an enticement for them to run. Perhaps it's Donald Duck's 50th birthday or the castle in the Magic Kingdom is being repainted or the thousands of unique clocks are all being turned back because of the seasonal time change. All constitute publicity angles. Maybe the frigid weather up north prompts us to send television weathercasters a tape of Goofy waterskiing that is personalized with their name saying "wish you were here." Or a photo is offered to newspapers that shows their local high school band performing in our parade. These and countless other examples produce publicity exposure for Disney that gives consumers a look at our product, which, we hope, gives them another thought about considering us for their vacation.

A name as recognizable and conveying as much magic as Disney signifies an obligation to uphold the image it has conceived in every possible manner, through the products it produces and from the value it offers to the way it is marketed. Understood, too, is the obligation the company has to its public at large, the community in which it lives, and helping those less fortunate.

Public Relations and Group Services

A department synonymous with the name Disney. An area whose responsibilities go hand-in-hand with the marketing task but are just as integrated with the entire Disney management philosophy.

Disney's public relations department permeates every aspect of the organization, but its specific functions deal with two general areas: community relations and government relations. What distinguishes it is its workings with the many communities it serves, for example, unusual corporate giving programs like community service awards, where annual cash gifts are given to hundreds of non-profit organizations by an independent group of outside judges, and Dreamers and Doers where school kids are honored for being not just the best, but the best all around.

Disney employees serve on hundreds of boards and organizations. There's even an independent board of employees which allocates funding for nonprofit organizations from proceeds generated by lost and found items.

Perhaps it is the in-kind giving that Disney does that is most beneficial to the company from a marketing standpoint. It serves to represent our company as the generous, concerned organization it is. Disney characters visit hundreds of hospitals and orphanages around the world each year with Mickey and friends, bringing smiles to kids who doctors tell us haven't smiled before or since. Hundreds of terminally ill children are granted their last wishes, quietly and inconspicuously, by visiting Walt Disney World.

It all serves as a reminder to us what a different role the company plays in a public relations vein than most other companies. What we have to offer of utmost importance isn't money, but human resources that bring goodwill and laughter throughout the world.

The various communities we serve offer a myriad of submarkets from which to offer special theme park events and activities, so much so that a special markets department is engaged to capitalize on all of them. This area identifies these opportunities, market segments, and then develops activities for them. Events include grad nites — all night graduation parties in the Magic Kingdom for thousands of graduating high school seniors, senior citizens' days, Armed Forces Month, and Salute to Floridians; all utilize special value ticket offerings during limited periods to potentially lucrative markets.

The most lucrative of all these segmented markets is one created by the Disney organization in the 1960s. It's called the *Magic Kingdom Club* and is a club set up through various company employee relations areas to offer employees special discounts on Disney products (tickets, merchandise, travel packages) as a company benefit.

Some 22,000 chapters of the club, representing an employee base of more than 47 million people are members of the Magic Kingdom Club and can pick up their free membership card at their place of employment.

Disney's benefit from the club is access to this vast employee population base. Through the employee discounts, employers take credit for providing a tangible company benefit. Like most good ideas, it sounds too simple to work. But it does, representing more than 30 percent of the guests who visit the parks annually.

To implement all of the programs described in these line areas effectively requires creativity and it is the *creative services* area that accomplishes this, which rounds out the marketing division. Artists, writers, still and video photographers are all on staff to provide the essential creative elements for ads, brochures, television commercials, radio spots, posters, pamphlets, and supplements that communicate the many programs to the public.

With the same attention to detail and high Disney standards, these creators communicate uniquely and effectively in order to stand out among the tremendous clutter of messages and madness so pervasive in today's marketplace. Not to do so negates any and every good idea conceived.

The task of marketing such a large and recognizable organization is an exciting one, perhaps because Disney is an ever-changing company with unlimited creative resources for new and exciting additions to the product. All that brings fresh opportunities to develop marketing programs around them.

Walt himself remarked, "You've got to keep changing the show," and we always have and will, with exciting new attractions to entice people to revisit us and, for those who never have, to do so. Walt also stated that Walt Disney World would never be finished but would rather "be in a constant state of changing" to provide the public with continual new reasons to visit. If there were a long-term plan for marketing Walt Disney World, it would be in the additions, events, and activities we're currently working on for the future.

I assume you will agree then that our little friend Mickey and his boss have certainly traveled a long way since they paired up. And at each stop they not only provided all of us with wonderful experiences and memories, but with many chapters in the business book of success. It's a book that can be read and applied by any individual or company, no matter what their product or service.

It's not even Disney's way. It's the right way.

Hospitality Marketing

ONE OF THE LARGEST SEGMENTS OF THE travel and tourism industry is the hospitality business. It is also one of the most visible. Not only do large hotels with well-known names like Hilton and Marriott dominate the skylines of all the major cities, but they are found on every interstate highway and in every major resort area.

There are more trade magazines, newsletters, and trade associations for hospitality businesses that disseminate information and marketing ideas than for any other segment dealt with in this book. Yet, as our first author suggests, while the hospitality business is the oldest profession, marketing is still regarded as a new concept and one that is not at all understood in many quarters.

Marketing policies for much of the hospitality field are synonymous with pricing policies. In too many marketing meetings, the only topics on the agenda are related to pricing: Shall we extend our summer season, offer a shoulder season rate, lower our group rates, or increase travel agent commissions?

As stated earlier, long ago marketers of package goods learned that price-off deals and couponing are the least satisfactory and the least profitable ways of competing for market share. To begin with, they are short-lived. When the promotion is over and prices go back up, the market share decreases. Secondly, they cut into margin. Smaller margins translate into smaller dollars available for marketing and distribution activities, and ultimately, a lower level of profit. Finally, pricing tactics are preemptable. A competitor can and often will preempt your low price with a lower one.

Better pricing strategies include those that focus on unique positioning, perceived or real value, strong sales programs, and promotional ideas that have staying power. For lodging enterprises these can be summed up as the four A's: advertising, accommodations, activities, and amenities.

All the authors I invited to contribute to this section have a clear understanding of real marketing principles and how they relate to the hospitality business.

Dr. Ron Nykiel is the author of an authoritative textbook in the field and a senior executive with a leading hotel chain. His article focuses on the evolution of market segmentation and segmentation strategy as it is currently practiced. Readers should note Nykiel's reference to externally driven forces and compare them with Robert Shulman's earlier article on life-style trends.

A key concept Nykiel introduces is product tiering. Earlier, the only focus in the business was on having as many different rates for the same room as you could manage. This yield management concept was pioneered by the airlines and is discussed by John Eichner and Whit Hawkins in the section on transportation marketing. With the advent of computerized reservation systems, many large chains use similar techniques to adjust available room rates whenever possible on a controlled capacity basis; however, the flexibility that hotels and motels have to customize their plants has allowed a much more sophisticated approach that emphasizes offering new products to achieve different price levels.

Nykiel also discusses the new trend towards branding products with different names as a positioning technique. This is an area in which some hoteliers will probably change their approaches with more experience. Automobile marketers, such as General Motors, have learned that they need to subordinate their corporate name to that of the product; otherwise it is difficult to achieve a unique position for each product and almost impossible to avoid cannibalization.

Given the diverse ways for achieving growth in the business, we asked Jurgen Bartels of the Carlson Hospitality Group to write about Radisson's strategy in chapter 14. Carlson also owns controlling interest in T.G.I. Friday's and readers will be interested in noting the similarities between Bartels' article and the article by Dan Scoggin, the founder of T.G.I. Friday's. Both use a rifle approach towards marketing; they aim carefully at one market segment and then stalk it with the eye of an experienced hunter.

It has been observed by many of our authors that tourism and travel is a people business. People can and do make all the difference in the type of product or service that is delivered. Nowhere is this more evident than in the hospitality segment. The definition of hospitality is "the friendly reception and treatment of guests or strangers." With that in mind, June Farrell, an experienced human resource manager now with Marriott, has contributed an article containing sound advice on the hiring and training of customer contact personnel. Staffing is an integral part of the hospitality product. Sometimes that is forgotten and instead, too much emphasis is placed on the bricks and mortar.

Howard Feiertag of Servico, who has trained thousands of sales and marketing people and runs a respected marketing operation of his own, wrote the final article in this section entitled "Making Effective Sales Calls." This chapter contains practical useful advice that every sales manager needs. The ideas in this chapter can be put to work for your organization immediately. The section on sales blitzes is particularly helpful, not only to hospitality people but to travel agents, and sales representatives as well. In his article, Feiertag discuses tele-marketing in the framework of identify-ing prospects for group sales calls. Telemarketing has also become a major marketing tool in a broad spectrum of the travel industry for selling to individ-uals. The most obvious case in point is AT&T's 800 single number service that makes it possible for consumers to read an advertisement for a hotel anywhere in the world and, by the use of a single toll-free call, immediately reserve a room. In addition, they can order brochures, enter contests, and get more information about their destination. Most important-ly, by calling the 800 number, these con-sumers are identifying themselves as prospects. Smart marketers can capture their names and addresses and use them in future promotional mailings.

Chapter 14

Corporate Strategy within the Hospitality Industry

Dr. Ronald A. Nykiel
Senior Vice President,
Stouffer Hotel Company

Dr. Nykiel is Senior Vice President and an Officer of Stouffer Hotel Company, part of Nestle Enterprises, Inc. His responsibilities include advertising, sales, public relations, promotions, reservations, food and beverage marketing, and creative services. He is a member of the Executive, Policy, and Hotel Management Committees. Author of the book Marketing in the Hospitality Industry, *Dr. Nykiel holds a B.A. from the State University of New York, and a Ph.D. in Business and Government Administration from Walden University.*

Understanding corporate strategy within the hospitality industry requires insight into both internal (within the corporations themselves) and external (macro socio-demographic and psychographic trends) factors. The fundamental causes of the strategies are as varied as the propagation of segmented product, service levels, and development approaches in existence today. In some instances these fundamental causes disappear almost as rapidly as a chameleon changes its appearance. To use the analogy of the chameleon changing its appearance to reflect threats and changes to its environment is also appropriate for many corporations in today's hospitality industry.

Historic Base

A brief look at history is essential to understand the evolution of most corporate strategies in this industry that are based on the internal factors. Historically, the hotel was a product that served the traveler to urban centers. Synonymous with hotels was the name Hilton. In the 1950s, one of the very first alternate corporate strategies to hotels was the invention of the roadside motel product by Kemmons Wilson. His concept translated itself into Holiday Inns, which quickly became synonymous with the word motel. Thus, two major product segments had emerged in the hospitality industry — the hotel, a downtown product, and the motel, a highway/roadside product. One was geared for the business traveler, the other aimed at the family market. Thus, two major market segments emerged, and with them, the beginning of large-scale market segmentation in the hospitality industry.

Before we examine the evolution of these product and market segmentation strategies from their embryonic state just described to their explosive state of today, it is important to note one additional historic root of today's hospitality industry and its strategic thrusts. Just as Hilton and hotel were historic synonyms, Marriott, Stouffer, and others became known as companies that emerged from root beer stands, ice cream shops, coffee shops, and the like to restaurant companies. The evolutionary strategy that took William Marriott and Vernon Stouffer from one simple small food/feeding store to the full gamut of food serving facilities and preparation processes continued to internally evolve until it manifested itself in the next logical service — providing meals *and* beds. Thus, added to the single product strategy and to the market segment strategy is the third strategic corporate thrust — multiple service with integrated (admittedly attached) products. I am sure there are other historic or fundamental reasons for strategies, but these three represent what has emerged as the base from which many of today's corporate strategic thrusts have been launched. Before we look at the emergence of these and at their proliferation, there is yet another fundamental base we must touch upon. It is called *resources*.

The entrepreneurs who built the hospitality industry were not the wealthy, computer-age geniuses we see labeled as entrepreneurs today. These early entrepreneurs were hardworking men and women whose primary resources were their own skills, personal friendship, and often, borrowed money. As they began to succeed, demand for their concept or opportunity outweighed their resource ability to expand. The answer to bring more of their product or service to the market was quickly found in another pioneering corporate strategy called franchising. Holiday Inns' phenomenal growth best exemplifies franchising in its heyday. One need only look at McDonald's and Wendy's to see its application in the fast-food industry to further underscore franchising as a means-to-growth strategy.

Now these basic product, market, and expansionary strategies began to develop from the seed, to the tree, and eventually, to a forest of hybrid strategies. To place these in some neat logically ordered structure is not an easy task, especially if an audit trail that leads us to today's corporate strategy in the hospitality industry is expected. I will attempt to do this categorization a little bit later, but first must comment upon what makes these strategies active versus inactive or dynamic versus static. There are two such forces: the *internally driven* and the *externally reactive*.

Internally Driven Forces

The very early strategy of today's corporations was truly internally driven. Simply stated, it was the entrepreneur's drive and desire to see his or her business grow, and new idea(s) that comprised the principal corporate strategy. This internal strategy was driven by the age in which quantitative units and growth rates were the only buzz words known in hospitality companies. In fact, it really was not until the early-1970s that "strategic planning" even entered the vocabulary of hospitality corporations. This internal strategic drive resulted in further market and product segmentation. It took on different meanings for different companies. For Holiday Inns, it meant locations that were at logical stopping points along the highway. Later, for Hilton and others, it meant entering the marketplace with an "inn" product and expanding this product through franchising. For the hospitality industry, it meant the birth and emergence of what would, one day, be known as the age of *brand proliferation* — the 1980s. For the seed had now grown into a forest with emerging new growth manifested in names like Ramada Inns, Quality Inns, Sheraton, and Hilton Inns. There were also bigger trees such as Sheraton Hotels, Western International Hotels (today's Westin), Inter-Continental Hotels.

It certainly could be stated that there was a true dual strategic thrust — internally driven product diversification and externally demanded market segmentation. However, in the 1950s and early 1960s, the motivator or cause was internal, and growth in units the game.

Externally Driven Forces

Long before John Naisbitt wrote or even conceived of *Megatrends*, major external forces were in place that would have lasting strategic impact on the thought processes of corporations in the hospitality industry. These external forces were categorized as quantitative and qualitative trends of a magnitude to influence and shape corporate strategy as it relates to markets, products, quality, levels of services, and pricing strategies, among others. Those in sync with these trends would emerge as the industry leaders and growth companies of the 1980s. The key external forces can be succinctly listed as: 1. population trends (growth, mix, and movement); 2. growth of affluence (wealth, discretionary income); 3. emergence of classes (low, middle, upper-middle, and upper); 4. development of transportation systems (interstates, airports, hubs, and the like); 5. tier qualitative segmentation of values, tastes, and psychographics; and 6. the internationalism of commerce and simple global perspective versus national isolationism. What is significant is not the importance of each of these factors, but the fact that components of each, such as a wealthier America, an older population, and yuppies, for example, brought forth strong enough trends/forces to cause everything from today's building supply of luxury accommodations to a surge in the budget motel lodging segment.

Corporate Strategies

To understand corporate strategies and state the cause of such strategies soon draws one to the conclusion that multiple internally driven and externally driven forces on top of the specific company's historic roots frequently combine to cause reasons — versus *a* reason for the strategies espoused today.

Earlier I stated an attempt would be made to provide some logical categorization or grouping of strategies employed today and how they came to be. There are as many ways to group as there are corporate strategists in the industry. The perspective that follows is based on participation in the planning processes within some of the companies used as examples and from twenty years of study and observation of other corporations in the industry. I have already referenced some of those whose hospitality business expanded from a food concept to encompass lodging — Howard Johnson, Marriott, and Stouffer, for example. So, the first categorization might simply be termed *horizontal expansions*.

Corporate Strategy I — Horizontal Expansion

Taking the perspective that the hospitality business encompasses food, beverage, lodging, and travel-related services, one could say that horizontal expansion was simply expanding from one line or product/service of hospitality — say, food — to another — say, lodging. This was and still is a strategy developed by today's corporations. Marriott, for example, now encompasses many away-from-home, or hospitality, services — food, lodging, entertainment, cruise ships, and in-flight feeding (airline catering). Holiday Corporation now includes multiple lodging companies (more on this later in this article), restaurant chains, and gaming/casino operations. Ramada is now in lodging, restaurants, and gaming/casinos. I could go on with other examples of horizontal expansions but this is but one of the dynamics of the hospitality industry strategies.

Corporate Strategy II — Geographic Expansions

The hospitality industry, by nature, capitalized on geographic demand. At first companies developed within a relatively small radius of the home or origin base. Marriott was known as a Washington, D.C.-area company right up to the 1970s. In fact, it was its rapid growth in lodging west of the Mississippi that helped it develop into a national brand. Holiday Inns was a mid-south company; Ramada a southwestern company; and LaQuinta was a Texas company, to list but a few. It was from the market growth opportunities, sales of franchises, and unit growth mentality of the 1960s and 1970s that local and regional hospitality firms emerged to national, and ultimately international, status. The same holds true for restaurant firms; for example,

Denny's, Wendy's, Brown Derby, and Arby's. For airlines, where mergers and route system expansions created regional and then national carriers, remember "Southern"; "Mohawk"; "Northeast" with its "Yellowbirds"; and "Hughes AirWest"; were all absorbed by larger carriers. Now, this trend has accelerated due not only to geographic expansion, but also to the economics of the industry segment.

Corporate Strategy III – Product Hybrid

Perhaps due to Holiday Inns' phenomenal growth and the entry of other inn/motel developers in the marketplace, it wasn't long before traditional high-rise hotel companies entered franchising and began developing low-rise inns. Hilton Inns and Sheraton Inns are two examples of product hybrids that emerged in the late-1960s and early-1970s. Product hybrids also were natural strategies for those who started out with inns. It wasn't long until there were high-rise motels called Holiday Inns, Ramada Inns, and Marriott Inns. At one point in many of these companies' histories, their actual name was "Marriott Inns"; "Stouffer Inns"; "Quality Inns"; etc. Product hybrids continued to emerge as high-rise and mid-rise facilities, offering more services than the traditional motel. Marriott's lodging operations, for example, at one point changed its name to Marriott Motor Hotels, and there were Sheraton Motor Inns. And it wasn't long before there were Holiday Inn Hotels and Marriott Hotels – actual products designed and developed to offer hotel services and amenities. Product hybrids were but the seed of a much larger and complex segmentation strategy that would fully bloom in the late-1970s and 1980s.

Corporate Strategy IV – Specialization

Just as Holiday Inns began with the idea of offering families affordable accommodations, other entrants into the marketplace began as specialists, categorized by price or service levels. For example, Motel "6", Days Inns, LaQuinta, and Budget Inns began with a specialized product offering limited facilities – essentially a room and virtually no services. In the food segment of our industry came fast food, salad bars, pizza parlors, specialty restaurants, steak houses, seafood eateries, and other food categories. Specialization also went upscale in both pricing and services offered. Today there are Guest Quarters, Embassy Suites, and a plethora of luxury hotel chains. Interestingly enough, some of these specialized products/services were the result of what is, perhaps, one of the most commented-upon corporate strategies – *product tiering.*

Corporate Strategy V – Product Tiering

Product tiering was an initial corporate response to limitations of growth and/or aging of the then-prevalent product. These limitations could have been caused by market saturation or when the actual economics of the original concept no longer worked or were not as lucrative as an alternate approach. Ramada Inns developed a three-tier approach in the early 1980s — Ramada Inns, Ramada Hotels, and Ramada Renaissance Hotels. Each of these product tiers reflected pricing, levels of service, and operational variations. Holiday Inns, Holiday Inn Hotels, and Holiday Inn Crown Plazas represented Holiday's original product tiering. Others soon followed with various forms of product tiering. Usually in its early development product tiering manifested itself in a perceived movement up the scale — inn to hotel to super hotel. Product tiering also touched those like Marriott which de-emphasized inns and franchising, and opted to go in both directions to hotels, then mega-hotels (1,000 rooms plus) — called Marriott Marquis, followed by a low-rise lodging product, "Courtyards by Marriott," and most recently to an "all-suites" product. Radisson, Howard Johnson, Quality International, Hyatt, and other lodging chains all "placed product tiering designators" on lodging facilities that offered varying levels of services, amenities, and pricing structures. This was simply the lodging industry's response to the mega-forces of population, demographic, economic, and psychographic segmentation. Product tiering was rampant by the early 1980s.

Corporate Strategy VI — Product Branding

The most recent corporate strategy to emerge might best be labeled *product branding*. This was in part due to the proliferation of tiering and subsequent consumer and franchisee confusion caused by tiering. The confusion was the result of some very true product tiering mixed in with a whole lot of product relabeling. It looked like an inn/motel, smelled like it, but often had another name. As a result of this confusion and of an even stronger force of marketplace dynamic known as consumer awareness, product branding emerged. Ironically, the hospitality industry — one of the world's oldest industries — was just entering the product development era of brand industries identification. Product branding has a focus on clearly delineating what that product/service is in terms of price, level, and quality of service, location, and other key consumer-oriented factors such as the psychographic appeal of prestige or thrift. There are a number of clear examples of today's product branding. In viewing these, one might think of the hospitality corporation as analogous to General Motors and Mercedes. For example, Holiday Corporation has followed the GM product branding concept and now offers Holiday Inns, Hampton Inns, Holiday Inns Crown Plaza Hotels, Embassy Suites, and Harrah's Casinos. Everything from a Chevrolet to a Cadillac. Marriott has adopted a similar strategy choosing to keep the "Marriott" label on all its products — Marriott Hotels, Marriott Resorts, Marriott Marquis, and Courtyards by Marriott. Others have elected to utilize what might be analogous to the Mercedes, Porsch, or Jaguar concept — one product of high quality — one brand. No variations. Examples include Four Seasons, Stouffer Hotels, Ritz Carlton, and Westin, to name a few. These firms have room to grow their brand and currently do not need to adopt an alternate strategy. There are other corporate strategies that transcend product, brand, and market. These are the financial/developmental approaches of today's hospitality firms. They can be simplified into the following categories.

☐ Non-franchising Corporations. Usually, product quality control, ownership, and management control are the motivators behind firms that do not franchise and often these firms have strong enough financial resources or can attain such. Examples of lodging chains that do not franchise are few. Stouffer Hotels (parent Nestle), Westin Hotels (parent Allegis), LaQuinta, and Motel "6" are such examples.

☐ Restricted Franchising—Predominant Control Corporation. Marriott Hotels is perhaps a good example of one such corporation. It primarily is a hotel management and operating company; however, it has a few selective franchise operators that have hotels under the Marriott banner. These are limited in number and usually are viewed as offering the quality of service and adherence to standards that would be found in a parent-owned/operated facility.

☐ Franchising Corporations. These are more prevalent; Holiday Corporation, Ramada Inns, Inc., Quality International; and Howard Johnson are examples of lodging firms that are large franchisers. McDonald's, Wendy's, Dunkin' Donuts, and Arby's are leaders in the fast-food area. Today it is virtually possible to purchase a franchise for everything from a travel agency to a destination resort.

In addition to these developmental/financial growth strategies, there are additional emerging corporate strategies increasingly visible in today's hospitality industry. These are juxtaposed in that one incorporates vertical and horizontal integration of various or all components of the hospitality industry, while the other focuses on singleness or simplicity.

☐ Vertical and Horizontal Integration Strategy. This is a corporate strategy that is premised on involvement in more than one component of the hospitality business. Two examples are Allegis and Carlson Companies. Allegis is parent of an airline (United), a hotel company (Westin), a rent-a-car company (Hertz), and a sophisticated reservation system serving travel intermediaries—the Apollo reservation system. How many of these they will divest themselves of remains to be seen. Carlson is the parent of Radisson and its line of lodging products; "Ask Mr. Foster," a large travel agency group; and T.G.I. Friday's, a restaurant company. Unlike in the pre-1980s when integration in the hospitality business might have consisted of a firm with hotels and restaurants or a firm with an airline and hotel chain, deregulation has provided the opportunity to gain competitive edges by owning or investing in multiple components of the industry.

☐ Singleness Strategies.   Some industry firms have chosen to concentrate on one product/service and in developing that specific component solely — foregoing product segmentation, tiering, and vertical and horizontal integration strategies. Stouffer Hotels, for example, has opted for a product of all first-class hotels with ownership and management control. Four Seasons is another lodging firm following this singleness strategy.

Finally, I would be remiss if a number of other specific corporate strategies and trends were not highlighted. Granted, these are at random, much like the development of our industry — growth-oriented and in natural evolution.

☐ Values Related Products/Services.   Residence Inns, Compri by Doubletree, and Embassy Suites exemplify concepts developed to respond to specific value and psychographic trends. The residential approach, social environments, and suite concept are all aimed at specifically expressed needs of today's consumers. As consumers continue to develop their sophistication, expressed demands, and product service wants, corporations will identify and fulfill these with appropriate and timely strategies. These are but three of many examples available from within the hospitality industry. Others include the variety of credit cards and services — gold cards, Platinum cards, etc., the variety of air travel options — first-class, budget fares, and new brands like Midway and People Express.

☐ Global Product Strategies.   Today, the oceans, to some extent political ideologies, and other traditional trade barriers no longer seem insurmountable hurdles for the hospitality industry. Lodging firms have no imposed boundaries. Holiday, Westin, Marriott, Ramada, and Sheraton have product throughout the world. As the U.S. based firms expand globally, others have entered the market — Meridian, Trust House Forte, Sofitel, and New Otani, to name a few. Fast-food chains brands/signs can be recognized in most international cities. Airports around the world in gateway cities display aircraft with symbols and flags of dozens of nations. Investment reasons, risk levels, growth strategies, and reasons for expansion all vary by corporation and by market. These variances change or are influenced by many different social, economic, and political trends and events. These corporations' perspectives are as varied as the products, services, and markets they serve. An Arizona-based firm,

Ramada Inns, Inc., has product in Europe and Asia. A Memphis-based firm, Holiday, has product virtually surrounding the globe. A company like Stouffer Hotels with parentage in the global Nestle company, opts for only the U.S. market. And, a French lodging chain, Meridian, begins to emerge in the United States. United Airlines has affiliated with Swissaire, and Delta has affiliated with JAL to have more competitive frequent traveler programs.

☐ Sorting out Potential Winning and Losing Strategies. In a dynamic environment and industry, change becomes the only sure bet. To pick winners and losers is virtually impossible. There are, however, some winning characteristics to look for in making judgments. Such characteristics include financial strength, quality control, ability to change, brand identity, and broad-based and strategic orientation. Admittedly, these are terms most can readily identify as ideals. A close look at some emerging trends and likely scenarios, however, will reveal just how *key* each of these will be in our industry.

Trend 1	Overbuilding in Luxury Lodging Segments from Full Service Hotels, Suite Concepts to Resorts.
Scenario	Likely Survivors/Winners will be those with the: 1. deepest financial resources; 2. best quality and concept; 3. brand identity of critical mass.

The strong will absorb the small and weak. Supply and demand will be more in-line as affluence grows.

Trend 2	Population Bulges in Older Age Groups will cause strong demand for lower-priced "budget" facilities.
Scenario	Likely to be next overbuilt category as market demand is strong and aggressive development occurs in next five years. Longer-term market will desire upgraded lodging and dining experiences and inexpensively-constructed facilities will be converted to other uses.

Trend 3	Mega-Companies Emerge
Scenario	The Marriotts, Holidays, Carlsons, and others will continue to accelerate their growth through acquisitions and new product development and will truly emerge as giants with a distinctly competitive edge. Only those who are specialized, single-minded in strategy, and financially strong will be able to carve their own niche and prosper.

Trend 4	Concept Sort-Out
Scenario	Surprisingly, very few of the new concepts will survive. All-suites without all services will appeal to some, but not high-money spenders.

Trends away from socializing may hamper social/residential concepts too heavily banking on the club environment. Likely successors will have social/secure environment.

Trend 5	Loss Through Lack of Understanding
Scenario	As the population mix changes, so will strong value orientations and psychographic trends emerge. These will be more critical for the employer to understand in order to attract and keep employees. Old guard must recognize the new ways to survive and relate to the customer and to the employee.

Trend 6	Complexities Beginning
Scenario	The complexity of marketing one's product or service is about to explode. Incentives, promotions, tie-ins, media, technology, and consumer types all seem to be much more complex. Those who are sleeping or banking on old image may as well lower the flag. The game of bringing the consumer in will be equally important to the service/value/quality level offerings to keep them coming back.

Trend 7	Critical Mass Gets More Critical
Scenario	The baseline for survival will become larger — more locations, units, and size will be needed than in the past to be market and brand-aware competitive. This suggests incentives to merge, franchise, joint-venture, and joint market. The brand poliferation of the mid-1980s (more than 50 new brands in the 1984-1985 twenty-four month period) resulted in consolidation in the late 1980s — as the strong swallow the weak and go for mass.

All these trends and corporate strategies provide for a most moving and exciting period for the hospitality industry. For those who have been in this business and are amazed at how it has grown over the past twenty years, the next twenty will astound you.

It is just the beginning of one of the world's fastest growing and largest industries — the hospitality industry. The one industry whose corporate strategies as a whole result in bringing people together, in caring for others, and ultimately building a better world.

Chapter 15

How We View Marketing at Carlson

Juergen Bartels
President, Carlson
Hospitality Group

As President of Carlson Hospitality Group, Inc., Juergen Bartels is a respected international leader in the hospitality industry. He is responsible for all the hotel and restaurant operations of Carlson Companies, Inc., a company whose hospitality operations encompass approximately $1 billion in annual sales. Mr. Bartels has been the driving force behind the sweeping Radisson expansion program at Carlson, which has more than tripled the size of the company in the past three years.

One of the most significant economic trends of this century has been the explosive growth of the travel and tourism industry in America. While Americans have always loved to travel, a number of important sociological changes in the postwar era opened the exciting opportunities of travel to millions in the nation's new middle class.

The largest single generation in the history of the world is alive today in America — young adults aged 25 to 44. Besides sheer numbers, this generation is the most affluent, best educated, and most sophisticated group in world history. By 1990, they will represent one-third of America's population. They are also the most frequent travelers. There is nothing subtle about trying to find our market in the coming years. They are it.

In effect, we are selling to a sophisticated adult market, dominated by baby boomers, who pull every other group along in the broad wake of their choices, tastes, and desires. It is the spending power and recreational preferences of this generation that we expect will propel the travel and tourism industry into the single largest industry in the economy by the year 2000.

The overwhelming impact of the travel and tourism industry in America has already set the stage for this accelerated growth. Today, one of every fifteen Americans is employed by our industry, which is the first, second, or third largest employer in 41 of the 50 states. The travel and tourism industry contributes more than $225 billion to the U.S. economy, fueled by more than one billion personal trips per year. These trips are defined as trips of more than 100 miles with a layover of at least one night. Nearly 15 million Americans travel in this way every day. This figure includes travel for business, conventions, leisure, and recreation or travelers who combine business with pleasure by extending a business trip into a personal vacation experience.

Against the background of these statistics and trends, Carlson Companies, Inc. is committed to major growth in the hospitality and travel industries through the remainder of this century. Carlson Companies is currently one of the largest privately owned companies in America with sales in excess of $3 billion. The company's two main businesses are travel ($1.5 billion in 1985) and hospitality ($800 million in 1985). The hospitality group alone employs more than 30,000 people and the overall Carlson Companies, 50,000. By combining travel and hotels, we have a uniquely synergistic opportunity to continue this fast growth into the future.

One of the key elements in Carlson Companies' success has been the fact that it is customer driven and service oriented. The entire focus of the organization is aimed at serving the needs and desires of the customer. We are, therefore, closely attuned to the pulse of the marketplace.

What are some of the major trends and consumer needs that have an impact on our businesses? We have learned that the new American consumer is motivated by quality of experience rather than mere consumption. With increased prosperity, they have increased choices. We see more elitist choices in our markets, choices based on matters of time, convenience, and self-fulfillment. The operative fact for all marketers is that these new consumers have the discretionary income with which to pursue their self-expression.

From our position in the mid-1980s, we have the greatest of expectations. The creation of $1 trillion of additional value on the stock market, a substantial decline in interest rates (lower mortgages), and a decline in energy prices (gasoline and home heating costs), in addition to low inflation and higher take-home pay are expected to be the locomotives in the hotel industry that will increase occupancy and average room rate above inflation levels.

Also revolutionary is the role of women among these new consumers. Because of women's economic strides, the basic consumer unit of the family is getting a new look. The norm for the remainder of this century will be the two-income household whose discretionary income dwarfs that of single-career units. The two-income family has two or fewer children, tends to live in the suburbs, and tends to have its breadwinners in managerial or professional jobs. These new consumers are our business travelers and recreational travelers.

Fifty-two percent of all women, including mothers (up from 32 percent in 20 years), are now working and 20 percent of married working women now earn more money than their husbands. This is a social revolution and only the beginning. Their choices are based on matters of time, convenience, and self-fulfillment. These new consumers have the discretionary income with which to pursue their self-expression.

Also affecting our industry is the value these busy couples can afford to place on their scarce time — especially their time off. These consumers are constrained by time, not income — fairly opposite from the previous generation. They are not looking for the cheapest, the bargain-basement; they are looking for quality, and are highly disciplined in choosing it. Adults today prize their vacation time; the old-time vacation with a car full of children and cheap motels was a journey to get through. The new consumers gravitate toward product leadership, high-end goods, high service levels. Nothing about their time and selves is considered cheap. The best price value is beautiful to the new consumers of the 1980s.

These trends are reflected in the types of services offered by hotels. We at Radisson are an up-market hotel chain. Our customers are the achievers in America. Achievers include the leaders in business, the professions, and government. They are competent, self-reliant, and efficient. Achievers tend to be materialistic, hardworking, oriented to fame and success, and comfort-loving. These are the affluent people who created the economic system in response to the American dream. They are defenders of the free enterprise economy. They are supporters of technology and are open to progress, but resist radical change. After all, they are on top.

Twenty-two percent of the population is counted as achievers and creates 80 percent of the room nights in our segment. We also know that the top 24 U.S. cities create 66 percent of all room nights. There you are — our customers.

Thus, one sees a trend in the hotel industry toward upscale services and special amenities. The new Plaza Club floors, concierge services, amenities baskets, complimentary breakfast, and turn-down services are extra touches that reflect the hospitality industry's efforts to keep pace with the increasingly sophisticated demands of its customers.

Smart businessmen always practice a belief in the future, since they must give to the consumer before they can expect a return. This has been our policy, and of course it requires confidence. Proof of this is the fact that we have invested substantially up front.

We eliminated hotels that did not meet our image requirements and have grown from 20 hotels with 6,500 rooms to 115 hotels with more than 27,000 rooms. We added more than $1 billion of product under the Radisson banner and have $500 million worth under construction. We have invested $37 million in renovation.

We have kept our commitment over the past three years to improve quality and grow fast. We have also kept our commitment to compound profits by 25 percent annually, an absolute necessity to justify our future and ongoing growth at present tempo.

Radisson has a theory: Our triangle theory. There must be a balance between guests, employees, and ownership. Management companies that err in favor of guests (rates too low) or employees (salaries too high or over-staffed) will have to learn new tricks or they will be shown as ineffective managers.

Nationwide, there are 2.8 million guest rooms in the U.S. market. During the past decade, more than $30 billion were poured into the hotel industry, which increased capacity by 4 percent a year in the 1980s, while demand increased only 2 percent.

This has created the issue of the so-called overbuilding USA (hotels). If you believe, as I truly do, in the deep-rooted changes in consumers described earlier, then you also believe that at least 420,000 guest rooms, or approximately 15 percent of the U.S. offering, have very little in common with the consumers' desires and will eliminate themselves. Picture this type of room: shag carpet, block walls — painted, nickel and dime wall hangings, cheap light fixtures, stripes and flowers, red, yellow, and blue decor — and all in one guest room. This description and the connotations associated with it shall bring an increased obsolescence of these kinds of properties.

Increased obsolescence, a slowing of building, and increased demand make my outlook for the U.S. hotel industry increasingly profitable and healthy.

A final factor affecting the hospitality industry during the coming years will be its connection with the real estate industry. Hotels and real estate are tied closely together since our physical products represent a basic part of the American infrastructure. In light of tax law changes, real estate has lost its privileged position as the most tax-advantaged investment around. Emphasis will shift to the economics of a project. In the short run (two to three years), real estate and hotel values, built on tax advantages, will decline because there will be more sellers than buyers. If you believe in the future and its cycles, as I do, you also believe that great deals will be struck in the next two to three years. Patient investors will do very well. There will be less building of hotels, but there will be selling and buying. Naturally, income-generating projects will be more worthwhile because of lower tax rates, and because they will go up, not down, in value. Even older shelters, which have already taken most of their deductions and are now receiving taxable income, will benefit from the lower tax rate. Highly leveraged deals that rely on big borrowing to generate large yearly write-offs will be gone, and most of these existing hotels will change hands. The drop in individual tax rates, as well as the increasingly limited ability to write off losses, make it unlikely that the limited partners continue to fund cash shortfalls, although recapture has to be kept in mind.

New owners will more likely be corporations than individuals. For the first time since the start of federal taxes, individual taxes will be less than the tax levels of corporations. The new owners will also have different ideas:

superior marketing, getting higher occupancy, higher room rates, and good management. It will not be whose name lends itself best to sell a limited partnership. It will be who does the best job in running this particular hotel, with special emphasis on marketing.

The period from now to 1990 will be exciting years in the travel and hospitality industries. There will be tremendous opportunities for growth and advancement as we lead an increasingly mobile public into the 21st century. Look forward with excitement to embracing the opportunity!

Chapter 16

It's People That Build Success in Hotel Marketing

June Farrell
Director of Media
Relations, Marriott
Hotels and Resorts

June Farrell began her travel industry career in 1968 in the public relations department of Eastern Airlines. While at Eastern, she was credited with developing the successful "Woman on the Go" program, targeted to the female business travel market. She has written numerous articles on how to apply public relations techniques to the marketing mix and frequently lectures to industry groups on the use of public relations techniques. She joined Marriott Hotels and Resorts in 1984.

Like it or not, as a travel agent, airline executive, hotelier, attractions operator, or convention and visitor bureau official, you are in the "people business." If your organization is good at it, chances for success are greatly enhanced. If not, you have to make up for your deficiencies in other perhaps more costly and less effective ways.

With tangible alternatives to business and leisure travel proliferating around us daily, it makes sense that travel industry professionals concentrate on designing and delivering a service-oriented product that meets their customers' needs.

So why is it that researchers Yankelovich, Skelly, and White reported at the 1983 ASTA World Congress that one of the deterrents to someone taking a discretionary trip is a growing frustration among consumers with "travel hassle"? And, in a monograph about fearful flyers, Boeing reported that 40 percent of the people who avoid air travel do so because of an impatience with having to stand in long lines, cope with lost luggage, and suffer rude service at the hands of uncaring customer contact personnel.

As American Airlines' Chief Executive Officer, Robert Crandall, pointed out in his keynote address at the annual Discover America International Pow Wow, "a person traveling almost anywhere in the world is more likely to meet a surly bartender than a terrorist. He is more likely to lose a bag than encounter a machine gun, more likely to feel held for ransom by a fancy hotel or an overpriced restaurant than by a kidnapper. In short, those who deliver travel services have the ability, by failing in their responsibilities, to do more damage than those who seek through violence to harm our interests."

Usually low-paid, young, and inexperienced, the customer-contact employee in most travel companies spends more time with the customer than any other person in the organization. It is, therefore, essential that travel suppliers make every effort to ensure that their frontline customer-contact employees have the skills and interest to respond professionally to customers.

The first step lies in sound recruitment, backed by your commitment to in-depth training and recognizing a job well done. Sounds simple, doesn't it? However, not everybody has the ability and personality to be an effective customer-contact employee. Being a good service provider is not something that can be learned; it is inherent in the individual. Just as there are born salesmen, so too, are there born service providers.

During the interview process most candidates interested in forging a travel industry career will tell you they want to work for you because they "like people." But, do they really? Do they have the stamina to treat the hundredth guest or customer of the day with the same positive degree of freshness and interest as the first? Do they have the sensitivity to neutralize an irate customer without personalizing or worsening the conflict? Do they have the team spirit and the ability to work with other employees to provide service, even when it involves doing someone else's work or a service normally provided by another department?

When it comes to recruiting customer-contact personnel who will be good service providers for any position along the sales or service distribution stream, look for individuals of any age who:

☐ Have a high energy level.

☐ Are genuinely interested in others.

☐ Possess a mature entrepreneurial instinct that encourages them to go that extra mile to assure a sale or total customer satisfaction.

☐ Have good work habits, not only in terms of reporting to work on time, but in exhibiting solid follow-through on commitments, completed staff work, and attention to detail.

☐ Are flexible. If there is one given in our industry, it is unpredictability. Your successful candidate must be adaptable to changing conditions, environment, situations, and people.

☐ Have the ability to identify problems, understand their probable causes, and decide on a reasonable solution. Whatever the situation, the job role often requires prompt, on-the-spot decision-making. All the necessary information is not always available, so your successful customer-contact candidate must be able to make high-quality decisions, exercising his or her good judgment.

☐ Can prioritize tasks, set objectives, and work to the satisfactory completion of those tasks in a timely manner.

Other personality traits are equally important to look for when staffing your frontline ranks. Your customer-contact employees must all be able to make a good first impression. Studies have shown that we are perceived and judged within the first 40 seconds of eye contact. Oftentimes there is no second chance to correct a poor first impression, so your customer-contact employees should:

☐ Present a professional, well-groomed appearance and express themselves clearly and effectively in one-on-one and group situations.

☐ Establish eye contact with the customer and maintain a pleasant and friendly facial expression. They should be people with a high credibility level; in other words, the kind of people who are immediately believable.

☐ Personalize the transaction, either by using the customer's name or by reference to something that recognizes him or her as an individual.

☐ Treat the customer in an unhurried manner, even when harried themselves.

☐ Speak clearly. Enunciation, pronunciation, voice pitch and tone, as well as word choice play a big role in determining customer satisfaction.

☐ Make the customer feel as though he or she is number one, while acknowledging the presence of another customer requiring attention.

☐ Be able to form accurate impressions of people and their needs by observing body language. The key to winning with people is simply understanding how they like to be treated. Getting on your customer's wavelength creates the proper chemistry, which builds trust, credibility, rapport, and cooperation.

☐ Know how to listen. By listening carefully and objectively and providing accurate, complete, clear, and concise information, your customer contact employees will more than satisfy the needs of your customers. If any of these factors is missing, there is a very good chance your customer will misunderstand the information being imparted and will become increasingly frustrated.

☐ Have the technical knowledge of the job at hand and be thoroughly familiar with your product line.

Why should you emphasize recruiting good customer-contact personnel? Today's travel industry frontline employee can be tomorrow's senior management. Unlike some industries, successful travel executives start at the bottom. At Marriott, for example, 40 percent of our managerial positions are filled with people who at one point in their careers held positions such as swimming pool lifeguards and front desk clerks. A second reason is that, in the travel industry, we are marketing an intangible product in a business where repeat business is the backbone of our financial success—and where the product is delivered after the sale.

Looked at another way, ask yourself: Would you rather spend $1 to resell a "sold" customer or $115 to attract a new one? That is the impact on the cost of doing business when you lose a valued customer by not providing service or responding to a need.

In the lodging, car rental, airline, or attractions business, if a front desk clerk, park attendant, or in-flight cabin attendant does not respond warmly and professionally to a customer inquiry, it will irritate an already committed customer, and your repeat business can be jeopardized. On an assembly line, if a yellow door is hung on a red car, someone will notice and quickly fix the mistake. But, if one of your people does not respond appropriately to a customer's request, you may never know about it.

Throughout the travel industry, one of the most important things we have learned is that our customers usually do not know what they are getting—what is really behind Marriott's or any other component's promise of satisfaction—until those times when we do not deliver. Only then are our customers aware of what they believe they bargained for. This situation is dangerous. Because customers are usually aware only of dissatisfaction in our business, they are extremely impressed by the promises made by our competitors, who can always promise a more pleasurable travel experience and cite small visible failures of service that imply even more tangible product failures. That is why we at Marriott and other recognized successful travel suppliers like American Airlines, Tauck Tours, and others pay such close attention to hiring the right people to deliver the warm customer service for which they are noted. That is why we back up our recruitment process with an emphasis on training and recognition.

Now, we are not all perfect. As Peters and Waterman pointed out in *In Search of Excellence*, controlling quality in a service business is not easy. As they so aptly put it, "Unlike manufacturing in which one can sample what comes off the line and reject bad lots, what gets produced in a service business and what gets consumed happens at the same time and in the same place." In the travel industry, we call this the *weakest link theory*. Travel agent Bob McMullen, former chairman of the American Society of Travel Agents, once noted that during any successful trip there are 285 identifiable points at which something can go wrong that will destroy the entire experience for the traveler.

Human error is a fact of life. That is why it is critical that the frontline people in your organization reflect a caring, sympathetic attitude. One that exemplifies a can-do spirit. One that is interested in solving problems, not creating them.

All the sound hiring strategies, however, will not guarantee a motivated customer-contact team. That is where training and recognition come in. Companies like Eastern Airlines annually spend millions of dollars training their customer-contact personnel, including new employees and recurrent training of other employees.

At Marriott, we have just spent more than $1 million developing a five-level successful training program for marketing personnel, built on developing listening skills and on surfacing every conceivable need of the customer, because we know that if we can learn what is important to him or her, we can deliver.

First of all, almost no one gets into a sales manager position at Marriott without first completing a three-to-six month hands-on entry-level program focused on various operational functions at the hotel front desk, convention services, housekeeping, and other duties. It is in this phase that our sales people learn our product inside out. Similar frontline programs at the airlines in such areas as the airport ticket counter and in reservations prepare their customer-contact people for future sales and marketing positions.

At Marriott, our customer-contact people then progress through a series of training programs that coincide with their stage of professional development. But training does not stop with marketing. One of the major areas to which we have devoted a great deal of money and man-hours recently is in the upgrading of our service and hospitality standards.

In the food and beverage area, we have an extensive culinary training program underway in Europe and the United States. In the rooms and related areas part of our business, we are continually developing new technologies to ease the guest service process from check-in to checkout, so our people can concentrate on the people contact aspect of providing good customer service.

Management and executive development is another area to which we are devoting considerable attention. We follow up training with a strong recognition awards program for excellence and success — with quarterly and annual awards, mentions in our in-house marketing newspaper, and with recognition of the star performers at our annual marketing meeting.

Does paying close attention to sound recruitment and following it up with a strong training program and recognition pay off? You bet. Especially in the marketplace. In 1985, for example, Marriott people were voted "best sales force" by *Sales and Marketing Management* magazine; Meeting Planners International named Marriott "best supplier"; *Consumer's Digest* magazine awarded Marriott its "Hall of Fame Merit Award for Service Excellence"; and *Business Travel News* named Marriott the "best hotel system" in the United States. And, where it really counts, on the bottom line; Marriott has consistently increased its net income, per share earnings, and return on equity more than 20 percent each year for the past 10 years.

By picking the right customer-contact people and motivating your team with proper training and a commitment to recognition of jobs well done, travel suppliers can help guarantee their success. After all, travel is a people business. Thus, having the right people on your team can make all the difference.

Chapter 17
Making Effective Sales Calls

Howard Feiertag
Senior Vice President,
Servico, Inc.

Howard Feiertag is Senior Vice President of Servico, Inc., a Palm Beach, Florida-based owner/operator/developer of 58 chain affiliates and independent hotels. An active member of Hotel Sales Marketing Association International, he formerly served as President of two state chapters and has been designated as a Certified Hotel Sales Executive (CHSE). He is a monthly contributing columnist to Hotel Motel Management *magazine,* Meeting and Convention *magazine, and* Business Travel *magazine.*

A salesperson's job is, of course, to bring in sales. Prospects are developed, then sold (or encouraged to buy) something. In order to create a sales situation, sales calls as well as other marketing efforts are made.

Sales calls differ greatly in the hospitality and tourist industry. There are all kinds of sales calls and salespeople need to distinguish between them. There are cold calls, PR calls, appointment calls, presentation calls, telemarketing calls, inside sales calls, calls to get group business, and probably a few more types used by a variety of very creative salespeople.

Cold Calls

These types of calls are characterized as fact-finding or exploratory or prospecting calls. The objective of the cold call is to maximize the salesperson's time and develop additional leads for various types of business. Generally, these calls are made within a small geographical area with a minimum amount of time spent on each call. The objective is to fill out a fact sheet, whereby the salesperson can develop information that will be helpful in developing further leads. In these types of calls, the idea is really not to do any selling, but to gather information so that strategy can be developed, and then to follow through and get some sort of business as a result of the contact made. Many times a salesperson will run into a hot prospect who is really interested in doing some type of business with the salesperson. Of course, at that time, the cold call can be converted into an actual sales call to close a piece of business.

PR Calls

The public relations call is made to a company or a person that is already a customer. Someone drops by to say hello or to ask if everything is going all right, or sometimes, even to bring a gift during a holiday season. The problem with this type of call is that it's generally made by nonaggressive types of salespeople. This is a comfort zone type of call where the salesperson feels very comfortable visiting these people because they are known and are, in many cases, already providing business. There's no real pressure to make a sales pitch for more or additional business. There is a place for public relations type calls, but salespeople must remember that there's always an opportunity to sell more. Salespeople need to look for advantages when making this type of call—to increase sales either with other types of business in the organization or to provide business in addition to what they may already be providing.

Appointment Calls

There are always some people with organizations who refuse to see anyone unless an appointment is made, thereby giving the opportunity to the salesperson to make an appointment for a visit. It's very important that in making these calls that they be well planned. The salesperson should have as much knowledge as possible about the prospect and what his or her needs are so that information may be presented that will result in some type of sale. Business may either be booked or information developed so a follow-up call can be made at a future date. It is important to remember that when appointment calls are made, the salesperson should not turn this into a cold call or a prospecting call. The person being called upon usually is busy and that's the reason for requiring an appointment; therefore, as much information about the prospect and his or her needs must be obtained before making the call.

Presentation Calls

This type of call usually results after several previous calls where all the necessary information has already been developed. The prospect needs to have a presentation made to either one or several other people, such as a committee, so that the seller can be considered for business. It's very important during a presentation call that the presentation be conducted with some type of visual aid and handouts so that the time spent is maximized. This is strictly a sales situation where the salesperson is putting his or her best foot forward with the objective of having the committee or group make a decision at that time. During this type of call, it's important to know who the decision makers within the group are, as well as what their "hot buttons" might be. The salesperson must be in the position to have the courage and confidence to make a strong sales pitch to try to get business, be able to answer questions so that objections can be overcome, and then ask for the order.

Telemarketing Calls

There is a place for soliciting business by telephone; however, it should not be a substitute for other types of sales calls. The telemarketing call is sometimes used to develop information and qualify leads, then salespeople may follow up to make a presentation and secure some business. Telephone calls should be used only for prospecting and not to make a sales presentation, since the best sales pitch has always been and always will be the face-to-face visit.

Inside Sales Calls

Many hospitality organizations (such as hotels, motels, convention bureaus, and attractions) have what they call *inside sales people*. These are people who, for the most part, don't go out on sales calls. They feel very comfortable staying in, waiting for people to come by or call in and ask for information. There certainly is a place for this type of person; however, it would seem logical that there is always somebody around who should be in a position to handle visits or telephone inquiries.

It's good to remember that sales calls come in all shapes and forms, but the best sales call is always the one that is face-to-face with the prospect. And the ultimate objective, of course, is to close a piece of business. No matter what form it comes in, the sales call must end with a sale.

The Sales Blitz

Most salespeople already know what a sales blitz is. It's an intensive survey of a given geographic area to determine market potential. It is a fact-gathering mission to provide leads to a sales department for follow-up and booking. It is accomplished by asking certain key questions to as many people as possible within a short period of time. The overall objective is to improve business and total revenue. A key to a successful blitz is to make as many calls as possible within a short period of time with as many people as possible in a small geographic area. Another key to a successful blitz is proper organization, supplies, orientation, and follow-up.

The Blitzers

Anyone on the staff can participate since the objective is not to sell, but to gather information. With some instruction, most staff personnel should be able to participate. Sell it to the staff as survey taking, not a selling job. Use any staff member — secretaries, bookkeepers, whatever. Use the same people throughout the blitz period. Planning in advance is important because of scheduling problems.

Organizing the Blitz Calls

Someone needs to be designated as being in charge of the blitz and all phases of its operation. The director of sales or sales manager is usually the best prospect if the company is determined not to use an outside source. This person is called the *Blitz Director*.

The Blitz Director needs to start planning the operation 30 days in advance of the blitz date. Logical days to select are Tuesday, Wednesday, and Thursday. Three days of blitzing should be the maximum. With limited amount of blitzer time available, a one- or two-day blitz could be very satisfactory. In fact, a one-day mini-blitz would be a good place to start experimenting with the process.

In organizing the calls to be made, the most helpful system to use is a city directory. The directory lists all addresses in a city by street designation. It is important to concentrate calls in a small area at a time, so no time is lost by a blitzer from one call to another. Use three-by-five index cards to record addresses of calls to be made. These cards are then assigned to the participants by geographical territory. For a three-day blitz, each person may be assigned 100 calls. (A good day's work would be 30 calls per person.) Logically, in a business area of any city, the calls would be located right next door to each other, or, in the case of office buildings, all in the same building, floor by floor. Each index card has a specific call on it with information taken from the city directory — the address and name of the company.

Supplies Needed

An adequate supply of collateral material and forms are necessary. Blitz Survey Forms (padded) should be plentiful (you will need one per call, at least); brochures, fact sheets, and promotional material should be given out on each call. Low cost, imprinted specialty advertising gifts may be distributed, but are not necessary or important to the objective of gathering information; a street map should be provided to each blitzer with the assigned territory outlined.

Blitz Training

An indoctrination dinner should be held the evening before the first blitz day. The dinner itself becomes a motivational tool. It is the first time all blitzers are assembled. Following dinner, the Blitz Director explains the objective and purpose of the Blitz. The Blitz Forms are reviewed and explained, a demonstration is given reflecting how the survey call is made, starting with introduction, asking of the questions, and the close. This is followed with the Blitzers being paired off to try out the questioning on each other and completing the Blitz Forms. The Blitz Director then explains how the completed forms are reviewed and graded. Since the objective is to develop leads and make a volume number of calls, it is important to grade all participants and provide incentives for the best and most calls. Direction should be given that all forms need to be completed on-the-spot (at the time the interviews are conducted) and must be neatly written. All questions need to have a response indicated on the form. All reports are to be signed by the Blitzer. (See exhibit A.)

SALES BLITZ SURVEY SHEET

Organization_____

Address_____

_____ Zip_____ Phone #_____

Contact_____ Title_____

Contact_____ Title_____

1. How many meetings do you have a year?_____ When?_____
   Size?_____ Who plans them?
   Contact_____ Title_____.

   Contact_____ Title_____

   When is your next meeting?_____
   Where are meetings usually held?_____

2. Do you have incoming visitors that require sleeping accommodations?
   Yes_____ No_____   How many per month? #_____

   If yes, where are they housed? _____
   Do you reserve the room? Yes___ No___ (If not, who does?)

   Contact_____ Title_____

   Contact_____ Title_____

3. Does your organization plan such things as:
          Christmas Parties?   Other Social Events?
          Awards Dinners?
          Retirement Dinners?

   Are you the organizer, or is there a social chairman?
   Yes_____ No_____ Contact_____

4. Are you, or any of your associates, affiliated with any other organizations or associations that might have need for meeting or banquet space?   Yes_____ No_____

   Name_____ Contact_____

   Name_____ Contact_____

COMMENTS:

Taken by:_____   Date Taken:_____

Exhibit A

Questions

The Blitzers should use the fact sheet to record answers to questions and should not try to sell anything during the interviews. If questions come up, or if it appears the interview may result in a hot lead, the Blitzer should react by saying, "Someone from our sales department will be in touch with you." It may be important enough to call the sales department immediately and put someone in touch with the prospect right then and there.

Number of Calls to Be Made

No time can be wasted during or between calls if the Blitz Program is to be effective. The first call should be made at 9:00 A.M. and calls should continue until 12:00 noon. Then again from 1:00 to 4:30 P.M. In six-and-a-half hours, each person should be able to conduct 30 calls. Depending on the area assigned, the number of calls will vary. In a downtown office building, more than 30 calls may be made; in outlying industrial areas, less calls may be made.

Blitz Recovery

After the day's calls are completed, there is a Blitz recovery period. It is during this time that the forms are turned in and reviewed by the Blitz Director or a member of the sales department. It would be appropriate to serve cocktails and snacks to the Blitzers to help them unwind and discuss their day's work.

Grades are also assigned at this period, after the forms are reviewed. A score chart is kept on which each Blitzer is credited with the number of calls and the number of leads developed. Once tabulated, a daily winner should be announced and a prize should be awarded. After the last Blitz Day, a dinner may be planned with husbands, wives, and guests invited and more incentives awarded.

Motivation

The real key to a successful Blitz Program is proper motivation. Management and owners need to be behind the program, as well as participants in the program (no one is too good to go out and make Blitz calls). The Blitzers need to be excited and psychologically up throughout the program. Breakfasts with music, "Rah, Rah" Blitz Recovery Programs, signs, banners, and awards will all bring in great results. Exciting meal functions are a key to keeping people in a proper state of mind. At breakfast each day, do not linger too long after coffee. Everyone should want to get a head start. If you plan to have the Blitzers come back for lunch, it provides the opportunity to answer questions that may come up that could improve the afternoon performance. It is important to put everyone in a competitive mood so special luncheon tables may be set up for those that have gone over their quota.

The Follow-up

Since the objective of the Blitz is to develop sales leads, a good deal of time and money would be wasted if a poor follow-up job were done. After each day's calls have been tabulated and prizes given out, the forms need to be sorted by the grades received. The highest grades obviously go to the forms with the best leads — and usually are the ones that require immediate attention. The Sales Director determines which leads need to be followed up the very next morning and arranges the remaining forms in priority order for follow-up, based on the information received. Even while the Blitzers are out the next day, the sales department personnel should start on the follow-up of the previous day's work. It is important to check files first before the follow-up to see if more information on the prospect is already available.

If 10 people are making Blitz calls, it is conceivable that 1,000 calls could be made in three days. From these calls, approximately 300 could result in leads for business. Immediate follow-up by the sales department is important so that the leads don't get cold.

Although a successful Blitz requires a lot of time and effort on the part of the management, it *always* produces excellent results. Besides developing leads, it helps promote the property to the business community. In addition, it becomes a motivational tool for the staff members that participated — a team effort — which creates a healthy, cooperative attitude that lasts a long time.

The Student Blitz — Another Sales Opportunity

Now there's another type of Blitz opportunity — it's the low-cost type of sales Blitz known as *The Student Blitz*.

As its name implies, the Student Blitz uses college students as outside sales help, and thus doesn't interfere with your business by drawing from your employees to make the calls.

Youthful Energy

Energetic college blitzers can cover a lot of ground generating sales leads by face-to-face contact. The students fill out fact sheets for full-time sales staff to follow up later, besides scattering promotional literature.

One such Blitz in Chicago on behalf of a large national chain stirred up 178 firm sales leads from 986 calls made by 10 students. Immediate results totalled $156,000 — and the leads continue to work.

In a similar Chicago Blitz, another group of 10 students yielded 107 leads and more than $200,000 in business — from a batch of 1,012 calls.

In both cases, the company involved provided the students five double rooms for three nights, meals, incentive awards, and mileage reimbursement.

One plus connected with using student blitzers is that a student can, in many instances, get in doors that an experienced salesperson can't. A smiling, nervous student can disarm secretaries and executives by appealing to parental instincts or by convincing subjects that the cause of education is at stake.

Usually, a group of 10 people can make 1,000 calls within three days. It's important that time isn't wasted by indiscriminate running around. Calls must be planned, routes marked out, assignments made, information sheets developed, collateral material selected, briefings given and participants rehearsed. Out of 1,000 calls, typically 200 to 300 result in some type of sales lead.

Although students are doing the legwork, it's important to have your full-time sales staff follow up to make sure that no leads go for naught.

If well-planned and implemented, a student blitz can keep your employees in the house while outsiders drum up immediate sales leads. Student Blitz Programs will work for all facets of the hospitality industry, although they have been more frequently used for hotels.

Student Blitz Programs are not new. Using college students for Sales Blitz Programs goes pretty far back to the early days of the Hotel Sales Management Association and Frank Berkman's introduction of this very successful technique.

The new twist to Student Blitz Programs is to engage the services of an outside source, for a fee, to handle the entire operation. This takes the adminsitrative burden of doing a Blitz away from the hotel's sales staff, thereby allowing the salespeople to continue their usual daily sales activities without taking time away from selling.

The hospitality's staff's only involvement would include a Pre-Blitz Orientation Dinner, providing collateral material, arranging for incentive awards, and providing the service of a sales manager each evening of the Blitz period. Each day, upon the return of the Blitzers, the sales manager reviews each Blitz Call Report to determine the number of calls and leads turned in.

In a Student Blitz exercise for the Royce Resort Hotel, Palm Springs, California, 988 calls were made in Los Angeles, that developed more than 400 leads. The business potential available to the property amounted to $600,000. Two definite pieces of business were booked by Student Blitzers while the calls were being made. The total cost to the hotel for the entire program was less than $6,000.

In addition to the development of the leads, the amount of goodwill and promotion benefit for the hotel was virtually immeasurable.

The experience gained by making the calls and the exposure to hotel operations could only benefit the students in their future studies and career paths.

Servico operated hotels have had extensive experience with Student Blitz programs.

Purdue University students have been involved in such programs for the Royce Resort Hotel, Palm Springs, California to make calls in Los Angeles (mentioned earlier) soon after the opening of this all-suite hotel. They also performed blitz programs in Houston, Texas for the 450-room Sheraton Crown Hotel near Houston's Intercontinental Airport. Another Purdue Student Blitz was conducted in Detroit on behalf of Servico's three Hilton Hotels and The Michigan Inn in that area. All the blitz programs proved to be tremendously successful, generating immediate business for all the hotels.

Florida International University has provided students for two blitz programs on behalf of the Royce Hotel in West Palm Beach.

Servico, Inc., a West Palm Beach, Florida-based company, operating 59 hotels in 20 states and British Columbia, has an ongoing program of local blitzes throughout the company. An example of a post blitz report covering the Raleigh Holiday Inn Downtown follows as an example. (See exhibit B.)

Also following is an actual written report on a blitz program conducted at the Servico operated Holiday Inn Pittsburgh W. In this case, the program involved only local staff personnel. (See exhibit C.)

ITEM 5

Date: Wednesday 12/18/85
Thursday 12/19/85

RALEIGH SALES BLITZ

| | | | | Potential Revenue | | | | |
| | | | | | | Banquet | | |
Person	Sales Calls	Leads	Business Cards	Transient Rooms	Group Rooms	Food	Bev	Total
R. Ashton	50	13	7	1450	8750	7505		17705
J. Batchelor	52	25	30	40950	3000	10500		54450
W. Beard	51	12	0	28200	49000	224400		301600
A. Crumpler	51	12	11	17200	20750	10150		48100
M. Dunham	40	21	22	758550	26350	23600		808500
J. Hill	40	12	4	34600	53000	53180		140780
R. Hobbs	51	34	4	25300	111000	78375		214675
A. Keating	60+	8+	9	13200	2500	1900		17600
S. Laney	50	32	9	84000	20500	68015	5000	177515
R. Laudano	46	9	2	5900	2500	700		9100
D. Lickteig	53	23	11	4400	15000	7800		27200
D. Miller	58	27	7	22400		11700		34100
S. Moore								
G. Oliver	32	38	15	11200	30500	13625		55325
G. Quick	47	18	6	4000	6400	5520		15920
C. Renfroe	42	10	2	24300	8000	5000		37300
J. Rodl	72	24	9	12300	1500	900		14700
K. Starnes	46+	28	2			400		400
M. Tope								
A. Rom	42	25	2	44774	450	2900		48124
L. Webb	46	14	10	29500	4100	10000		43600
S. Kappeler	50	8	5	32500	8500	9500		50500
Total	979	395	167	1194724	371800	545670	5000	2117194

Exhibit B

MEMORANDUM

TO: Mrs. Uranker

FROM: Jill Holliday

DATE: October 23, 1986

SUBJECT: Recap of Sales Blitz Conducted October 7-10, 1986

The blitz personnel included three (3) department heads, myself and two (2) marketing students from Robert Morris College.

Tuesday, October 7th, we began with an orientation of the hotel. All of the department heads introduced themselves and explained the functions of their respective departments in relation to the entire hotel. Discussion on the blitz objectives, goals and the hotel in general was conducted. A property tour for the two students was conducted. (In order to familiarize themselves with the hotel, these two were required to stay overnight to experience what they would be selling).

Role playing for the purpose of learning how to make a correct sales call and how to use the fact finding sheets was conducted. The two students observed as the hotel personnel acted out various situations they would, no doubt, be confronted with. They then also participated. Tuesday, then ended with a group dinner in the dining room.

Wednesday and Thursday, October 8-9th, followed the exact same format beginning with breakfast and a question and answer period. Territories were then assigned and from 9 AM - 3 PM everyone was on the road making sales calls. During recovery, the sales calls were classified into two groups: those requiring a call back within one month and those which have no immediate business or none at all. Each person briefed us on his/her day.

On Wednesday, seven people were out making calls, however only a total of 108 calls were made. The territory locations were within a seven mile radius of the hotel, however included: Airport Area, US Air Operations Base, Airport Office Park, RIDC Parkwest, Parkwest I & II, Campbells Run Road and Vista International Park. In addition, one person was assigned to the Mobay Complex. We did not hit our "goal" this day for calls. I feel this was due to the fact that with both Mobay and US Air, it was difficult to speak to anyone without an appointment and too much time was wasted at both of these locations.

Thursday was an extremely busy day in the hotel; therefore, after lunch, all department heads returned to the hotel thus leaving only three (including myself) making sales calls in the afternoon in relation to five in the morning. Our concentration this day included: Penn Center West, Campbells Run Road again, Calgon, Hightower Office Complex, Parkway West Industrial Park and a brief contact with the Carnegie Office Complex. Only a total of 104 calls were made.

Exhibit C

Although only 212 calls were conducted, I still feel the blitz proved to be successful. 66 good leads were generated and I will be following up on them within the next month.

Upon planning the blitz, I had anticipated having seven people on the road making calls for two full days with a goal of contacting around 350 businesses. I feel this goal was not reached for several reasons:

1. The department heads could not stay on the road for two full days (6 hours/ day) due to business in the hotel.
2. I noticed that the two students from Robert Morris were "burnt out" the second day, thus being tired and less enthusiastic.
3. The area blitzed on Wednesday is an area where I normally do not make many calls, however a good number of leads generated from here. In addition, as mentioned earlier, much time was wasted at Mobay and the US Air Operations Base due to our not having appointments.

We have already experienced some positive results from the blitz:

1. Three new companies (Shandon Corporation, Genix and Chrysler) have all booked meetings for 1986.
2. Transient sleeping rooms have been booked by Safety First, Elkem Metals, Chrysler and Westinghouse. **Safety First and Elkem had been heavy transient users of our hotel and had stopped using us for awhile. However, after hearing of the construction enclosing the rooms, etc, they have decided to try us again.
3. Approximately eight new people have expressed an interest in our ERS Club. (Secretaries Reservation Service)

Friday, October 10th was the last day of the blitz with everyone meeting at the hotel for an awards luncheon. Three awards were given out to the top three people generating the most leads and potential. The following Friday, Ocotber 17th, a "Customer Appreciation Party" was held to thank everyone for their time during our blitz and to show prospects our hotel in general. This party proved to be a tremendous success.

I feel the following improvements could be made for the next blitz conducted by the hotel:

1. Emphasize strongly that the calls are only for the purpose of fact finding. Only 3-5 minutes should be spent in each office. If a person can not see you, move on to the next call.
2. Have more personnel, either from within the hotel itself or outside resources, out on the road making calls enabling greater exposure.
3. Reserve the areas which I knew would be difficult to speak to (Mobay and US Air) for myself at another time. Not during a blitz.
4. Screen territories. A lot of time was spent on Campbells Run Road trying to locate companies which turned out to be only warehouses, not offices, with no potential at all.
5. Conduct the blitz during a less busy time of the year.

Exhibit C

Mastering Sales Methods — A "Do-It-Yourself" Proposition

No matter how many times we try to establish sales training programs for entry-level salespeople, or even provide advanced training programs for seasoned sales people, it really all boils down to a self-training situation. There are, of course, company policies and training manuals that set standards for salespeople at a property or corporate headquarters. And there are certain forms and records that must be kept and systems for establishing and maintaining files. These are standard requirements established by companies for their people. When it comes down to basic selling techniques, however, it's a do-it-yourself thing: the more you do it, the better you get.

We need to challenge our salespeople to learn more about customers and their businesses. It's very important that they learn what's going on in the customer's world so they can be better prepared to do business with that customer.

By making face-to-face sales calls, we are able to learn more about the prospect and what his or her needs are. This is really what selling is all about — and it's easy to do. It's merely a matter of asking; most people are more than willing to tell you about themselves, their businesses, and what it is they're looking for. Then it comes down to knowing and introducing the product.

Once we know what the customer wants and have a thorough knowledge of our product, it's just a question of relating the customer's needs to the services our hotel or motel has to offer.

An important selling technique developed in the field is finding out what we do that our customers appreciate, what makes them want to come back to have more meetings and conferences with us. We should ask our existing customers why they like our property and its services. Learning why present customers use what we're selling is very valuable to us in seeking new customers.

What serves well for one group can also serve well for another group. This is where the salesperson must know the benefits a client realizes from coming to a property. Most of the time, we already know (or think we know) the benefits to a group using our property; however, by asking repeat customers what they enjoyed, we'll no doubt discover additional benefits we may not have been aware of earlier.

There's no question about it, the more calls we make, the more sales we make. Becoming an effective salesperson requires more calls, more inquiries, more leads followed up, more rejections, more digging, more effort in finding out what the client's needs might be, and more analysis of previous successes that can be applied to present selling situations; in short, a continuation of hard work and the selling process.

There's no real selling unless the seller and the prospect end up face-to-face, which means going out and making the calls or having prospects come in to look at the property.

Before a sale is made, multiple calls usually must be made. It's unlikely a sale will be closed with the first cold call to a prospect. It probably will take four, five, or six calls on a prospective customer before an actual sale is made. So it's a question of making as many calls as needed to get the job done.

Salespeople can learn as they go by asking prospects certain questions and listening to their responses. What works for one customer may not work for another. The idea is to be comfortable in making sales calls, comfortable in asking questions, and comfortable in the relationship with the prospect.

Becoming a professional requires an extended learning challenge. There are no short cuts to knowing your customers. Developing selling skills is a self-training process that's accomplished in the field.

Restaurant Marketing

WHILE MOST CONSUMERS ARE NOT FRE-quent or heavy users of the large majority of products and services in the hospitality industry, the restaurant business is a different story.

The average American spends 40 percent of his food dollar away from home. Just 20 years ago the figure was only 25 percent. The explanation for this phenomenon is to be found in Robert Shulman's earlier article on social and lifestyle trends that have influenced the entire hospitality industry and will continue to do so. Baby boomers and working women have clearly affected it.

The average person eats out 3.7 times a week. Our choice of restaurants is as varied as their menus. According to the National Restaurant Association, the quick service restaurants (primarily fast-food) get the lion's share of our business on 64.1 percent of the occasions. Mid-scale table service restaurants that are popular with families get 27.1 percent of the occasions, and upscale full-service restaurants receive 8.8 percent. All these visits to all these restaurants generated a $144 billion industry in 1985.

As Mark Lawless and Christopher Hart point out in their article, which focuses on strategic planning, however dy-namic this industry might be, it is not one in which marketing has played a large role until very recently. Indeed such concepts as positioning are just now emerging and others, like the value of a brand name, are just a few years old. With the exception of hotel restaurants, franchises, and chains, the business is still highly fragmented and consists of small entrepreneurial units. The number of classifications of products, each with its own market segment, is substantial. The quick service segment alone can be broken down into hamburgers, pizzas, chicken, ice cream, sandwiches, donuts, Mexican, fish/seafood, and Oriental restaurants.

Only the largest chains have even been able to think about the four Ps of marketing as they apply to their business. In most cases the product has been a given. French chefs open French restaurants and Oriental chefs open oriental restaurants. Demand is not researched or considered. "There's always room for a better one," the owners believe, but their criteria for better is purely subjective.

Pricing strategy, too, is relatively simplistic and often naive. For this reason, as many as 50 percent of all restaurants fail within the first year. Their owners have not considered or have failed to understand food and labor costs, productivity, and competitive pressures.

The third "P," Place, often does get careful attention, but sometimes operators have asked the wrong questions or failed to get the right answers. Restaurants in shopping centers, for example, are dependent on the success of the center — and many smaller centers don't make it. Roadside restaurants catering to travelers are dependent on the ultimate fate and success of the route. When he was already 65 and ready to retire, Colonel Sanders was forced to find a new concept and a new location when his only restaurant lost all of its customers because of the opening of a new interstate.

Promotion has for the most part been minimal because of the small profit margins and marketing budgets. Again, only the chains and successful franchises have been able to generate enough dollars for it. Some have caught on very well. McDonald's is one of the most marketing oriented companies in the world and has built its business by researching customer demand and delivering what the market wants, where they want it, and what they want to pay for it. Their promotion has been a classic case of good advertising carefully targeted to various market segments: businessmen for breakfast, children, teens, adults, and even the handicapped!

Given the undeveloped state of the industry, the second article in this section, by Dan Scoggin, founder of T.G.I. Friday's, is particularly relevant. Scoggin started with one small restaurant and a concept in 1972. He now runs an organization of 130 restaurants. He offers no magic formulas for success nor did luck play an important role in his growth; instead, a solid understanding of market demand and target marketing combined with an acute sense of how to make a profit brought Scoggin success.

I consider this section to be extremely important to the overall concept of the book. For most travelers, whether they are on business or at leisure, food is an important component of the trip. For a hotel, destination, cruise, or tour to succeed, it needs to understand the trends and the future of this segment. Lawless and Hart and Scoggin have done excellent jobs of putting all of this material into perspective.

Chapter 18

Forces That Shape Restaurant Demand

Mark J. Lawless
Vice President,
Corporate Planning,
Ponderosa

Having a B.S. and M.S. in Economics from Southern Illinois University at Edwardsville, Mark J. Lawless is vice president and director of corporate planning for Ponderosa, Inc. Prior to this he was the Manager of R&D Finance and Administration for NCR Corporation.

Christopher W. L. Hart
Professor, Cornell
University

Christopher Hart, whose specialty is management of service businesses, is a visiting professor at the Harvard University Graduate School of Business. He is on leave from the Cornell University School of Hotel Administration, where he received a B.A. and Ph.D. He received his M.B.A. from Harvard University.

This article was originally published in the November, 1983 issue of The Cornell Hotel and Restaurant Quarterly, *and is reprinted here with the permission of the Cornell University School of Hotel Administration.*

I f we can know where we are and something about how we got there, we might see where we are trending — and if the outcomes which lie naturally in our course are unacceptable, to make timely change.[1]

Just as a fish doesn't know that it's wet — because it has been in the water all its life — managers often lose track of the environment in which their businesses exist. The crush of day-to-day operations frequently locks managers' attention onto short-term concerns to the exclusion of long-term considerations critical to the success of their firms. Indeed, one of the most difficult tasks managers face is setting aside time to take off the hat of the operating manager and put on that of the strategist.

The distinction between efficiency and effectiveness underscores the need for a longer view. Peter Drucker put it simply, but elegantly: "Efficiency is concerned with doing things right. Effectiveness is doing the right things."[2] In Drucker's view, *efficiency* involves improving what is already being done (an internal, operational orientation), while *effectiveness* is concerned with

---

[1]Attributed to Abraham Lincoln in Arthur A. Thompson, Jr., and A.J. Strickland III, *Strategy Formulation and Implementation* (Plano, TX: Business Publications, Inc., 1983), p. 189.
[2]Peter F. Drucker, *Management: Tasks, Responsibilities, Practices* New York: Harper & Row, 1973), p. 45.

what *should* be done — with directing a firm's resources to the opportunities that will optimize long-run profitability.

Managers' tendency to focus on day-to-day operating tasks is often reinforced by accounting and management information systems. The data made available by these systems draw managers' attention to problems (inefficiencies), but are incapable of identifying opportunities. A case in point: *The cost of missed opportunities is never revealed by accounting data or the output of management information systems.* To overcome the natural tendency toward a short-term operational orientation, many corporations have formally incorporated the *strategic-planning process* into the structure of their firms, forcing their managers to engage in some semblance of long-range thinking.

Strategic Planning — Pro and Con

Strategic planning has probably been more widely heralded than any other business concept in the last 20 years. A report published in 1962 by the Stanford Research Institute, for example, hailed strategic planning as "a systematic means by which a company can become what it wants to be." By 1971, strategic planning had become, in one author's view, "the manifestation of a company's determination to be the master of its own fate . . . to penetrate the darkness of uncertainty and provide the illumination of probability."[3] Although most would agree that strategic planning falls short of the poetic heights described by this writer, the concept has undeniably had an enormous impact on the business world.

Strategic planning is not without its detractors, however, as the following comments by CEOs indicate:

— "Strategic planning is basically just a plaything of staff men."

— "It's like a Chinese dinner: I feel full when I get it, but after a while I wonder whether I've eaten at all."

— "Strategic planning? A staggering waste of time and money."[4]

One prominent consultant even went so far as to state that, "in the large majority of companies, corporate planning tends to be an academic, ill-defined activity with little or no bottom-line impact."[5]

How can these critical comments be reconciled with the obvious popularity of strategic planning? The criticisms reflect the considerable confusion that surrounds both the definition and the implementation of strategic planning. Although a wealth of articles and texts deal with these issues, they are usually written for a broad audience, and therefore employ generalizations in

[3]Sam R. Goodman, *Taking the Guesswork Out of Long-Range Planning* (New York: Prentice-Hall, 1971), p. 42.
[4]Louis V. Gerstner, "Can Strategic Planning Pay Off?," *Business Horizons*, December 1972, p. 5.
[5]Ibid.

an attempt to address a wide range of industries. This is unfortunate, because every industry embodies a unique set of economic and competitive characteristics; as a result, many "generic" strategic-planning concepts fall short when they are applied to specific situations.

The wholesale application of general strategic-planning principles is especially problematic in the restaurant industry. Not only does food service possess elements of manufacturing, retailing, and service industries, but it is also highly fragmented (as opposed to industries in which a few firms dominate). Few of the major strategic-planning concepts (e.g., scale economies, the experience curve) have been specifically applied in the business literature to industries with these characteristics. As a result, the "pillars" of the strategic-planning discipline can be a shaky foundation indeed in strategy formulation for restaurant companies — as many have already discovered.

This article begins with an overview of strategic planning before moving to an analysis of the forces that affect restaurant demand. The "big-picture" view offered in the following pages is intended to help readers expand their perspective — to take off the operating manager's hat that can constrain one's thinking about the nature of the industry, and to begin wearing the strategist's hat.

Some Definitions

Definitions of strategic planning abound; some use the terminology of classic military theory, while others are couched in the arcane language of academe. But a simple definition is possible: *Strategic planning is the managerial process of developing and maintaining an optimal "fit" between the deployment of an organization's resources and the opportunities in its changing environment.*

One critical facet of strategic planning that grows out of this definition is the concept of *competitive advantage*. Briefly, a firm's strategy should be designed to gain an advantage over its competitors. (Part of Red Lobster's strategy, for example, is to maintain a cost advantage over its competitors through volume purchasing and a vertically integrated supply chain.) To identify strategies that will yield a competitive edge, one must first understand the forces underlying competitive behavior in a given industry.

Consider the competitive forces at work in a *commodity industry* — one whose product represents a high percentage of the raw-material costs of products made by other firms. An example is the beef industry, whose product is essential for such familiar end products as steak dinners and hamburgers. The major demand-based forces underlying the competition among beef suppliers offering comparable product quality are purchasers' concerns regarding price and delivery service (with heavy emphasis on price); consequently, the competitive behavior of supplier firms would emphasize price and, to a lesser extent, customer service. To gain a competitive advantage, therefore, a beef supplier's overall *strategy* must be directed at achieving cost reductions and maintaining an adequate level of customer service.

Numerous other forces influence the nature and intensity of competition in an industry, including *barriers to entry*, the availability and price of *substitute products*, the industry's *cost structure*, and its evolutionary *stage in the product life cycle*.[6] Understanding these forces, and the interrelationships among them, provides the conceptual framework needed to identify and analyze a firm's strategic options and, ultimately, to develop a strategy that capitalizes on a firm's strengths while defending it against its weaknesses.

Well-formulated competitive strategy will grow increasingly important in future years — if for no other reason than the increasing percentage of firms that will acquire and use sophisticated planning techniques. To develop such a strategy, a firm's managers must fully understand both their industry and the competitive position their firm holds in it. The process of formulating competitive strategy also requires managers to assess critically their firms' strengths and weaknesses, in light of both the strengths and weaknesses of competing firms and of available business opportunities.

In this perspective, we will now analyze several issues fundamental to understanding the competitive environment of the restaurant industry. This discussion will serve as a foundation for future articles on more specialized topics, such as economies of scale, experience-curve effects, the product life cycle, and the concept of company mission.

Restaurants Are Not Buggy Whips

The first step in developing a "big-picture" view of an industry is to consider the general nature of the need it fills. Imagine an industry providing a product or service that fulfills an enduring human need for which no suitable substitute exists. Imagine further that the need is universal and must be satisfied on a recurring basis. The characteristics you just imagined are those of a huge and stable market — one that should provide ample business opportunities.

The provision of food certainly meets the above criteria. Humanity's need for food has provided a host of lucrative business opportunities over the centuries — many of which fall into the familiar category of restaurants.

The reason that we state what is fairly obvious is to underscore a critical point that is rarely given any thought: *It is highly unlikely that the restaurant product — food prepared and served away from home — will ever be made obsolete by technology.* This is not generally the case in the rest of the business

---

[6]For an especially good discussion of the forces underlying competition, see: Michael Porter, *Competitive Strategy: Techniques for Analyzing Industries and Competitors* (New York: Free Press, 1980).

world, where products and entire industries are routinely replaced by products based on new technologies — as electronic calculators replaced slide rules, for instance.

This is not to say that technological obsolescence has not occurred in various *sectors* of the food industry. Salting and smoking as methods of preservation, for example, have largely been replaced by refrigeration; aseptic packaging could eliminate the need for canning; the microwave oven has replaced more time-consuming methods of food preparation; and giant supermarket chains have eclipsed thousands of smaller, less efficient retail grocery operations.

Despite such changes in production technology, however, the fundamental manner in which humans satisfy their eating and drinking needs has remained unaffected. While food-preparation techniques and the popularity of different foods may change over time, it is highly probable — contrary to what some futurists might think — that the human species will be eating and drinking thousands of years hence. Moreover, as long as humans are able to leave their homes and move about, some portion of their eating and drinking will most likely take place in restaurants — especially in view of the basic human need for social interaction. In short, restaurant firms are in no danger of going the way of buggy-whip manufacturers.

Having established that the nature of the restaurant need is an enduring one, let us consider the forces that have affected the *size* of the eating and drinking market over time.

The F&B Market: A Broad View

In simple terms, food and drink can be purchased either in a retail store or in a food-service establishment and, once purchased, can either be consumed *at* home or *away* from home. Combining these options presents consumers with the four basic eating alternatives shown in Exhibit 1. Each business that competes for consumers' food and beverage (F&B) dollars can be placed in one of the matrix's quadrants. From this overall perspective, restaurants are merely a part of a much larger industry that caters to people's eating and drinking needs.

We take this broad view of the food-service market to stress the importance of avoiding "marketing myopia," which occurs when management's focus becomes too centered on its existing business. We hypothesize, for example, that many food-service firms have failed to give adequate consideration to opportunities in the "take-out service" quadrant, despite strong consumer interest in time-saving products and services. (In Japan, the two fastest-growing restaurant chains *specialize* in take-out meals.[7])

[7]"Share of Leading Restaurants and Catering Firms Drops, Check Shows," *The Japan Economic Journal*, May 10, 1985.

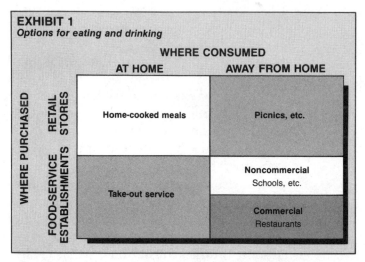

Another reason for taking a broad perspective of the food-service industry is to raise the issue of how broadly the industry should be defined — always a topic of considerable debate in strategic-planning circles. Many writers have encouraged managers to define their businesses as broadly as possible, usually in terms of an underlying consumer need, so that potential sources of competition will not be overlooked (e.g., recognizing teleconferencing as a potential threat to transient hotel accommodations).

Defining an industry broadly in no way implies that a firm should attempt to *compete* in every industry sector thus identified. A firm's particular strengths and resources will determine which of the numerous potential opportunities the firm should consider pursuing. Different strengths are required to compete successfully in the fast-food market than in gourmet restaurants, for example, although both are segments of the food-service industry.

One way of categorizing different restaurant types along these lines is shown in Exhibit 2, which classifies operations by menu variety and service level (or check average, which parallels service level). There are profound differences in the competitive characteristics of the restaurant segments represented by different cells in the matrix. As a result, different strategies are required to compete effectively in different cells, and different factors determine which firms will succeed in each. Consider, for example, the operational problems that beset such major food-processing firms as Pillsbury and General Foods when they first diversified into fast-food restaurants — in theory, a logical extension of their existing food businesses, but in practice, a business requiring many skills these firms lacked. In summary, defining the boundaries of an industry for purposes of analysis is very different from formulating strategies (i.e., from determining where a company should compete in that industry).

EXHIBIT 2
Restaurants categorized by service level and menu variety

SERVICE (CHECK) LEVEL		LOW	MEDIUM	HIGH
HIGH		Concept Restaurants *Benihana*	Upscale Dinnerhouses *Red Lobster*	Fine-Dining Restaurants *Four Seasons*
MEDIUM		Specialty Restaurants *Tony Roma's*	Family Restaurants *Ponderosa*	Casual Dining *The Good Earth*
LOW	Service	Pizza Parlors *Pizza Hut*	Retail Stores *Bloomingdale's, K-Mart*	Delis and Diners
	Self-service	Fast Food and Convenience *Church's*	Cafeterias *Morrison's*	

Food-Service Growth and Market Share

Let us now classify the food-service industry in another way to begin our examination of recent demand trends.[8] At the broadest level, the industry may be segmented into the commercial, institutional, and military sectors.

The commercial-feeding group includes establishments open to the public and operated for profit. This group encompasses freestanding restaurants, food-service contractors, hotel and motel restaurants, and restaurants in department stores, drug stores, etc.

The institutional-feeding group is composed of business, educational, government, and institutional organizations (e.g., hospitals and schools) that run their own food-service operations rather than assigning them to food-service contractors. While some of these establishments operate at a profit, institutional cafeterias are often operated as a service (e.g., for one's employees) rather than primarily as a profit-making venture.

The military-feeding group, which is largely nonprofit, comprises sales of food and beverages at military clubs and exchanges, as well as food service for the armed forces.

Between 1970 and 1980, the food-service industry as a whole grew at a 10.3-percent compound annual rate. As shown in Exhibit 3, most of this growth occurred in the commercial sector, which expanded from $35 billion in 1970 to $113 billion in 1982. Much of this growth was the product of inflation, however; real sales growth in the commercial sector over this period was a more modest 2.0 percent per year.

---

[8]Much of the following material draws heavily from "Past, Present, and Future Trends in the Food-Service Industry and Their Implications for Hospitality Management Development," a report prepared for the Cornell School of Hotel Administration by Christopher W. Hart, recent Cornell M.P.S. graduate Gary Spizizen, and Joan S. Livingston, executive editor of *The Quarterly*.

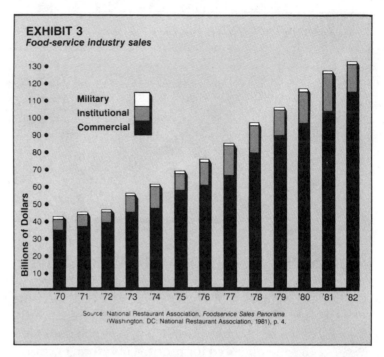

EXHIBIT 3
Food-service industry sales

Billions of Dollars

Military
Institutional
Commercial

'70 '71 '72 '73 '74 '75 '76 '77 '78 '79 '80 '81 '82

Source: National Restaurant Association, *Foodservice Sales Panorama* (Washington. DC: National Restaurant Association, 1981), p. 4.

EXHIBIT 4
Regional food-service sales

	Real Annual Rate of Change
Western Region	5.8%
Southern Region	5.4%
Northeast Region	.8%
North Central Region	−6.0%
Total U.S.	1.4%

Source: 1983 Annual Report, *Restaurants and Institutions*, March 15, 1983, p. 72.

Growth has varied not only by segment but also by geographical area. As shown in Exhibit 4, sales grew fastest (in real terms) in the western and southern regions of the U.S. between 1979 and 1982. The northeastern region experienced no growth, while sales declined in the north-central region.

While the commercial sector has been growing in size, it has also been growing in concentration. Between 1970 and 1980, the top 100 restaurant companies' share of total commercial sales increased steadily, as shown in Exhibit 5, rising from 24.0 percent in 1970 to 47.8 percent in 1982.

When the sales of the top 100 are broken out by industry segment, the "separate eating place" group (of freestanding restaurants) emerges as the sector with the most growth in both sales and units over the past ten years. Within that segment, during the ten-year period between 1970 and 1980,

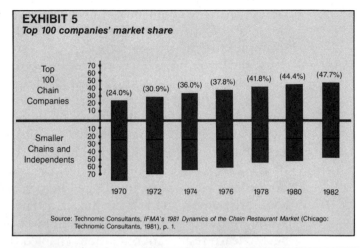

EXHIBIT 5
Top 100 companies' market share

Top 100 Chain Companies / Smaller Chains and Independents

(24.0%) 1970 (30.9%) 1972 (36.0%) 1974 (37.8%) 1976 (41.8%) 1978 (44.4%) 1980 (47.7%) 1982

Source: Technomic Consultants, *IFMA's 1981 Dynamics of the Chain Restaurant Market* (Chicago: Technomic Consultants, 1981), p. 1.

EXHIBIT 6
Top 100's sales and units by restaurant type

	Percent of Total Sales		Percent of Total Units	
	1970	1980	1970	1980
Separate eating places				
Fast food	52.0%	56.1%	61.8%	60.3%
Specialty	14.3	23.1	10.4	20.0
Family	12.7	10.1	5.7	7.6
Total separate eating places	79.0	89.3	77.9	87.9
Hotels and motels	14.4	8.4	8.5	5.8
Retail stores	6.6	2.3	13.6	6.3
Total Sales/Total Units	$6.9B	$35.4B	36,199	75,624

Source: Technomic Consultants, *IFMA's 1981 Dynamics of the Chain Restaurant Market* (Chicago: Technomic Consultants, 1981), p. 3.

the only subsegment registering an increase in its share of both sales *and* units was specialty-type restaurants (see Exhibit 6).

There is one overriding reason for the increasing concentration of the restaurant industry: namely, the competitive characteristics of the largest industry sector — restaurants providing inexpensive food and fast service in convenient locations (i.e., fast food) — are well-suited to the growth of large chains. Fast-food operations offer the greatest opportunities for achieving economies of scale and experience-curve efficiencies — and whenever an industry segment presents these opportunities, the level of concentration increases until the segment is dominated by large firms.

Industry concentration is related to potential economies of scale for the following reason. Larger firms generally can gain cost advantages over their smaller competitors, and these cost advantages enable them to sell their products at lower prices with no sacrifice in profit margins (or at comparable prices with higher profit margins). Thus, larger firms make more money that can, in turn, be spent in various ways to increase their market share even more, leaving the smaller firms further and further behind. In fast food, for example, the gap between the large and small companies has widened because the larger firms have applied their profits to rapid expansion and large-scale advertising — creating a formidable competitive advantage.

Another important reason for the increasing concentration of the restaurant industry has been the entry of such large corporations as Heublein (which acquired Kentucky Fried Chicken), PepsiCo (Pizza Hut and Taco Bell), Pillsbury (Burger King and Steak & Ale), Ralston Purina (Jack-in-the-Box), General Foods (Burger Chef), and General Mills (Red Lobster and York Steak House). As mentioned before, most of these firms initially encountered unexpected difficulties in attempting to run the operations they acquired, but their financial staying power, marketing muscle, and willingness to learn restaurant operations enabled them to prevail (except for General Foods, which never overcame its problems with Burger Chef). The entry of these firms into the restaurant industry substantially altered the nature and intensity of the competition in the segments in which they chose to compete. Many of the other restaurant firms operating in these segments found themselves ill-equipped to compete against the sophisticated and well-heeled newcomers.

At Home vs. Away

We will now look at the food-service market from another angle by investigating the factors that have altered demand for food consumed at home and for food consumed away from home.

Food and Beverage at Home

Exhibit 7 shows total U.S. food- and liquor-store sales between 1960 and 1981, corrected for inflation. Sales jumped dramatically from 1960 to 1970, but were basically flat from 1970 to 1981. The lack of growth in the latter period is puzzling in view of the concurrent increase of more than ten percent in the U.S. population; more mouths to feed would logically be expected to translate into an increase in F&B purchased for home consumption. In fact, however, expenditures per capita for F&B at home declined from $516.10 in 1970 to $474.90 in 1980. (These figures seem low because they are in constant 1972 dollars; inflationary increases have been removed.) Moreover, this decline occurred in a period when per-capita disposable income increased from $3,665 in 1970 to $4,538 in 1981. As a percentage of disposable personal income (DPI), F&B at home decreased from 17.1 percent in 1960 to 14.1 percent in 1970 and to 10.4 percent in 1981.

What caused this drop? Fundamental changes in Americans' eating and drinking patterns. In short, consumers were spending more on F&B away from home.

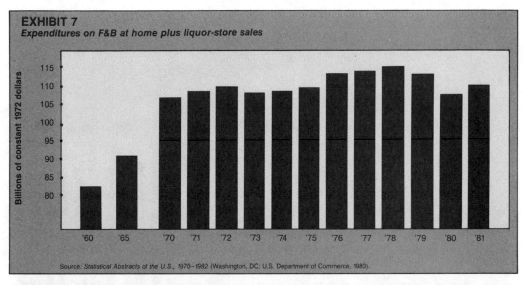

EXHIBIT 7
Expenditures on F&B at home plus liquor-store sales

Source: *Statistical Abstracts of the U.S., 1970–1982* (Washington, DC: U.S. Department of Commerce, 1983).

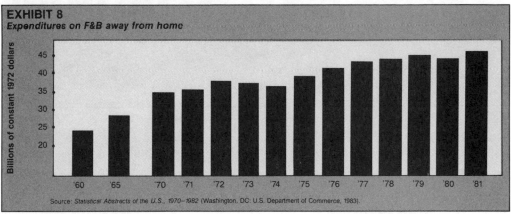

EXHIBIT 8
Expenditures on F&B away from home

Source: *Statistical Abstracts of the U.S., 1970–1982* (Washington, DC: U.S. Department of Commerce, 1983).

Food and Beverage Away from Home

Exhibit 8 shows total expenditures on F&B away from home between 1960 and 1981. Although sales dipped during several years (reflecting the impact of recessions), a definite upward trend is still apparent. In contrast to the general decline in F&B at home, uninflated expenditures per capita on eating out increased from $165.40 per person in 1970 to $190.30 in 1981.

Interestingly, as shown in Exhibit 9, while expenditures per capita for F&B at home were declining as a percentage of DPI, the percentage of DPI per capita represented by F&B away from home was stable, ranging between 4.1 percent and 4.5 percent. Since the percentage of F&B away from home remained constant while the percentage of F&B at home declined, it is logical to question what was happening to total per-capita F&B *expenditures* during this period.

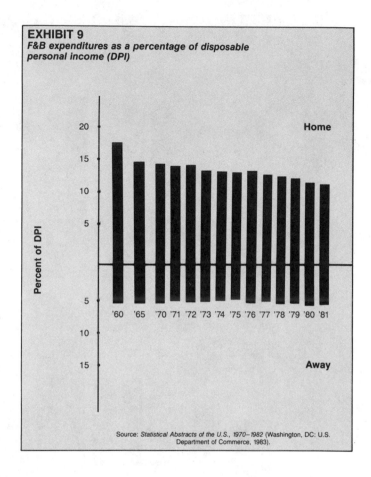

One might presume that the decrease in per-capita F&B expenditures at home was more than offset by an increase in per-capita F&B expenditures away from home — at least if people were eating the same number of meals — due to the generally higher unit cost of meals eaten away from home. In fact, however, total per-capita F&B expenditures were relatively *flat*, in spite of the increase in the dollar amount spent on F&B away from home. Assuming accurate data, the only possible interpretation is that people are eating and/or drinking less than they used to. More research is needed to test this interesting hypothesis; if true, it is empirical evidence for the widely publicized trend toward consuming fewer calories.

This possibility notwithstanding, the fact still remains that both total and per-capita F&B expenditures away from home have registered real increases. A host of supply and demand factors account for this increase. The supply-based factors include the following:

☐ the proliferation of low-priced, consistent-quality, fast-food operations,

☐ an increased number of restaurant units, and

☐ the adoption of large-scale, sophisticated marketing techniques.

Proliferation of Fast-Food Operations

The growth of large fast-food chains has been a tremendous stimulant to restaurant demand. Efficient, assembly-line restaurant operations enabled the chains to charge prices far below those of competitors, and — true to the law of demand — lower prices led to a dramatic increase in the demand for food away from home. (Much of this growth came at the expense of retail grocery chains — whose failure to enter the fast-food market is one of the worst cases of marketing myopia in history.)

Increase in the Number of Restaurant Units

The more restaurant units there are in a given area, the more convenient it is for consumers to choose to eat out; as a result, more units bring higher demand. The number of commercial food-service establishments in the U.S. jumped from 336,000 in 1970 to 407,000 in 1982, an increase of 21.1 percent.[9] (The importance of the fast-food sector again becomes apparent; it accounted for 78.9 percent of this increase.)

Sophisticated Marketing Techniques

The entry into the restaurant industry of large firms possessing enormous financial resources and marketing expertise (e.g., Pillsbury and General Mills) has had a huge impact on restaurant demand. Skills in such areas as market research, new-product development, advertising, and promotion enabled these firms to (1) define the needs of restaurant market segments, (2) develop products closely matched to the needs of their target markets, and (3) build strong brand images (or "brand franchises").

The demand-based factors that have fueled food-service growth include these:

☐ stability of demand,

☐ a reduction in household size,

☐ the increasing participation of women in the work force,

☐ the entry of the enormous, consumption-oriented baby-boom generation into the work force,

☐ a better-educated population,

☐ the growth in dual-income families,

[9]"1983 Annual Report," *Restaurants and Institutions*, 92, No. 6 (March 15, 1983).

☐   general population growth, and

☐   growth in disposable income.

Most of the demand-related factors are familiar to food-service operators; in fact, they have become mundane in the trade press. But the behavioral causes underlying the statistics are rarely examined, and these offer implications for our conceptual understanding of the restaurant industry's competitive nature.

Demand Stability

Although many restaurant operators complain loudly during recessionary periods, sales are robust. As shown in Exhibit 8, sales declined significantly only once in 12 years — during 1973–74, a period of severe economic upheaval and limited gasoline availability. The most recent recession affected restaurant sales only slightly.

Why have restaurant sales not dropped as precipitously as sales in other industries (e.g., durable-goods production) during recent recessions? First, as pointed out earlier, people *need* to eat — many restaurant meals are far less discretionary than, say, purchases of new automobiles. Second, especially in bad economic times, consumers may feel a need for the "occasion" aspect of dining out and the opportunity to socialize. In fact, a restaurant meal may be one of the few self-indulgences a financially pinched family can afford. A recent survey of 1,000 consumers revealed that half were reluctant to reduce restaurant patronage as a way to save money. (Consumers ranked it 12th out of 14 possible ways to cut back.)[10] For many, the restaurant experience apparently more than compensates for the cost of dining out.

Another reason for the food-service industry's relative stability is the high percentage of dining-out occasions that reflect necessity, rather than personal choice; travelers, of course, are simply not able to dine at home. Two-thirds of all McDonald's sales, for example, are to customers who stop at the fast-food unit as part of a trip made for another reason.[11] Similarly, much of the higher-end meal market is composed of businesspeople who are either traveling or entertaining; for these customers, dining out is less a matter of discretion than of exigency. Finally, there is evidence that, in times of recession, people in high-income groups tend to "trade down" from expensive entertainment (especially vacations) to meals in high-service restaurants.

[10]Laura Wolda, "Consmers Less Likely to Cut Back Dining Out," *Nation's Restaurant News*, July 4, 1983, p. 55.
[11]Robert Emerson, *Fast Food: The Endless Shakeout* (New York: Lebhar-Friedman Books, 1979), p. 15.

Reduction in Family Size

Household size is frequently cited as a factor with a major effect on the demand for restaurant meals; in general, smaller households spend more dollars per capita on F&B away from home than do larger households. However, the behavioral reasons underlying the relationship between restaurant sales and household size are rarely given any attention. First, cooking meals at home in a small household is generally more expensive per person than for a larger household, since smaller households are unable to achieve larger households' economies of scale. This is true despite the narrowing of the price gap between dining out and eating at home caused by the advent of inexpensive, limited-menu restaurants. Second, one- and two-member households without children usually have more freedom and more opportunities to dine out — and often more discretionary income. Finally, large families dine out less because the price of a restaurant meal as a percentage for disposable income is greater for a larger household. In economic terms, demand for restaurants becomes more elastic as household size increases.

Historical trend data indicate that, since 1960, the percentage of larger households has been decreasing while the percentage of one- and two-member households has risen. And indications are that this trend will continue at least through 1995, fueled in part by the dramatic growth of single-person households, which will rise from 23 percent of the population in 1980 to 27 percent in 1990. By 1990, single individuals' share of the food-service dollar will increase from 23 percent to 29 percent.[12] All of the foregoing is good news for the restaurant industry, particularly for those firms that target this market and effectively meet its needs.

Women in the Work Force

Working women have a positive impact on food-service sales, because they:

☐ increase the amount of disposable income in a household,

☐ have less time to cook, so their families eat out more often, and

☐ often dine out during the workday.

Labor-force participation by women has been climbing and will continue to climb in the future — although admittedly at a slower rate than in the past. A full 59 percent of all women 16 years or older will be in the work force by 1990.[13] Their pattern of participation is approaching that of men; soon, most women will either remain in the work force throughout life or re-enter it after having children.

[12]"Demographic Forecasts: Household Consumption," *American Demographics*, July/August 1981, p. 47.
[13]"Demographic Forecasts: Labor Force," *American Demographics*, February 1981, p. 47.

The increase in the number of working women has led to growth in the number of two-income families. The number of married couples in which both spouses work full-time is projected to increase in every age group but one (householders under the age of 25), and the largest increase will be for householders aged 35 to 44. It follows that this group's disposable income will increase, as will its expenditures on F&B away from home. (In fact, the number of families earning $30,000 or more should increase 48 percent by the end of the decade.)[14]

Increase in Population

Increased population, with all other factors held constant, increases the demand for food. Although U.S. population growth is slowing down (10 percent growth during the 1970s, 9.7-percent during the '80s, and 7.3-percent during the '90s), the absolute number of Americans is still increasing. By 2050, it is estimated that the U.S. population will reach 309 million.[15]

Change in Age-Group Composition

Although the population as a whole is growing, growth rates vary across different age-group segments, as shown in Exhibit 10. The post-war baby boom is surging like a gigantic wave through our society. By the 1990s, the median age of Americans will be almost 35, compared to 28 in 1972. The baby-boom generation has had — and will continue to have — a profound impact on the food-service industry.

During the '60s and early '70s, the population of 18- to 34-year-olds was growing at an average annual rate of three percent — more than twice the average of the total population. An important reason for the rapid growth of fast-food restaurants in this period was their appeal to the baby-boom generation. Compared with the slow growth of full-service restaurants during this period, the growth of fast-food chains was astounding. Since 1980, however, the percentage of 18- to 34-year-olds has declined to 30 percent of the U.S. population, and by 1990, they will constitute only 21 percent of the population. The fastest-growing segment will be the 35- to 44-year-olds, a group that will be 40 percent larger in 1990 than it was in 1980.

The gradual maturing of the baby-boomers has important implications for the food-service industry. According to the Conference Board, the middle-age group is "by far the most promising sector of the market for the goods

---

[14]"Demographic Forecasts: Families by Size and Income," *American Demographics*, March 1983, p. 50.

[15]Gregory Spencer and John F. Long, "New Census Bureau Projections," *American Demographics*, April 1983, p. 50.

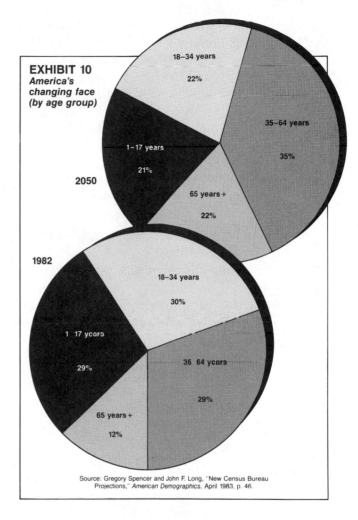

EXHIBIT 10
America's changing face (by age group)

18–34 years
22%

35–64 years
35%

1–17 years
21%

2050

65 years +
22%

1982

18–34 years
30%

1–17 years
29%

35–64 years
29%

65 years +
12%

Source: Gregory Spencer and John F. Long, "New Census Bureau Projections," *American Demographics*, April 1983, p. 46.

and services required for everyday needs as well as for luxury and top-of-the-line products generally."[16]

This sector will be particularly promising when the baby-boom generation enters its years of greatest productivity and earnings. Partly as a result of the increase in the earning power of this group, per-capita income, adjusted for inflation, is expected to increase 15 percent by 1990.[17] Moreover, these individuals, having grown up in the fast-food environment, have made eating out a fundamental part of their life-style — and they are now in a position to influence future generations as heads of households.

[16]"Two Incomes Will Lift More Families to Middle-Class Affluence in Decade," *The Wall Street Journal*, June 27, 1980, p. 8.

[17]"Demographic Forecasts: Income Distribution," *American Demographics*, September 1981, p. 46.

According to Sandra Shaber of Chase Econometrics, the impact of the baby-boom generation on the food-service industry could be "awesome":

> Advertising, menu choices, and formats will all have to be totally upgraded or at least changed. The two-income couple will be an especially powerful force; they will value convenience, status, and sophistication.[18]

Firms that can position themselves effectively to tap this market segment should do extremely well during the next decade. The market will, however, be hotly competitive.

As the population has aged, the size of the elderly segment has grown accordingly. On July 1, 1983, for the first time in U.S. history, there were more Americans over 65 (27.4 million) than teenagers (26.5 million)[19] — and the growth of the 65-plus segment will be enormous over the next 70 years. Even though today's older Americans spend a relatively smaller proportion of their total food dollar on meals outside the home than other segments, restaurant meals already account for nearly one-fourth of their weekly food budget.[20] Because of their specialized needs (e.g., nutritional requirements, need for special physical facilities, etc.), as well as the existence of a large subsegment with major financial resources and few financial demands, the elderly represent a unique marketing opportunity — one that will grow continually more fertile as the population continues to "gray."

Level of Educational Attainment

Educational levels are rising; at least 35 percent of Americans will have attended college by 1990.[21] This trend means better-informed, more-discriminating consumers who seek quality, who are interesting in experimenting with new brands and products, and who are both more willing and better able to pay premium prices.

Consumers' growing "health consciousness" and desire for more nutritious food, for example, probably represent a long-term phenomenon with major strategic implications for food-service firms. To name one, there appears to be an unmet need in the fast-food segment, among others, for low-calorie and nutritious menu items. A similar phenomenon is consumers' increased emphasis on quality rather than quantity — in other words, a desire for less food of a higher quality (for the same price — or a higher one).

---

[18]"State of the Industry," *Restaurant Hospitality*, September 9, 1982, p. 52.

[19]Claudia Wallis, "Slow, Steady, and Heartbreaking," *Time*, July 11, 1983, p. 56.

[20]Ken Rankin, "Americans Spending More for Restaurant Food," *Nation's Restaurant News*, August 1, 1983, p. 42.

[21]Richard Leviton, "Soyfoods Soar on Demographic Trends," *American Demographics*, March 1983, p. 37.

Although the *need* for food and beverage has remained relatively stable over time, the ways in which consumers attempt to satisfy that need are anything *but* stable. The economic, demographic, and life-style trends enumerated above yield one conclusion: The restaurant market is turbulent and continually changing. To succeed in this turbulent and increasingly competitive environment, restaurant managers must now systematically monitor trends, anticipate threats and opportunities, and formulate effective strategy to gain a competitive advantage. It is hoped that this article will help managers develop the analytical perspective needed to accomplish these objectives.

Chapter 19

How They Pack 'em in at T.G.I. Friday's

Daniel R. Scoggin
*Former President and
CEO, T.G.I. Friday's*

Daniel Scoggin mixed business acumen with a healthy dose of philosophy when he first took T.G.I. Friday's concept national in 1972. Today Friday's has more than 140 restaurants in 33 states and the United Kingdom and enjoys the highest per unit sales volume of any national restaurant chain.

When you hear the words "dynamic industry," what examples immediately come to mind? Computers, no doubt; semiconductors; biotechnology.

If "restaurants" isn't on your list, add it. The restaurant industry today is growing at a faster rate than at any time in history. Consumer tastes are changing so quickly that many restauranteurs can't keep up. Sophisticated market research and product development are keys to survival in this fiercely competitive business.

How did the industry evolve from the days of Joe's Bar and Grill and the local drive-in to the multiunit chains that crisscross the country today? More important, where will the industry be tomorrow?

The Industry since 1945

The evolution of the modern restaurant industry parallels social changes that occurred after World War II. In the late 1940s, families almost exclusively ate at home. Eating out was an occasion. Coffee shops and cafeterias began to spring up, but most restaurants were what we would consider mom and pop operations: family-owned businesses that could be either very good or very bad. If you weren't a local, you had no way of knowing what to expect when you walked in the door.

As postwar prosperity boosted the average American's disposable income, eating out became more common. In fact, with more and more families able to afford automobiles, Americans took to the highways and eating away from home became a necessity.

Chain restaurants sprang up. In a new city, travelers needed restaurants they could depend on for consistent quality, whether they were consistently good or just mediocre. "This mom and pop place might be excellent," they reasoned, "but how can we be sure? Let's go to the cafeteria down the street. At least we know what to expect there."

Automobiles quickened the pace of American life during the 1950s. Early fast-food restaurants like the *American Graffiti*-style drive-ins filled a demand for quick, inexpensive food. Hotel-chain restaurants were preferred for more formal occasions. Segmentation in the industry continued and by the 1960s steakhouse chains had emerged as an alternative to expensive, white-tablecloth restaurants and inexpensive coffee shops, cafeterias, and fast-food establishments.

The industry continued to mirror American life-styles into the 1960s. Changes came rapidly. Liberal sexual mores and advances in birth control encouraged young Americans to postpone marriage and family life. Many eschewed the traditional ways of the previous generation in favor of a more hedonistic life-style.

For these consumers, everything, including their favorite restaurants, had to be exciting and different. The opening of the first T.G.I. Friday's in New York City in 1965 heralded the new age. With its chalk-slate menus, over-sized burgers, and active bar scene, Friday's became known for good food and fun. Friday's-type establishments became known as *casual theme restaurants*.

In the 1970s and into the 1980s, the influx of women into the work force accelerated, which meant less time for cooking at home and more money for eating out. Restaurants proliferated, and consumer tastes ruled. If customers wanted Mexican food, for instance, scores of Mexican restaurants opened to satisfy them. There was a concept to suit every taste, and lots of money to be made.

Casual theme is an umbrella term that has harbored countless restaurant concepts in the more than 20 years since T.G.I. Friday's began. Consider how quickly life-styles have changed in the past two decades, from the hippies through the me-decade to the yuppies. Now think back on all the restaurant concepts and gimmicks these changing life-styles have given birth to: fern bars, discos, sushi bars, pizza parlors, and home-cookin' restaurants, to name a few. As consumer tastes changed, the industry raced to keep up.

T.G.I. Friday's rode the crest of the restaurant boom into the 1970s. Sales in our three base restaurants at the time topped $60,000 a week. Then, in the mid-1970s, those figures suddenly dropped 50 percent. Naturally we asked why.

"There's a lot more competition on the block," our managers said. "Everybody is getting smaller slices of the pie." "That's the restaurant business these days," the experts said. "With life-styles changing as quickly as they are, a restaurant can't expect more than five to seven years of success."

We were convinced this was not the case. The market was still there; we were just not getting a big enough share of it. So we traveled the country, studying restaurants on their way up, restaurants that had peaked, and restaurants in decline. From that knowledge we reshaped our marketing strategy. We developed a number of management theories that we instilled in our employees and within 90 days sales in our three base restaurants were back up to $60,000 a week.

Those theories are now time-tested. Since 1975, Friday's has grown thirtyfold, from a $10-million, six-unit operation to a more than $314-million, 120-restaurant chain. Per-unit sales are the highest of any national restaurant chain in the country.

Theories and Strategies

How has Friday's survived for more than 20 years while other restaurants have peaked and died out in less than seven? To put it briefly, we do it by paying attention to product, package, and service.

We have a theory at Friday's called *The Success Syndrome*. Any business is susceptible to it, but let's consider a restaurant as an example.

When a new restaurant opens, managers and employees are aiming to please. They will do anything to make the restaurant a success, because they need a job to pay their bills. The customer is king. This attitude continues for a few months, but after the restaurant is a proven success and customers are lined up outside, attitudes shift. The employees aren't concerned if service slows down a bit or if they get a little surly with the patrons sometimes. If a few customers leave, there are plenty more to take their places. With business going so well, the staff might start cutting corners in the kitchen and neglecting to clean up just a little to save the time and effort, thinking the customers won't notice. But they do notice. Then the restaurant staff wonders what happened when the customers stop pouring in, and nothing — not advertising, nor promotions, nor neon signs — will get them to come back.

It all goes back to the bottom line in the restaurant business: product, package, and service.

1. Product

Survival in the restaurant business means always providing top-quality food. But more than that, you've got to provide the product your customer wants. Since the proliferation of casual theme restaurants in the 1970s, the market has been zigzagging. Consumer tastes change constantly and restaurant concepts are hot only until the next concept comes along. For example, consumers may be hungry for ethnic foods (zig), so ethnic-food restaurants spring up; then consumers may turn to health foods (zag), and off they go toward the new hot concept, with the rest of the industry scurrying to catch up.

What happens to the restaurants that are left behind? If they haven't prepared for a shift in consumer tastes, they die with the trend that bore them. The restaurant industry is not unlike the fashion industry in the respect that trends come and go. The fashion industry expects styles to change and prepares for it. The death of the Nehru jacket, for instance, probably didn't put many clothing manufacturers out of business. Yet failure to anticipate and respond to changing food tastes has hastened the decline of many casual theme restaurants.

Because consumer tastes continue to change rapidly, T.G.I. Friday's menu is in a constant state of evolution. Since the first T.G.I. Friday's restaurant opened in 1965, our menu has grown from a chalk slate with less than 50 items to a 25-page listing of more than 200 choices. Our test kitchens are constantly researching and testing new foods and drinks.

Why the diversity? Because customers have what we call a *palate range*. Let's say you get up in the middle of the night and start prowling around the refrigerator. You're thinking to yourself, "It's hot out. I want something cold and light. Maybe some cold cuts or a salad with vinaigrette." Then again, you might think, "It's cold out. I want something heavy and meaty that will warm me up inside." A diverse menu that covers the palate range ensures that we can serve almost anything our customers want. That diversity is our buffer against the zigzagging that means boom and bust for many other restaurants.

Anticipating the consumer is crucial. Restaurants that do nothing but respond to the market always remain a step behind it. At Friday's we anticipate changes in several ways. For example, every day we track the sales of every food item we sell. This constant barometer helps us monitor the popularity of each item so we can adapt our menus accordingly.

We also listen to our employees and our customers. One of our employees in Miami is a fan of our chicken sandwich and used to experiment with different ways of preparing it. She shared some of her concoctions with her customers, and chicken sandwich sales in Miami started to grow. We noticed. We introduced Miami Chicken along with a number of other gourmet chicken sandwiches in 1985 and the line became one of our top sellers.

2. Package

Another of our management philosophies at Friday's is called the *Oyster Theory*. An oyster, so the theory goes, is happy in his shell when all the elements are just right. But let a grain of sand invade the shell and the oyster is irritated. A pearl may form, but the oyster dies.

A good atmosphere is essential to a good dining experience. If the silverware is dirty, if there's dried catsup on the lamp, or if the air conditioning is too cold, a restaurant risks losing a customer. Friday's managers periodically sit in every chair in the restaurant to experience the place from the customer's perspective.

Menus and furnishings are part of the package, too. Friday's menus have won scores of industry awards for graphic design. A recent Sunday brunch menu featured Impressionist paintings; customers took it home and framed it. We also build our restaurants to last. We invest in hard woods, brass, and real stained glass because we plan to be in business more than five to seven years.

3. Service

Yet another of our management theories (there are more than 20 in all) is called *Plus, Minus, Zero*. Think about the two most common topics at the dinner table or at cocktail parties: Seen any good movies lately? Been to any good restaurants?

No amount of advertising can top a solid recommendation. Therefore, the customer's dining experience has to be a good one. If something goes wrong and management does nothing about it, customers will leave with a minus. And they will talk about it.

If the experience is adequate, they will leave with a zero. They probably won't think to mention it, and they may or may not come back. If the experience is a plus, they will proselytize.

Making that dining experience a plus is a matter of good service. If customers want a substitution, make it. If they want an item that's not on the menu, get it. If they're dissatisfied, pick up the tab.

Another of our management philosophies is the *Four Walls Theory*. A restaurant's long-term success does not depend on any outside factors such as competition, the economy, or the weather. It depends on what goes on inside the four walls. In other words, the way to attract and keep customers is to concentrate on the basics: product, package and service.

Current Challenges

Today the restaurant industry is experiencing the most challenging period in its history. Not surprisingly, the proliferation of restaurants that characterized the 1970s and the early 1980s eventually overshot the market. Between 1960 and 1980 the expansion rate for new restaurants was 2.3 percent a year. Since 1980, the rate has jumped to 4.4 percent, while the growth in the American GNP in 1986 has grown just 3.5 percent. As a result, there are more restaurant seats than there are patrons.

Competition has intensified and not just among restaurants. Many restauranteurs have failed to realize who their competition is. We are competing against each other, sure, but the fact is that, ultimately, we are all competing with the grocer.

Grocers realize that Americans don't have time to cook every night, so they now offer quick and easy gourmet foods that can be prepared in a microwave in a matter of minutes. Many operate deli sections with freshly prepared foods one can take home. These alternatives to eating out cut directly into restaurant revenues.

Restaurant sales traditionally are tied to growth in disposable income. While disposable income remains high, consumers are spending it on such items as videocassette recorders and televisions — items that encourage them to stay home rather than eat out. That's good news for the grocer.

Meanwhile, a labor shortage is developing among teenagers and young adults — the primary pool for restaurant employees. As the number of 16- to 24-year-olds continues to shrink over the next 10 years, restaurants will be forced to pay higher wages, well above the minimum wage and at the expense of their profit margins.

Economic factors are also affecting the industry. The nationwide insurance crisis hasn't spared restaurants. Liquor liability premiums shot up 110 percent industry-wide in 1985, and many small operators now cannot afford insurance at all.

The customers themselves represent another challenge. They are more sophisticated than ever, which means they are harder to please. Compared with restaurant patrons of the past two decades, they are better educated, more widely traveled, and more discriminating. They know quality and they demand it. They expect restaurant food to be at least as good, or better, than homemade.

Customer tastes continue to set the pace for the industry, and at a more rapid clip than ever. There has been as much change in customer preferences in the last year as in the three years before it, and as much in those three years as in the decade before them. Pasta? Fajitas? Cajun? Today's customers have tried all the hot concepts in the industry and are eager to see what's new. Palate ranges are broader than ever. The challenge for the industry is to keep pace with the customer, if not one step ahead, while maintaining top-quality standards.

The Future

Rapid changes and intense competition in the market foretell a shakeout in the restaurant industry in the next decade.

The shakeout will closely resemble what happened to the grocery industry. Twenty years ago, most groceries were family owned. Now smaller operators are virtually nonexistent, having been replaced by large grocery chains whose immense inventories and economies of scale eliminated most of their competitors.

Similarly, large restaurant chains will supplant the mom and pop businesses, and smaller chains will merge or consolidate to survive. Through their sheer size, the larger chains will be able to contain costs by managing multiple restaurant concepts with a single corporate staff, purchasing in bulk quantity and operating their own food distribution systems.

The large chains also will gain a competitive advantage through:

☐ Real estate. As smaller operations fold, real estate opportunities will arise for larger companies with the capital available to take advantage of them.

☐ New technologies. In response to the labor shortage, restaurants will develop new systems to streamline kitchen operations and allow them to operate with fewer employees. Small operators who cannot afford to develop or acquire such systems could be forced out of business.

☐ Research and development. Sophisticated research efforts will enable restaurants to spot new trends in the marketplace and develop new foods and drinks to meet customer demands. Again, small operators who cannot afford large-scale R&D efforts could fall behind.

Undoubtedly the tug of war between grocer and restauranteur will continue. Restaurants must have strong management teams and effective marketing tactics to operate efficiently and capture market share.

The $144-billion restaurant industry is just a part of the much larger, $450-billion food industry. A 10 percent shift in this market represents a share of $45 billion. The customer will weigh the quality, value, and convenience of grocery products versus restaurant food; the operator who is more creative and proactive in meeting consumer needs will come out on top.

Car Rental Marketing

To understand the marketing problems faced by the car rental industry we need to start literally on square one with the first "P" of marketing, the product.

While car rentals can be defined as a service industry, delivering that service involves acquiring a large fleet of new automobiles. Consequently the car rental business is dependent on economic trends with its roots in Detroit and Tokyo. The used car market is a good example of this. Used car sales are an important source of revenue for such major companies as Hertz, Avis, and National. Hertz sells roughly 125,000 used cars every year and Avis reported that it turns over approximately $500 million annually selling its rental cars. They are usually retired after a year and a half. Without these sales the companies could not easily finance the acquisition of new cars every year, and without new cars their product quality suffers. When the large auto manufacturers can't sell new cars they offer such consumer incentives as low or free financing and that dries up the used car maket. In 1985 and 1986 car rental firms were forced to cut the prices of their used cars drastically.

Another trend that has had serious implications for car rental firms is the trend toward higher insurance rates. Avis, for instance, pays out at least 15% of its operating costs for coverage. Most car rental companies reported that their insurance costs doubled in 1986 and the crisis in that sector is far from over.

As a result of these obstacles to profitability, the trend toward vertical integration in travel and tourism as a whole, and in Avis's case an attractive leveraged buy out situation, three industry leaders changed hands. UAL (currently Allegis) bought Hertz from RCA in 1985. Wesray Capital Corporation acquired Avis from Beatrice in 1986, and Gibbons Green van Amerongen purchased Budget from Transamerica the same year. The situation remains unstable at this writing.

The new management in all cases shifted marketing strategies immediately and put top emphasis on profitability as opposed to market share as a first priority. Price cutting and promotional incentives were de-emphasized. In their place, companies instigated city surcharges, increased daily and weekly rates, and reinstated mileage caps.

Companies also started taking a closer look at their mix of leisure and commercial business and the costs of doing business in both of these sectors. Over the years corporate accounts had succeeded in bargaining down rates to levels that the new owners considered unprofitable. Moreover, with companies trying to save costs in travel, there is good reason to believe that commercial accounts will not be where the growth is in years to come. Consequently there appears to be a renewed interest in the leisure segment in some companies. This has caused a new look at the travel agent's role, and while some car rental firms are putting more emphasis on working with agents, others appear to be stressing direct marketing and sales, devising promotions and programs that bypass agents, and restructuring commissions.

In our first article in this section Brian Kennedy, Executive Vice President of Hertz, tells how his company is responding to all these new pressures and strategies. The reader will recall that in the preface I pointed out the symbiotic relationship that exists between various sectors of the travel and tourism industry. This article begins, not surprisingly, by pointing out that "it is impossible to separate air travel and rent-a-car." Kennedy touches on all four Marketing P's: Product, Price, Place, and Promotion. In Hertz's case locations are particularly important. In 1986, *Travel Weekly* reported that 75% of the major firms' bookings came from airport locations. Hertz had 33.8% of that market, Avis 25.4%, National 20.6%, and Budget 15.8%.

Our second contributor, Henry Dominicis, International Vice President of National, explores the international market and the domestic one. He points out the similarities as well as the differences between them. He then focuses on the car rental business in some specific international markets including the People's Republic of China which Dominicis opened up for his company a couple of years ago.

Chapter 20

How Hertz Plans for Tomorrow's Rent-A-Car Market

Brian J. Kennedy
Executive Vice President
and General Manager,
The Hertz Corporation

Brian J. Kennedy is executive vice president and General Manager of The Hertz Corporation. Prior to joining Hertz, Mr. Kennedy was vice president, advertising and sales, for Trans World Airlines, Inc., and previously was assigned a number of marketing and sales positions with TWA. He served with the United States Army Intelligence following graduation from Georgetown University's School of Foreign Service in 1963.

In 1918, when Hertz founder Walter Jacobs opened his Chicago rent-a-car business with a dozen rebuilt and repainted Model-T Fords, the business was virtually without precedent. The startlingly new concept that Jacobs pioneered has, however, become an integral link in modern business and leisure transportation.

Domestically, the rent-a-car industry is a better than $4 billion a year business, growing at double-digit rates since the 1950s, and expected by industry observers and analysts to continue to do so. Worldwide, it amounts to more than $7 billion yearly.

Growth in the rent-a-car industry has tracked growth in business travel. Approximately 60 percent of rent-a-car business is commercial in nature, covered by corporate contracts.

Industry expansion, however, has also paralleled increased air travel. It is impossible to separate air travel and rent-a-car. For example, approximately 70 percent of Hertz rentals step off or onto a plane. Worldwide, this industry leader has approximately 5,000 locations in nearly 130 countries, but the bulk of its revenues are generated at its 2,000 airport locations.

Indeed, broad industry research shows that the airlines' most frequent users (the 30 percent that account for 80 percent of airline revenues) are also the most frequent renters.

Moreover, in recent years, with an increasing number of corporate offices moving out of urban locales and close proximity to airports to suburban and exurban settings, rent-a-car has become an integral part of the nation's transportation system.

This close relationship with air travel also meant that deregulation of the domestic airline industry, which started in 1978, would have a direct impact on the rent-a-car industry—and it has.

On one hand, deregulation produced a more price-sensitive traveler, attuned to bargain fares and discounts. For a time, it shifted the travel focus from service and value to price and nothing else, a development that was detrimental to the industry and ultimately to travelers. But deregulation was a cloud with a silver lining and while for a short period it caused a myopic focus on price to the exclusion of all else, it opened the discretionary or leisure travel market and introduced new segments that simply had not been a factor before. Now, discretionary travelers, some of whom had never flown before, are boarding planes, flying to vacation destinations in the United States and abroad, deplaning, and driving away in a rented car.

This beneficial impact was compounded through expansion in the number of carriers and increases in the number of routes flown. For rental companies such as Hertz, who established a coast-to-coast rental network as early as 1925 and unveiled "rent-it-here/leave-it-there" service in 1933, the increase in carriers and routes further boosted growth.

Advances and innovations within the car rental industry also furthered acceptance of a rental car as a means of transportation and pushed out the market's limits. Hertz, over the years, compiled a long list of industry firsts, introducing the first rent-a-car charge card just eight years after its founding, followed that same year by advance reservations. In 1959, Hertz established the first centralized billing system and three years later, the first booking system for travel agents. Today, more than half of Hertz's reservations come from travel agents. In 1971 Hertz introduced the toll-free reservation number. Its reservation system now handles more than 15 million calls a year, for rentals in all corners of the world. The following year, 1972, Hertz started the first club for frequent travelers, the #1 Club, which now numbers well over 7.5 million members.

Yet, with all the growth and advances, the booming rent-a-car business is utilized by only a fraction of the adult population. In the United States, the estimate is that only about 15 percent of the adult population has rented a car. In Europe, the percentage drops to 2 percent of the adult population. All of which is to say that, as far as the rent-a-car industry has come, it has a lot further to go in terms of an untapped potential market.

Growth, of course, can breed problems of its own and in the wake of deregulation, some people within the rent-a-car industry, recognizing emerging expansion opportunities, made grabs for market share through price wars on the commercial side. These costly and short-sighted strategies have abated and there has now been a return to the fundamentals of rent-a-car, which are rooted in service and value.

Several factors are critical to a rental company's long-term success, which the company measures in terms of profitable performance and the customer measures in terms of satisfaction.

Fleet is the first and most obvious. Fleet management is at the heart of a rent-a-car operation and, for the renting customer, that translates into availability of the desired class of car when and where the customer needs it. For commercial renters, the peak demand period is Monday through Thursday. Effective utilization of the fleet means encouraging leisure rentals during the Friday-through-Sunday weekend period, which explains the inducements frequently offered for weekend rentals nationwide or in select geographic markets.

A broad selection of models and, more important, low-mileage cars, are two other aspects of fleet management.

In line with this, maintenance is extremely important. The commercial customer and the leisure customer want reliability in a rental. At Hertz, for example, a thorough maintenance check each time a rental is returned coupled with a periodic preventive maintenance check helps ensure the reliability of our cars.

An adjunct of fleet availability is, naturally, location. How many locations does a rent-a-car company have and where?

At a black-tie dinner in New York, the head of a worldwide financial institution remarked to a Hertz executive that he always rented from Hertz on his globe-hopping treks because Hertz was the one company he could count on being wherever he was. That is the essence of location, being ubiquitous in travelers' eyes. Certainly Hertz, with the largest fleet and the most locations worldwide, has achieved that objective.

Location, however, is not simply a matter of numbers; it must also be strategic. While each location has an underlying strategy, a fundamental locations issue divides the industry. That is the question of on-airport versus off-airport.

The major rent-a-car companies, having recognized early on the direct and important link between rent-a-car and air travel, moved quickly to establish themselves on-airport. This not only placed them at major transportational crossroads of modern travel, but enabled them to provide greater convenience and service to their customers.

On-airport service not only means counter space in the terminal facility, but airport rental lots, speed, and convenience in picking up or dropping off, plus a host of other advantages. For the on-airport rental company there is the cost of concession fees for maintaining such an operation.

Off-airport rental companies, often local or regional, do not maintain facilities on airports, do not pay concession fees, and do not offer the renter the convenience of on-airport operators. They do, however, compete with on-airport rent-a-car companies, vying for a share of the market. For the customer, the off-airport location means he or she must leave the airport—

by bus or cab — and travel to the rental office, sometimes distant, sometimes isolated. Once there, the customer has little recourse if he or she is not satisfed. By comparison, with on-airport rental companies situated side-by-side in the terminal area, if the customer is not satisfied, he or she need only walk to the next counter.

Another important factor influencing the success of a car rental company and the satisfaction of its customers is its reservations capabilities. Via an 800 phone number, renters can reach Hertz's Oklahoma City Reservation Center and secure a reservation anywhere in the world, seven days a week, 24 hours a day. In addition, travel agents can book rentals for companies such as Hertz via automated airline reservation systems, and developments at Hertz such as Direct Link and Direct Access are making reservations even easier.

In the highly charged and competitive arena of car rental, innovation is essential to staying on top, meeting evolving customer needs and expectations, and continuing to grow. Hertz has initiated efforts to assist travel agents in booking rentals, in answering customer questions, and in resolving problems that may arise. ANSWERLINK™ enables travel agents to get fast responses to a host of questions via their automated systems. Questions may relate to PNR problems, systems procedures, special services, or rental policies. Through automated systems it is even possible now to order brochures or other supplies, or process a #1 Club application or update.

Looking toward the future, airports and air travel continue to be pivotal to rent-a-car growth. Hertz Express Service™ rentals and Hertz Express Return® speed #1 Club customers on their way at major airports. Links with airlines through frequent flyer programs provide an added incentive for busy business travelers, as do similar arrangements with hotel and motel properties through frequent traveler programs. Hertz has more than a dozen frequent flyer partners and eight major hotel chains with which it participates in frequent traveler programs.

For leisure travelers, Hertz's Affordable packages are extremely popular, here and abroad, pulling together in one program attractively priced car rental, hotel accommodations, and airfare.

In 1984, Hertz introduced a new and unique service that has yet to be matched: Computerized Driving Directions. To paraphrase an old cliche, getting there is only half the fun, it it's not fun at all if you can't find your way.

Available at more than 60 major airport and downtown locations in the United States and more than 30 locations in 10 European countries, Computerized Driving Directions provide the renter detailed yet easy-to-understand directions that take him or her from the Hertz location to the customer's chosen destination. The user-friendly, self-service computer terminals typically store about 250 area destinations, including hotels and motels, tourist attractions, corporate and government offices, historic landmarks, exhibition centers and convention halls, sports arenas and stadiums, and even shopping malls, and nearby cities and towns. In Europe, directions are available in English as well as more than six other languages.

Among the fundamentals of service is dependability. That extends to back-up when something goes wrong. At Hertz, 24-Hour Emergency Road Service, available virtually anywhere in the United States, evidences such dependability. Inaugurated in 1978, the service is available to customers via a toll-free number, day or night.

The same kind of dependability is evident in Hertz's Special Services Desk in Oklahoma City, which can help provide prequalification for cash rentals, arrange special billing at corporate locations for companies not covered by a contract, handle group bookings, and confirm reservations for special vehicles.

Looking toward the future, rent-a-car industry growth is very likely to be sustained with the industry, domestically reaching the $12 billion mark before the end of the century.

This continued dramatic growth will not be without problems and setbacks. Steep rises in liability insurance costs could jeopardize the continued operation of small rent-a-car companies. Mercurial fuel costs could rebound, depressing driving and travel and negatively affecting car rentals. A recession could reduce business travel. Terrorism or shifts in the foreign exchange rate could dampen in-bound travel overseas from the United States.

In short, any view of the future is necessarily cloudy. In 1981, Walter Jacobs quite likely hadn't anticipated the advent of the jet age and the deregulation of the U.S. airline industry.

What can be said is that corporate rental activity will continue to dominate the market mix, with corporate contracts priced more accurately and intelligently than has necessarily been the case in the price-cutting, market-share-grabbing past.

Discretionary travel, however, will become an increasingly important factor in the rent-a-car equation. Discretionary travel will encompass not only the leisure traveler on vacation, but the noncontract business traveler, perhaps an entrepreneur member of a small firm. Both will be sensitive to price, but will place a premium on service, on the perceived value that comes from a coupling of price with service delivered.

With travel agents, rent-a-car companies will focus much more attention on this discretionary side of the rental business, which offers greater profit potential. The key to more effective fleet utilization and improved levels of return from this most important asset will, in large measure, be the discretionary traveler who takes up the off-peak, weekend slack in fleet use. Aggressively competing with the majors for this discretionary renter will be the regional rent-a-car companies, who will hold out price alone as the primary incentive.

Improved financial performance from the industry leaders, stemming from more accurate pricing, will provide returns necessary to reinvest in fleet, facilities, people, and services. For the renter, this will mean an improved rental product.

Primary factors in the rental decision, especially among the business traveler, will continue to be—not necessarily in order—convenient/on-airport location; reasonable rates; clean, recent-model, low-mileage cars in good condition; fast, easy check-in and return capabilities; and participation in frequent-renter programs.

The successful strategy for the future depends upon a commitment to service rather than bargain pricing. That will be the basis for product differentiation. Those with a reputation for service, such as Hertz, and those with globe-spanning size in terms of fleet, locations, and service delivery capabilities, again such as Hertz, will be in the best position to capitalize on the opportunities that arise, while riding out the difficulties and absorbing short-term shocks, thereby achieving real growth.

Chapter 21

International Car Rentals — A Growing Business

Henry Dominicis
Vice President,
International, National
Car Rental System, Inc.

As divisional Vice President, International for National Car Rental, Henry Dominicis is responsible for the development of National's international licensee network, offering technical assistance and sales and marketing direction. He joined the company in 1970 and has served as director of international operations and vice president of international sales. A native of Cuba, he holds a pharmacy doctorate from the University of Havana.

In an age of jumbo jets and space shuttles, international travel is no longer a novelty. It's commonplace for many people and a necessity for others.

Americans, however, are spoiled. They think that goods and services must be the same overseas as those here. This becomes especially apparent when they travel. They look for hotels in which the sheets are changed daily, shop at places that accept credit cards, and expect the very best in table service when dining at fine restaurants.

The same holds true for travelers using rental cars. They often expect the car rental situation to be the same worldwide, despite the wide differences in local customs, laws, and economic conditions.

The international car rental market has grown dramatically over the past ten years, but there still are many parts of the world in which car rental is far behind that in the United States.

Before I talk about the variations in car rental around the world, I'll look at the similarities. The car rental industry originally developed from the growing need for ground transportation to complement the increased popularity of air and rail travel. Consequently, as international air travel became more popular, the need for international car rental services became more important.

National Car Rental's total rental service could no more exist today without international representation in major cities of the world than it could exist without car rental locations in the United States. The company learned long ago that if it wanted to compete locally, it had to compete internationally as well. The availability of international outlets is a necessity when signing contracts with major corporations.

The international car rental market differs from the domestic market. Each system operates in a unique manner, and National believes the best way to run an international operation is through local businesspeople in each area. They understand the business conditions in their country and have an active interest in running a profitable operation.

That's why National's international activity is handled through such affiliates as Tilden in Canada; Europcar in Europe, Africa, and the Middle East; and licensees in Latin America, the Caribbean, and the Pacific. Other companies prefer to own their outlets overseas, and still others prefer to franchise their entire system.

Regardless of the method of operation, the four car rental companies that operate on a worldwide basis provide their customers with some important benefits.

One is a central reservation system. Renters can make a car rental reservation in the United States for more than 140 countries.

There are some things to ask about, however, when placing that international reservation. Check prices in U.S. currency. Ask about tax. In France, for example, value-added tax can be very high. Drop-off charges will vary from country to country and insurance is apt to be different around the world.

Another service offered by international car rental companies is the privilege of charging a rental on any one of a number of credit cards. Such major credit cards as American Express, Diner's Club, MasterCard, Visa, and Carte Blanche are honored around the world. For those customers who choose to pay cash, some companies have a cash identification card, too. Without it, cash customers may have to be verified at the time of rental, and may be required to pay a deposit at check-out time. This amount will vary from location to location.

Because local conditions dictate variations in some countries, reservation agents have to be well versed in the details of foreign car rental. For instance, in most countries the minimum age requirement is 21 years, but this can vary (up to as high as 30 for the larger cars in some countries).

Car types, too, can vary. Renters may not be familiar with models such as the Seat in Spain or the GM Commodore in Australia.

Any valid drivers license is acceptable in most countries, but here again reservation agents can point out any special license requirements.

Public liability, property damage, collision insurance with a deductible are often included with all rentals at no additional charge. This coverage, however, may vary from country to country.

A collision damage waiver is also available at international locations, but the terms and conditions can vary widely. For instance, in some countries you can purchase a CDW and still be responsible for some of the damages. In other countries, theft of such things as windshield wipers and spare tires are not included.

In most locations, gasoline is not included with the rate.

Now that I've explained the similarities between international car rental and operations in the United States, let's look at some of the differences.

Earlier I said that customers can make a car rental reservation in the U.S. for hundreds of countries. In most cases these travelers will find their car rental location at the airport, but sometimes they will have to take a taxi to the hotel because of local laws that do not allow cars to be received at airports. This is most common in the Caribbean and is dictated by political protection for taxi drivers. In other areas, customers will find car rental facilities at railroad stations, ferries, or even at the dock of the QE II.

Cars, themselves, will also vary. Automatic transmission is not always so automatic. There are many countries in which travelers can rent only standard transmission cars. What may be called a subcompact in the United States may be even smaller in other countries.

Many European and Pacific/Asian countries offer chauffeur services along with the rental, and in some areas, such as the People's Republic of China, it's mandatory.

Probably the car rental situation most unlike that in the United States is in the People's Republic of China. National Car Rental is the only car rental company represented there and is the only company in China whose credit card is accepted. Customers can procure cash only with American Express, Visa, or MasterCard. They get the cash in advance from a local bank in order to pay their bills.

In the People's Republic of China, cars rent for approximately $30 per day for a compact, or $50 per day for a luxury car. Cars are either manufactured in China or imported from the United States or Japan. The days are 8-hour days, and all cars must be driven by a chauffeur. The car rental market here is 100 percent foreign, with most of the people being tourists. National Car Rental estimates that only 15 percent of the business comes from business travelers.

In another Pacific location, Australia, the situation is the reverse, with about 90 percent of the business coming from local sources. This market is very conservative and price-conscious.

The first car rental operation in Australia began in 1953. Today, there are about 10 car rental companies with 17,000 vehicles competing for business. Compact cars rent for $33 per day; luxury cars for $55 per day.

In Latin America, a growing car rental market has emerged in countries such as Venezuela, where there are 14 different car rental companies. Most of the business comes from business travelers, generally from Venezuela. Of those business travelers who come from somewhere other than Venezuela, about 90 percent are from the United States.

Cars in Venezuela are less expensive than cars in the United States. A compact car, for example, sells for $4,000, while a luxury model costs only $8,500. Car rental began in the late 1950s, and today includes 5,500 units.

In the United Kingdom, where National's affiliate is the official rental car company of the royal family, the business is split evenly between business and leisure. Eighty-eight percent of the total, however, comes from local business. Car rental in the United Kingdom is indeed booming. More than 800 car rental companies serve customers with a combined fleet of more than 100,000, according to National Car Rental estimates. The four major U.S. companies are represented here, as well as several European systems.

Prices are not cheap. Compact cars sell for $5,000 and rent for $20 per day, with unlimited mileage. Luxury cars sell for $20,000 and rent for $100 per day, with unlimited mileage. Ford and General Motors products are popular.

While car rental around the world may not be as sophisticated as car rental in the United States, it is a growing business. International travel will continue to increase during the coming years, placing new demands on car rental companies to serve this expanding portion of the business.

The important thing to remember is that every country is different, and you should not be afraid to ask questions when you place your reservation.

Cruise & Tour Marketing

IN HIS BOOK, *THE MARKETING IMAGINATION*, Professor Theodore Levitt of Harvard discusses "the industrialization of the service sector." He uses McDonald's as an example of a service industry that has brought industrial methods (such as the assembly line) to service industries.

The entire cruise and tour business is, as Levitt points out, another example of industrialization in the service sector. Cruise and tour operators take many different components of the travel experience: transportation, lodging, food, and recreation and package them together. The result is a product that can be marketed more efficiently and in considerably higher volume than the individual parts by themselves.

The consumption of the product has also been industrialized. Instead of delivering their packages on an individual basis, cruises and tour operators seek to provide them to larger and larger groups at the same time.

All of these activities have led to a much greater interest in mass marketing. In the cruise industry, for example, current annual sales fall somewhere between $5 and $7 billion. But a study completed in 1986 by Cruise Line International Association (CLIA) projects a market of at least $32 billion, or nearly $60 billion if all income and age brackets are included. "Ships have that very basic primitive pull, that of the ocean and the sea," says David Sutherland, vice-president of Home Lines Cruises.

The problem is to translate that pull into sales. Currently, fewer than 5% of Americans have ever taken a cruise. The CLIA study found that the prospective market has almost 28 million prospects. The best ones fall between the ages of 25 and 39, and are both families and single travelers as well as older men.

Here we can see the chicken and egg paradox mentioned in the preface of this book in clear view. In expectation of this huge potential, the cruise lines have already built and refurbished more ships than demand currently warrants. Their reasoning is that if the right product is offered at the right price, people will want to buy it. That may not be true. Many landlubbers think that seven days at sea will be boring no matter what happens on board, that they will get seasick, or will have to spend time with a group of people they don't like. The truth is that this is a product-oriented industry in some quarters, and until the product line has been refined to the point where a real market demand exists, the supply/demand ratio will remain unbalanced. Marketing is having what people want, not getting rid of what you have, and one might argue that many prospects as defined by the CLIA study, haven't taken a cruise because they don't want to. Indeed, some cruise lines refused to participate in a generic advertising campaign to create demand on the grounds that it wouldn't and couldn't work because the chicken has to come before the egg!

Howard Fine, President of Costa Cruises, has laid out very concisely Costa's strategy for survival and growth in this uncertain marketplace. Readers will note that Costa has designed a product for a very specific market segment and that Costa has a well-designed strategy in place to capture that market.

The next article has been contributed by John Martinen, Managing Director of Globus Gateway/Cosmos Tours. Martinen's company is one of the leaders in escorted motor coach tours. One senses immediately that while there are similarities in the marketplace between cruises and tours, a huge difference exists as well. A cruise ship can cost $150 million or more and takes two years to build. Motorcoaches aren't even comparable.

Motorcoach operators can therefore afford to approach their markets in much more conservative manner and are clearly doing just that. But there is a growing recognition among operators that they are competing for the same discretionary time and dollars that cruise lines are after, and they share some of the same problems. At a 1986 meeting of the National Tour Association in Hawaii, a key topic was how to change the negative images many people have about their tours. The association presented the results of a survey that found many consumers still regarded a motorcoach as a bus and perceived it as an unglamorous, old-fashioned way to travel that often bears the stigma of cheap transport.

Edward Rudner, who contributed the third article in this section, sells a different kind of tour. Certified Tours packages and operates all of Delta's Dream Vacations as well as a line of tours under its own name. Like other kinds of tours, this is a risky business and in recent years several established operators have gone under by overestimating demand and underestimating costs. Rudner's mention of McDonald's therefore is not surprising. Like McDonald's, Certified offers to its clientele a limited menu of consistent quality that represents a good value. Because of Certified's link with Delta, the reader of this section might want to refer again to the article by Whitney Hawkins in an earlier section, which discusses Delta's marketing strategy. Although the two articles were written independently, they dovetail nicely in comparing problems and opportunities.

Chapter 22

How Costa Cruises Creates Demand

Howard A. Fine
Former President
and CEO, Costa
Cruises, Inc.

Howard A. Fine, former president and CEO of Costa Cruises, Inc. rapidly and successfully moved Costa into a unique industry niche by underscoring its "Cruising Italian Style" ambience on all cruises to the Caribbean. He holds a B.S. from New York University and an M.B.A. from the New York University Graduate School of Business Administration. He has been named "Man of the Year" of the World Travel Committee and the A.J.C. and has received the Sales and Marketing Management Magazine's *"Distinguished Award."*

While many cruise lines predict a devastating overcapacity of cruise vessels through the 1980s, Costa Cruises is moving ahead to create increased demand. This increased demand will continue to fill Costa's six luxury vessels and many more to come in the future.

The secret of success in this business is no different than in any other competitive industry. To solve the problems of the business, one must first see the situation from the customer's point of view.

As the overseas sales manager for a West German machinery company, I was traveling around the world every two months visiting most major capitals in Africa, Latin America, Asia, the Pacific, and the United States. Although I had an almost unlimited expense account, I was surprised that most luxury hotels catering to top-class business travel failed to understand the needs and pressures of the busy traveling executive.

On one particular trip, my complaints about the inefficiency of a five-star luxury property and its failure to deliver messages on time, which may have cost a potential of more than a million dollars worth of sales, caught the ear of a hotel executive aboard my flight, who urged me to stop complaining about inefficiency in the industry and join it to solve the problems that I had recognized. I did as he suggested.

Throughout my 15 years in the international hotel industry, I never forgot that the product was simply a tool to satisfy the needs of business travelers, vacationers, honeymooners, incentive winners, conventioneers, and any other markets that we could gear our product to satisfy.

As executive vice-president for the world's largest hotel and catering organization, I was responsible for the profitability of more than 900 hotels, 3,000 restaurants and catering outlets, and a number of unique leisure products firms that virtually lived off the business and vacation traveler — products such as airline and institutional catering, duty-free shops, travel and tour companies — all providing a service in a competitive world environment.

The dramatic success of TrustHouse Forte hotels was achieved by placing clear and strong identification on each of its unique hotel properties. This identification was accomplished by carefully researching the business traveler market and adding value to each product by offering individualized services rather than discounts.

Overseas restaurants presented a special challenge in marketing to the American traveler, and we received the *Sales and Marketing Management Magazine's* Distinguished Award for packaging various combinations of restaurants for the use of travel agents, incentive houses, business corporations, and consumers. The "Eat Like a King" dining program produced millions of dollars of added profitable revenue, on an initial launch of just several thousand dollars in advertising and brochures.

In the 1980s and the 1990s, the cruise industry will continue to provide the greatest marketing opportunity of any segment of the travel industry.

When I joined the cruise industry as president of Norwegian American Cruises in 1981, I realized that a strong brand identity was necessary to succeed, and that could only be achieved by establishing and promoting the "unique selling propositions" that the company offered.

The product was immediately examined, both through external market research and internal examination of the physical plant of the company's ships. After improvements were made in both the physical plants and the services offered to passengers, both the Sagafjord and the Vistafjord soon became "the world's top-rated ships." *Fielding's Worldwide Guide to Cruises* by Antoinette DeLand bestowed its coveted 5-plus star rating for the very first time on both vessels, which was followed by the "Ship of the Year" award by the World Ocean and Cruise Liner Society, and similar recognition from Garth's profile of ships, and other critics of the industry.

The "world's top-rated ships" became a philosophy of management as well as a popular marketing slogan, and every crew member worked to sustain the prized gradings. In a period of 18 months, the ships became highly profitable and were sold for nearly double the asking price of a short two years prior.

Costa Cruises' product line was far larger and more diverse than any other company in its field when I took over the helm in 1983. Costa's image was confused by the fact that many of the ships operated under various flags and no clear identification had been created in the market. Research indicated that Costa's unique Italian staff and style were clearly unique among its competitors and were considered highly desirable images to promote and strengthen among all segments of the market, including experienced passengers and those who had never cruised before.

The "Cruising Italian Style" slogan was created, and a series of on-board activities to support that slogan were developed in its execution. Costa's new Caribbean ship, the CostaRiviera, was developed entirely around the idea of a Caribbean cruise ship with a European flair. Every shipboard element was examined and European designer shops and pizzerias were installed along with an array of day and night activities, including impromptu entertainment throughout the ship and unique theme nights—topped off by a grand finale, a Roman Baccanal, on the last night of the cruise. The CostaRiviera has been received as a great success and a most intelligent alternative to the usual Caribbean cruise experience. The elements that made the CostaRiviera so successful have been installed on all six Costa cruise ships in the Caribbean, South America, Trans-Panama Canal, the Mediterranean, and on the cruise that helped Costa prove its worthiness to the deluxe market, its yearly successful Around the World Cruise.

Having developed a strong following for its unique cruising style, Costa has been highly successful in retaining clients by marketing, through the travel agent, to its long list of repeat travelers. Obviously, one of the factors that has made Costa a favorite for repeaters is that many different cruise destinations are available on Costa ships, with the guarantee of the Costa quality in food service, entertainment, and accommodations.

Costa's variety has also played an important role in its ability to interest groups and charters to its ships, through the use of a comprehensive incentive cruise program that includes full-ship charters on ships of 400 to 1,000 passenger capacity, full-deck charters for those groups who may not be large enough to charter an entire ship, yet may wish the exclusivity of having specific facilities available to their group alone, and a long-term lease of cabins and suites for the use of corporations wishing to reward their dealers and employees on an individual basis. The personalization of each incentive cruise, from ice carved in the shape of the company's logo and such individual room gifts as travel bags, bathrobes, and golf shirts are an ever-present reminder of who is paying for the trip that the winner receives.

Costa has become a leader in the incentive cruise business and has had hundreds of major corporations on its vessels throughout the world. No two incentive programs are identical and the company prides itself on its individual design for each corporation's program, arranged to meet specific needs in a manner different from any other incentive program performed on that vessel before. The individual design and execution of each incentive program assures the corporate organizer that he will never offer a "me-too" program to any of his winners, and no one will be able to say that he or she previously had a similar experience.

The importance of themed activities that capture the magic of a myriad of worldwide destinations in a single cruise has been most popular on incentive programs, not only as a means of delivering a high-impact activity, but also as a dramatic introduction to the next year's incentive cruise destination. Themes such as Costa's unique Roman Bacchanal have lent themselves to unforgettable entertainment experiences, with the head of the company or top salesman charging into a banquet of hundreds of toga-clad incentive winners aboard a chariot drawn by other corporate executives or Costa's own "slaves." Similar, but equally dramatic entries have been made aboard rickshaws, elephants, and an expensive Italian sportscar.

Leadership in the incentive field as well as in catering to all cruise markets depends heavily upon a great deal of creativity, willingness to take risks, and an eagerness on the part of the staff to accept new challenges and flexibility. At Costa Cruises, I was blessed with an extremely capable and talented Italian-trained staff. From the Captain to the dishwasher, everyone was (and is) an expert in his own profession, highly trained and confident in his or her ability to predict and satisfy the needs of the most demanding clients. Our well-trained and highly motivated staff is what makes "Cruising Italian Style" more than a slogan; it's a commitment to our personalized service in the pursuit of excellence in each operation, with the objective of encouraging passengers to rebook future Costa cruises, and bring friends, relatives, and neighbors with them.

There is a direct relationship between the degree of customer satisfaction and the amount of future bookings received following a Costa cruise. Therefore, a great deal of time is spent motivating the members of our staff aboard each of our ships, reminding them of their importance to the overall success and profitability of the organization.

Although we are determined to perform programs that we are committed to, I also believe highly in management by consensus, and a continued review of all operations is made aboard each ship by observing the results of the operation and interviewing passengers and staff to qualify the results.

Staff participation is encouraged, which results in increased motivation and personal commitment toward success of each program.

Passenger participation is most significant, since the product cannot succeed unless it passes the test of those who ultimately purchase the cruise tickets. Passenger surveys, review of comment forms, and personal interviews with passengers determine not only customer approval of the current product, but also indicate future trends and preferences for all aspects of the product, from cruise destinations to menus, entertainment, and activities both onboard and onshore.

Costa's now-famous "Resort Cruising" is a product of consumer and passenger research that indicated that many past passengers would cruise more frequently, and other people would take their first cruise if they were able to play their favorite sport each day. Resort Cruising does this and more. On Costa's Caribbean Cruises aboard the Daphne, each port is a sportman's paradise where, upon arrival, Costa's Resort Cruising passengers are whisked away to a world-famous resort or golf course that normally caters to the rich and famous—or those who would like to be.

Arrangements for golf starting times, tennis court rentals, horseback riding, scuba diving, deep-sea fishing, yachting, sailing, or just relaxing on a world-famous beach, are made by Costa's sports director, who also gives lessons in each port while the ship is at sea and supervises the results of these lessons in port.

Resort Cruising has greatly increased demand for the Daphne and for cruising as well, since most passengers aboard this unique, low-capacity luxury vessel would have opted for a land-based vacation had Resort Cruising not been available.

Consumer and passenger research has influenced Costa's cruise product from every point of view and has made Costa the ultimate user-friendly cruise product to purchase. No longer is the prospective passenger intimidated by nautical terminology or complicated pricing. As the appeal of cruises becomes more widespread, so must the ease of purchase and confidence in the purchase decision by both experienced cruise passengers and novices.

The travel agent plays a crucial role in the booking of cruises and therefore receives intensive attention from management and the sales staff in researching the travel agents' needs in satisfying their individual cruise markets.

Travel agents were quick to respond to Costa's "Crusing Italian Style" philosophy. They commented that "Cruising Italian Style" made it easier for them to identify the unique differences in selling a Costa cruise as opposed to any other cruise product. Results of primary research indicated that Costa has developed one of the few niches in the industry, and that 78 percent of the market indicated that "Cruising Italian Style" would be preferred to any other existent cruise line philosophy in making the cruise purchase decision.

As in any other industry, it appears that this is the age of niche-makers, and the future looks very bright for those who are able to identify specific market segments and create a product that caters to the market more specifically and successfully than any general cruise product can.

It is ironic that of the many new entrants into the cruise market in recent years, only two have decided to cut out a specific niche in the market for themselves, mainly Sea Goddess Cruises, whose ships carry a very small number of passengers on a tiny ship that can get into smaller harbors than traditional cruises, and Windstar Cruises, which is launching the first wind-powered cruise ship, also to the luxury market.

Niches for the cruise ship market are as numerous as the number of special-interest and ethnic markets that exist. The 1990s will bring a new era of cruising, with as many people taking holidays at sea as those who buy packaged holidays on land. Several large cruise lines will compete for the general interest market on a low-cost basis to generate thousands and thousands of passengers per week. Larger cruise lines will use their market weight to create a need and an awareness for cruising while smaller cruise lines that cater to a specific market segment will prosper by doing a better job for that segment than the larger, all-purpose cruise line can do.

New technology will make a cruise vacation experience available to specific handicapped or sports-oriented markets with all of the latest equipment on board the cruise vessel. Other new or converted ships will be geared to specific ethnic or special-interest markets by means of entertainment, cooking, language of staff, and itinerary.

Costa Cruises, with its unique "Cruising Italian Style" ambience, will grow in quality and profitability faster than simply the number of ships we own. Although Costa now has more ships than any other world cruise line, we feel it is important to control the size, and therefore the quality, of not only our ships but the organization, to cater to each passenger in a very individual manner, and offer a luxury product at a popular price. Costa's Resort Cruise program has become so successful that a natural expansion into luxury full-service resorts at popular vacation spots around the world is planned, along with a line of Costa Cruisewear Italian Style, which will eventually be carried in boutiques and department stores around the country to provide that extra amenity of Italian-designed cruise fashions for passengers bound on Costa ships, as well as ships of other cruise lines.

The future of cruising is guaranteed, as is the future of Costa—the original niche-maker in the market.

Chapter 23

The Growing Market for Motor Coach Tours

John Martinen
Managing Director,
Globus-Gateway/
Cosmos

John Martinen graduated with highest honors from Michigan State University in 1960 with a B.A. in economics and received his law degree from New York University in 1963. From 1963-69, he was with Grace Line. As a consultant to Empresa Turista Internacional (Galapagos Cruises) in 1960-70, he developed the first steamship tourist cruises in the Galapagos Islands. He joined Globus-Gateway/ Cosmos in 1970 and was named chief executive officer in 1978.

The marketing of tours grew up like Topsy, adapting to local conditions in a hundred countries. Even today, in the 160 years or so since Thomas Cook took his first group to Ramsgate by train, his method of promotion is followed by tour brokers and ground operators who put together local groups through the organizations in which the participants are affiliated.

The advent of large, fast, long-range aircraft in the 1950s coincided with the spread of affluence through the United States, Canada, Western Europe, and other countries with relatively high standards of living, and travel began to take on mass aspects. At the time, tour wholesalers had established the rudiments of an international marketing and distribution system by using the services of their travel agent colleagues—travel agents appointed by the steamship lines and adopted by the airlines. Under an arrangement with carriers belonging to the International Air Transport Association, they were able to add a three percent override commission to the then standard seven percent airline commission, and pay agents 10 percent on packaged trips that qualified as pleasure travel. Airlines accepted the wholesalers' rationale that by this means they would develop new business for the carriers—and they certainly did.

In the main, the marketing machinery in place then remains undisturbed today, whirring away fairly smoothly and productively. What has changed, of course, is the amount of machinery and the degree to which it is used—a simply stupendous growth produced with minimal travel industry promotional effort. One thing that has not changed is the innocence of our marketing approach; the wealth of the market and its prodigious natural growth have protected us from the normal results of competition, and the extremely narrow margins on which we work don't provide us with the cash to support any but the most limited market research.

Discussion of marketing motor coach tours—or marketing any travel service—must therefore consider both what we do and what we should do. Though other industries claim to know in extensive detail their customers' motivations for buying, we admit we don't. We do understand that travel, to most people, is a dream, and we try to fulfill the expectation of that dream. Though other industries know which segments of the market are attracted by this offer or that, we don't. What we do as an industry, because it works well enough, is periodically to shoot arrows in the air by the swarm; if one finds its target, we have a customer.

I say that our method works well enough. My company markets motor coach tours internationally and domestically in two categories, first-class and budget. Of course we know that our first-class product, Globus-Gateway, is designed for the middle-of-the-road, middle-income, middle-everything American, Canadian, Australian, or any other relatively well-heeled, English-speaking person. More than half a century of experience has brought us to understand our market in these broad terms, and our choice of hotels, the element that most differentiates tours, is directly related to this understanding. We have also come to understand some of the characteristics that make up the prototype of this middle-of-the-road buyer: a putative lack of self-confidence, a preference for company, a limited acquaintance with travel, and a willingness to be managed. Cosmos customers, we also know, are very different. They like company, too, but they're much more self-reliant; they've usually seen more of the world, and they submit themselves to the discipline of motor coach touring a mite reluctantly—they do so because, at Cosmos prices, they are seeing what they want to see at rock-bottom expense, a price they couldn't match unless they backpacked. And that's what attracts them—price. We also know that Cosmos attracts travelers from all age groups and a high proportion of professional people. But neither we nor any other company in our segment of the industry grasps the demographic nuances of our markets, and we won't until we find a way to place market research into our price structure, which may mean when the limits of the market are reached and before competition becomes so cutthroat as to inhibit the investment.

Generally speaking, the operators of escorted motor coach tours are outstanding planners and organizers, eager to maintain and improve their offerings with quite sophisticated quality-control methods and product experimentation. Considering the millions of people they carry every year (and the propensity of some people to find fault with the Archangel Gabriel), the number of complaints is stunningly low; considered as a percentage, invisible. This, in a sense, is an element of marketing: excellent word-of-mouth promotion. At our company and several others, inspectors are on the road incognito throughout the season, checking reception and performance at the hotels, attractions, dining establishments, and places of entertainment that we include on the tour. Questionnaires returned by people on tour are cross-referenced in computers with inspectors' findings; if a pattern of poor performance emerges, a warning is issued; if it persists, the hotel or other establishment is replaced. Hotels are chosen first for those characteristics that make them first-class, and next for their capacity to handle groups with the personal attention that any good hotel gives to individuals. The sightseeing attractions we include are those the world wants to see, from Westminister Abbey to the Pyramids; they have to be attractions of the broadest appeal, for that's our market.

If marketing internationally turns on the factor of insecurity, marketing domestically carries no such motivator. Joseph Doakes, the diffident American abroad, is Joseph Doakes, the confident leader at home. Likewise Josephine Doakes. Confident leaders get into their automobiles and take off; they don't need a motor coach and a tour escort at home. So who tours by motor coach in the United States and Canada, other than visitors from abroad? First, let me say that we wish we knew; second, we think they're the same people who are introduced to motor coach touring by local operators a la Thomas Cook, find it companionable fun, and graduate to longer trips. Mainly the older set travels on Globus-Gateway, men and women evenly mixed. But it's surprising how many younger people travel on Cosmos, a fact whose significance we are still debating. Part of the motivation that takes North Americans to Europe is "roots"; a desire on the part of older people not to hibernate seems to be the underpinning of motor coach travel at home. But these are seat-of-the-pants assumptions, unsupported by scientific evidence and, in common with all such speculations, should be treated by the reader, especially the student reader, as possibilities, no more.

We do watch trends that are evident in our bookings. Our product mix, as with those of our competitors, includes traditional, multicountry itineraries, regional packages, even a few city and resort stay-overs. From year to year, there's a shift of emphasis in bookings between or among these categories; so, for the upcoming season, we provide what the market seems to favor. What we have found is that the best-seller of the 1950s—the two-week grand tour of eight countries—was the best-seller of the 1960s, the best-seller of the 1970s, and is the best-seller of the 1980s. The wit who poked fun at us all in the 1960s by saying, "If it's Tuesday it must be Belgium . . ." spoke for and to the snobs of the world. Obviously our products are not for them. The grand tour of Europe has never ceased to outsell any other kind of tour. It's not only the number of countries that attracts people but the fact that many of the greatest tourist attractions in the world can be seen up close on the one trip. No person can honestly say he's bored at the thought of riding in a gondola on Venice's Grand Canal or cruising past the Lorelei on the Rhine River. These are experiences that, transmitted from generation to generation, send millions of travelers to Europe to see and to wonder.

A great deal of unwarranted criticism is aimed at travel agents, criticism that I feel parallels complaining that an apple is not or orange. A travel agent, if he or she is indeed an agent, represents a host of commercial enterprises that comprise his or her product line: carriers, accommodations, sightseeing attractions, and the rest. An agent is also regarded as a customer's man, a broker for the purchaser. That's an impossible position to be in, but travel agents, by and large, acquit themselves well. No, they're not always experts on faraway places or airline fares — far from it. They shouldn't be expected to be. If we put all the computers in the world together, they still wouldn't have the combined capacity to contain every fact needed by today's travel market, nor would we ever have the information flow to keep them up-to-date. The travel agent serves the industry's purpose, if not ideally, then most practically, as an outlet for all the industry has to offer. The best travel agents know where to find the facts they don't have at hand and what choices to offer their clients. We certainly don't expect travel agents to be able to analyze in detail every Globus-Gateway or Cosmos tour; what we expect them to know is the potential market for our tours within their clientele, the difference between the two products, and how to book them. With agencies that promote aggressively, we advertise cooperatively and have found it mutually productive. We don't believe in organized *fam* trips for agents; a fam trip and its inevitable red carpet gives an agent an inaccurate impression of a product, and we want agents to have exactly the same experience as their clients. So we offer a 50 percent discount and positive space for any travel agency that has sold a Globus-Gateway or Cosmos tour within the current or previous year. Any qualifed member of the staff can go and bring a companion along at 25 percent off. We give a courtesy 25 percent discount to any agent on all tours at any time. How many agents take our tours on this basis? The average is 700 or so a year, which we think speaks very well for their interest in equipping themselves professionally. Most, if not all, travel companies using travel agencies as outlets will admit there is no cheaper nor more effective way of getting their products into the hands of the public.

Perhaps when we know more about market segmentation, advertising will become a more important factor in our marketing. As it now stands, we do very little advertising outside the cooperative efforts with agents. Advertising to so broad a market, even supposing it was successful, would require an outlay not feasible in the price and profit structure of motor coach tour operations. With public relations, however, we have achieved recognizable growth; it is inexpensive, as befits our pricing policy, and long-term, which suits our planning.

The future, in this industry, is no further than a figurative tomorrow. Change is endemic to it; changing technology outdates our methods with cavalier disregard for our conservatism, the changing values of currencies demand a master juggler. A society in explosive change threatens our very existence. Who would predict what will happen the day after tomorrow?

Chapter 24

Selling Value and Convenience in Organized Tours

Edward B. Rudner
President and CEO,
Certified Tours

Edward B. Rudner is the President and CEO of Certified Tours, one of the nation's largest wholesale travel companies. In the three years that Mr. Rudner has been associated with Certified, the company has grown from 40 to more than 350 employees. Prior to joining Certified Tours, Mr. Rudner helped found Alamo Rent-A-Car, where he held the position of Executive Vice President and COO. Mr. Rudner has been instrumental in the development and building of both companies into very large, profitable businesses.

Before the turn of the century, Abraham Lincoln was quoted as saying, "If you once forfeit the confidence of your fellow citizens, you can never regain their respect and esteem. It is true that you may fool all of the people some of the time; you can even fool some of the people all of the time; but you can't fool all of the people all of the time." Today, we deal with customers far more sophisticated and wary than in Lincoln's day, making the challenge of marketing a product, any product, very difficult indeed.

Today's customer demands value. Neither low price nor extremely high quality by itself is enough. A combination of price and quality is essential. Customers understand the equation, Value $= \frac{\text{quality}}{\text{price}}$. Therefore, a very low-priced product with marginal quality can have the same value as a very high-priced product with extraordinary quality or vice versa. At some point in the lower end of the quality scale, however, a product or service has no value at any price. In the wholesale travel business, combining a variety of services that *are* a value in the marketplace is our first and foremost objective. It is very important to understand that the array of services we offer must honestly and truly have a high degree of value and not a mere illusory value, in which value originally perceived turns into disappointment. As Lincoln pointed out "once (you) forfeit the confidence of your fellow citizens, you can never regain their respect and esteem." I think you can safely assume that they don't buy your product again either.

Obviously, value is subjective and since the spectrum of subjectivity varies incredibly in this business from people who are willing to pay any price for the finest travel accommodations available to people on the tightest of budgets, I think it is very unwise to attempt to serve everyone all of the time. The choice is clear: serve some of the people all of the time or all of the people some of the time, but forget about serving all of the people all of the time. When I make this statement to associates, I am often told that in order to grow we must serve as many people as often as possible. Knowing where to draw the line is essential, for when a company goes beyond the customers it knows and the product it produces well, it inevitably starts to falter.

At Certified Tours, we have used what I call a McDonald's approach, named after a company whose accomplishments we have all come to respect. In all of my travels, I have yet to meet anyone who eats a hamburger with ketchup, mustard, pickles, and onions. I know many who eat them with ketchup and onions, nearly as many who prefer mustard and pickles, but not one solitary sole who looks forward to their burger with all four ingredients. In fact, I have often inquired at large gatherings whether anyone even knows of anyone else who prepares a burger with those four ingredients and, yes, I can tell you that not only have I not met anyone who prepares a hamburger with ketchup, mustard, pickles, and onions, I have yet to meet anyone who knows anyone who makes a hamburger in that particular fashion. That is, until they proceed through those doors beneath the golden arches. How then does McDonald's sell billions of hamburgers in a manner very few, if anyone at all, would choose? By *consistently* serving them fast, hot, and at a very good value. I would also note that although McDonald's will make your hamburger any way you want it, it does not take long to realize that the small group of frowning people standing against the wall with white slips in their hands are not McDonald's bread and butter. McDonald's serves a large number of people some of the time, always doing what they do consistently and incredibly well.

Even my most optimistic views do not foresee Certified Tours selling as many tours as McDonald's sells hamburgers, but I like the concept. McDonald's gives up the additional benefit of variety both in entrees available and product preparation, but adds efficiency and consistency. Obviously, a large number of consumers are happy to make that trade.

At Certified, we don't have tours that fit everyone's travel requirements. We do not serve every destination nor do we serve any destination completely; however, we offer a reasonable variety of destinations and have some variety within these destinations. We think that if someone wants a tour (or a hamburger) and is willing to be somewhat flexible (ketchup, mustard, pickles, and onions), we'll provide that tour at a better, more complete value than anyone else.

Over the past few years I have encountered many so-called marketing professionals as well as very experienced travel industry afficionados who have told me that airlines have to be able to serve all classes of customers from all originating cities to all destinations, that hotels have to become large chains located everywhere serving customers as variant as business executives and high school students on vacation, and that sellers of wholesale travel have to have gigantic offerings with unending variations in order to be successful. In my opinion, the marketplace has determined the opposite. Every industry, including the travel industry, has many successful companies that fill niches, sometimes large niches, but very few, if any, that are all encompassing. If you are a glutton for punishment, you can try to serve everything to everyone, but I'll take the other road. McDonald's has sold billions of hamburgers by offering their menu, their way, and this year, after only a few years in existence, we will serve more than 300,000 people at Certified Tours using a similar concept. And if you thank we are the only ones, look at companies like The Limited, IBM, Honda, and Sears who do what they do well. Their customer base is not only growing, but is fiercely loyal.

I think by now you can appreciate that I believe one must identify a reasonably sized market and stay in touch with it, as well as serve that market in a way that provides consistent value. Therefore, Certified looks to people who operate their businesses in a similar way when choosing with whom to do business; we seek out companies that are looking to serve a similar market at a similar value quotient. The best example of this is our relationship with Delta Air Lines and its evolution to other suppliers. Having been granted the privilege and opportunity to operate Delta Dream Vacations®, we set out to identify the target market, value quotient, and business partners that fit the perception that Delta Dream Vacations® had in the marketplace. What we found was that a decade of award-winning service on Delta's part had become the standard expected of every aspect of a Delta Dream Vacation®. Customers figured, rightfully so, that those associated in supplying a combined service like a tour ought to be consistent (Consistent Value Quotient). If you are going to promote a brand name synonymous with the finest quality service at competitive prices and therefore, the best available value, you had damn well better live up to the billing. To my chagrin, I heard this bit of constructive criticism far too often.

It was at this point we realized that we had a large market ready for a product that was not necessarily the least expensive, but one that was of greater value by virtue of its quality. Having started with outstanding air service, we then sought to upgrade the rest of our services dramatically, beginning with the service we had control over ourselves. We began to upgrade our entire staff of more than 300 by increasing our training as well as setting higher standards of service than previously practiced in our industry. We developed ways to handle bookings more quickly and accurately than ever before. We improved our documentation process to the level where we now issue documents 24 hours after payment with greater than 99.5 percent accuracy and at the same time have the capability to ticket more than 5,000 people a day if necessary (I hope we get to test this one frequently in the years to come). I've been told we pay our bills faster and more completely than anyone in the industry. When we have had customer problems, we completely resolved them in 48 hours. And when we came up with a product or service that we could not handle within all of our standards, we just plain did not offer it. That's right, we regretfully said "We're sorry, someone can do that for you better than we can and we look forward to serving you in the future." You cannot make many exceptions to a standard if you expect to maintain that standard as part of your business philosophy. We missed some business in the early times—maybe even more than we got with our new philosophy—but we kept growing to the point where today we still forgo some business, but we have built a very firm foundation of business from an aspect of profitability, respect, and demand in the marketplace.

We also carried this value concept to our suppliers of hotel rooms, car rentals, and amusement features. We consolidated our relationships with businesspeople who shared our zeal for quality and value, not price alone. And we concentrated on these relationships to the exclusion of others even though we again left some business on the table for others. At the time, I was hopeful that by picking the right partners in our experiment we would gain some momentum in the marketplace. What resulted exceeded my wildest expectations. Our product became simpler and easier for customers to understand and travel agents to sell. We found it ensured an even higher level of quality control over more limited offerings and really sold.

Several years ago, one of the people I most respect in the travel business told me he was having terrible problems with the phone system at his wholesale travel company. The phone company could not install promised lines properly and it kept cutting off many of his existing lines in the process, all this during the height of his busy season, when almost a whole year's worth of business is conducted in a couple of months. Desperation set in and he decided to throw the phone company out until the season was over because they were causing more problems than they were fixing. He then had the phone numbers on all his lines changed with no forwarding message left on the old numbers. Then, by a stroke of genius, he only told the top 25 percent of his producing accounts the new phone numbers. These people were overwhelmed with the easy access they now had and poured in their business. In fact, they used the new phone number so much and became so familiar with his product that they called less frequently for information and used less time for actual, and more frequent, bookings. At a month's end, this gutsy man's business had nearly doubled over the year before. He found the right people to distribute his product and serviced them beyond their wildest expectations. He unquestionably lost some business from people who had called in the past and now could not find him. I guess it is one step backward and then three steps forward. One often gives up something to gain something else. The trick is to make sure you give up much less than you gain.

The same concept worked for us in finding partners to sell our products, and when we looked for suppliers of the services in our tours. We sought businesspeople who had the same standards of service and aggressive attitudes toward selling what we believed was the best product in the marketplace. Then we developed joint marketing and sales programs with these people to consolidate our efforts, combining the best aspects of two organizations' services and ideas.

In this objective, we had a very low success rate—often failing twice as often as we succeeded. However when we hit it right, business just poured in. Frequently the one success turned out to be more successful than we had projected the two or three unsuccessful attempts to be combined. This phenomenon has enabled us to continue to grow at a very substantial pace.

In the past three years, we have been very fortunate to have enjoyed success. We have also been inspired by the wonderful relationships we have developed and look forward to many more years with these business partners. The converse of Lincoln's statement has turned out to be as true as the statement itself, for as one maintains the confidence of his fellow citizens, he or she can relish being the object of their respect and esteem.

Travel Agency Marketing

A PARADOX EXISTS IN THE TRAVEL AGENCY business that is difficult to explain. On the one hand, deregulation, lower fares, and decreased corporate and overseas travel have spelled ruin for many retail agencies. Record numbers closed or were declared insolvent in 1986. At the same time, new agencies and other ticket outlets are proliferating at a rate that would put to shame any respectable rabbit hutch. In 1987 there were an estimated 30,000 travel agencies in America, up from 17,000 in 1980.

An understanding of the travel agency business requires another look at the four fundamental Ps of marketing. The preceding articles have dealt mainly with Product and Price. The third P is Place. The place in travel and tourism where the sale is consummated, in the large majority of transactions, is the travel agency.

Distribution channels are by definition mechanisms that bridge the gap between producers and consumers. They are marketing intermediaries or middlemen. As Nicholls and Roslow point out in their article, many agencies act as both wholesalers and retailers. This phenomenon sometimes produces an identity crisis that makes it difficult to develop effective business strategies.

The crisis is compounded by the added confusion in the minds of consumers as to whom travel agents really work for. For years everyone, including the agents, believed their first obligation was to their clients. But that was before their major suppliers pointed out the true facts of life and started replacing standard agency commissions with service fees and market share overrides.

At the heart of all of this turmoil lies the real question on the ultimate long-term value of the current travel agent system as a distribution mechanism. The airlines who have the largest stake in it tend to be ambivalent. From their point of view, there are 30,000 agents in the marketplace licensed to issue their tickets. That means 30,000 locations that need to be supplied with timetables, tour brochures, and notices of fare and schedule changes. It also means 27,000 agencies to collect money from on a weekly basis and to send sales reps to visit.

Do all of those 27,000 agents generate enough business to warrant that level of service? Hardly. At best the old 80-20 rule applies here—80% of the tickets come from only 20% of the agencies. And yet as pointed out earlier, travel agent commissions represent airlines' third largest operating expense.

Agents are terribly concerned about the long-term implications of this situation. Many survival strategies have been proposed and are being implemented, but everyone's crystal ball contains different pictures. Some experts feel that all future agencies will be large discount operations like K-Mart or small highly specialized boutiques. Others say that scenario is not likely because travel is a service based enterprise.

The new mega agencies, with sales of $500 million and over, are already causing a tremendous impact in the business. For the first time airlines and lodging operators are dealing with a unified, well-directed entity that can exercise real clout. These could turn into master agencies in the future that could provide tickets to smaller agents and get paid as distributors do in other fields.

Alternate distribution forms are springing up rapidly as well: consolidators, bucket shops, and non-conference outlets. Indeed the entire agency appointment system of ARC and IATA is still under attack. Some corporations, like McDonnell Douglas, have asked for and received accreditation to run their own agencies and more are considering it. In the struggle to become more efficient, agencies are upgrading their technology, adding back office systems, and studying productivity and scientific management with a fervor that is reminiscent of the days of Frederick Taylor and the Gilbreths.

Because of small profit margins, automation has been slow in coming to the travel agency business. Given that agents are middlemen and distributors of information, and that their sources of supply have been spewing out the information they need in megabytes per second, sophisticated and integrated computer systems are now a necessity to compete. Sadly, many smaller agencies still do not have very much back-office hardware and are not in a financial position to obtain it. Some have turned to fashioning their shops into "cruise only" operations and thus do not feel that automation is such a critical element. The cruise industry, however, is now moving towards more computerized reservation systems, and the handwriting is probably already on the wall.

The next two articles' authors explore the changing role of the travel agent and survival tactics for the years ahead. John Nicholls and Sydney Roslow discuss the impact of automation on the travel agency business. Both men are marketing oriented academics and their perspective is that of outsiders looking in.

The second article is the product of two insiders who are probably the most respected teachers of travel agency survival tactics. Besides owning their own travel agency, Phil Davidoff is National secretary and Vice Chairman of the American Society of Travel Agents, and Doris Davidoff, his wife, is one of the most prolific writers and speakers in the business.

Chapter 25

Travel Agency Marketing in a Computerized World

Dr. J. A F. Nicholls
Florida International University

Dr. J.A.F. Nicholls, who earned his doctorate from Indiana University, is Distribution/Transportation Coordinator in the College of Business Administration, Florida International University.

Dr. Sydney Roslow
Florida International University

Dr. Sydney Roslow, who received his Ph.D. from New York University, is a professor of marketing and associate dean of College of Business Administration at the Florida International University.

Marketers are concerned with the delivery of products to ultimate consumers. Travel agents supply a special sort of product — a service — that is an intangible item. Regardless of the nature of the product, whether it be a tangible good, like a package of detergent or a service, such as providing a tour, its success depends on the degree to which the customer's needs and wants are satisfied.

In the delivery of tangible goods to consumers there are usually several intermediaries. These intermediaries form a distribution channel. For example, a manufacturer may use wholesalers, brokers, and retailers to deliver his product to the consumer.

Travel agents are part of the distribution channel in providing a unique service that includes transportation and lodging. Both transportation and lodging reservations can, however, be supplied to the consumer directly by airlines, hotels, and nowadays, other services. Why then does the consumer utilize a travel agent? Similarly, why does an airline or hotel use an agency's services? The reason is that transportation and lodging are the means by which the consumer satisifes his requirements for travel, entertainment, business, education, adventure, relaxation, vacation, and so forth. Consumers believe that travel agents better understand their needs and are more informed than any individual industry provider. Travel agents are community based and perceived as trustworthy. They are, in a sense, brokers, acting as an intermediary between two parties. After all, travel agents have access to a plethora of alternatives. They have the ability to match very particular consumer wishes.

For their part, airlines, particularly, and hotels have found that it is both efficient and effective to have agents distribute their reservations services to individual travelers. An overwhelming proportion of airline reservations are made through travel agents. Airlines and hotels still, however, maintain their own centralized reservation systems. These systems sell directly to individuals and organizations, thus competing with their own travel agents. This system is used when the transportation is specific and limited, such as for a business traveler or an individual attending a funeral.

Nevertheless, even business travelers frequently employ the services of a travel agent, perhaps a captive one. This phenomenon is similar to a manufacturer utilizing an outside advertising agency to promote a product, despite the fact that the manufacturer has the financial capacity to operate his own internal advertising department.

The Role of Travel Agents

Just like the ultimate consumer, travel agents have their needs and wants. For example, if the travel agent is thoroughly familiar with all airline schedules, he or she can more easily meet the requirements of the traveling customer. One contemporary tool is computerized reservation systems (CRS), such as American Airlines's SABRE, or United's APOLLO. SABRE, alone, has more than 11,000 U.S. travel agencies subscribing to its service. The computer allows for the storage and efficient retrieval of vast amounts of data. Additionally, new uses are now being developed that are having a large impact on the delivery of agency services. Particularly with the emergence of the personal computer (PC), travel agents have access to the data banks of transportation providers. In addition, the PC provides the capability for word processing, data base management, and statistical analysis. The PC increases the travel agency's capacity and efficiency to conduct business. Subscriptions to any one system, like Eastern's SODA, make access to all the other systems possible. This permits worldwide reservations, including hotels, car rentals, and cruises.

Transportation and lodging must be delivered to the consumer in such a way as to yield the utmost satisfaction.[1] The travel market is not just one amorphous market; it is segmented into several smaller markets. For instance, there is the individual business traveler, the retiree, the frequent user, the youth market, and so on. Their needs can differ significantly. Computerization enables the travel agent to function as either a retailer or wholesaler in any of these market segments. As a retailer he or she meets the require-

[1]Gilbert H. Harrell, "Market Planning to Increase Travel Agency Profits," *The Cornell Hotel and Restaurant Administration Quarterly*, 7 (17), February 1977, pp. 44-48.

ments of each individual customer directly. As a wholesaler he or she provides for the needs of groups with similar requirements. Computers also improve communication between retail-oriented agents and wholesalers. Additionally, a travel agent can wear both a retail and wholesale hat simultaneously.

How does the emerging electronic delivery system enable the travel agent to enhance the consumer's satisfaction in the areas of transportation and lodging? The consumer needs reservations most convenient for his plans, covering travel dates and time schedules. Because the computer can access considerable detail quickly, the travel agent is able to answer the consumer's questions, providing him with pertinent detail of the trip being planned. In addition, the travel agent is able to provide the consumer, particulary the corporate consumer, with a management tool — hard copy printouts of individuals who have traveled on company business, whether bookings were made at the lowest available fares, and so forth. In this role, the travel agent is, in effect, an extension of corporate management in making the most effective use of a company's personnel and financial resources. This utilization of the computer will not displace the use of brochures concerning the trip, at least for now. With the exponential development of the computer, immediate color reproduction of brochures, for instance, may become a real possibility by the 1990s.

The computer provides immediate tangible confirmation of reservations from its data bank. Changes in the traveler's itinerary can be made rapidly, as can the airline's schedules. In addition, inventory control of availabilities and load factors for both air travel and lodging is continuously monitored and therefore, up-to-date. Seat reservations made at the PC terminal facilitate check in for the traveler. The force of competition will make hotels provide customers with specific room assignments, too. Price changes are virtually instantaneous. In the first three months of 1986 alone, there were hundreds of thousands of price changes made by airlines. Issuing and reissuing of tickets comes practically automatically, too. By the late 1980s, it will be possible to request and obtain information on in-flight movies, menus and meals, provision for storage and retrieval of a mother's infant foods, business aids such as typewriters for personal computers, and so on. It is currently possible for travel agents to book hotel rooms, cruises, theatre tickets, and even restaurant reservations in select cities around the world. Agents subscribing to American Airlines' SABRE already have access to 18 different reservation systems, including Club Med., with the capability to book British and German railroad and ferry seats expected in the near future.[2] By the 1990s these services will be more prevalent and sophisticated than they are now.

[2]"Survey: Information Technology," *The Economist*, July 12, 1986, p. 26.

The Needs of the Traveler

All travelers have needs. Some of their needs are general, others are quite specific. They vary, according to the particular traveler and the circumstances of the trip.

General needs include such items as convenient departure and arrival times, appropriate seating arrangements, the interconnections between the several legs of a journey, and accommodations. Specific requirements vary widely from individual to individual, but can still be broadly categorized. Such requirements include airport characteristics and location, availability of telecommunication, car rentals, travelers' checks, the ability to supply a complete tour, and hotel location. Consider the traveler who intends to visit Miami, Atlanta, New York, Chicago and Los Angeles. Such a journey may involve four different air carriers and may also include hotel reservations and car rentals. Travel agents can handle all these segments and arrange for specific requirements at each stopover using a computer system. They can search for the lowest combination of fares and other details wanted by the customer. This eliminates the use of a hotel guide and numerous telephone calls to confirm travel details. In some instances, a travel agent may be asked to book conference rooms and other facilities. While they can now reserve theatre tickets and restaurant seatings, later it will be possible to supply actual tickets and menus.

In effect, the successful travel agent becomes a consultant for the traveler. As such, the travel agent is in a position to provide the traveler with information concerning local restaurants, places to go, things to do, likely weather outlook, shopping, and so on. The computer is able to store and retrieve this information with consummate ease.

Serving the Travel Provider

The travel agent serves airlines and hotels as an extension of their reservation systems. With CRS there is no need to talk to anyone—just deal directly with the host's computer. Rapid developments are taking place, for instance, in the cruise industry which has been adding new ships on a continuing basis. Most cruise line reservations are still made over the telephone; however, the emerging CruiseNet will make it possible to eliminate voice communication. Eastern Airlines has already made agreements with several cruise companies and has them listed in its SODA system.

The travel agent can become an entrepreneur, wholesaling blocks of tickets to his or her own retail customers. Of course, the retail customers may be other, smaller, travel agents. He can now organize a whole trip and provide his customers with a total travel and entertainment package, entailing coordination between the travel modes, lodging, education, and recreation. Without the computer this would be a very cumbersome integration effort. In the 1990s, the travel agent will be able to schedule the most complicated plans by punching a few keys.

The PC used for reservations also enables the travel agent to develop a profile of customers, their likes and dislikes, and their past travel experiences — all with an eye to the customer's future travel plans; in effect a travel history exists. This concept applies to individuals, corporations, and associations and functions as a marketing tool for the travel agent. The agency can periodically review a client's status and suggest new and interesting travel ventures. The agent needs enough providers to make possible all the facilities required for the travel arrangements. As a merchant middleman, he matches particular customers, actual or potential, with particular service suppliers. To satisfy providers and passengers, the travel agent must have access to all reservation systems available. This has become important because charges of discrimination have been made when airlines are not equitably included in a particular reservation system.[3] Woodside Management Systems, one of the large consortiums, currently has a chain of 70 agency representatives and more than 1,250 branch offices in 37 countries on six continents. Their computers are tied into all airline and hotel reservation systems.

This matching of consumer needs and supplier capabilities can be done at an elementary or a more sophisticated level. On an elementary level it involves the matching of past history with present needs. On a more thorough-going basis, it involves fitting a combination of needs with the services available. For example, an association seeks a site for its annual meeting. In the future, a travel agent will have the capacity to provide a total package, on a one-stop shopping basis, as opposed to now, with the association dealing with hotels and a series of other providers.

Fully computerized travel giants, such as Ask Mr. Foster, American Express, and Thomas Cook, that can do everything connected with travel, will most easily survive. Indeed, they may be in the process of acquiring a competitive advantage as the International Air Transport Association (IATA) proposes the setting up of *superagents*, those agencies that agree to invest heavily in computerization and marketing, and in return receive an enhanced commission of 15 percent.[4] Smaller ones may be gobbled up as franchise operations or may need to join cooperatives to compensate for their low capitalization. Some of the smaller agencies may be able to survive as specialists filling a particular market niche. Other small agencies may be able to carry on because of an advantageous location. Also, larger travel agents may find it unprofitable to provide such small scale services as local sightseeing tours or a shuttle ticket from New York to Washington.

[3]Marvin A. Brennen, James O. Leet, and Elihu Schott, *Airline Deregulation* (Westport, CT: Eno Foundation for Transportation, 1985), p. 67.
[4]"Travel Agents," *The Economist*, July 5, 1986, p. 59.

What Travelers Would Do for Themselves

Microcomputers are becoming increasingly widespread. Projections are being made that there will be as many households with computers as there are now houses with telephones. In France, the Minitel system already has almost 1.5 million subscribers, projected to be 8 million by 1990.[5] Minitel is a combination of a telephone with a cathode ray tube (CRT). With this there is a loss, however, of the personal touch through the absence of voice contact. Because of this loss, consumers may prefer to stay with travel agents. Can, however, the loss of the personal touch be compensated for by an individual's sense of control over his travel destiny? Perhaps some of this loss of contact may be overcome by travel videos supplied by the agency for home VCR viewing. Such systems would enable an individual to make his own travel arrangements, either directly to the various providers, or through a travel agent. In advanced systems, other services could emerge to replace the travel agent altogether. This process is already happening with the introduction of the EAASY SABRE personal reservations system from American Airlines. This PC software enables an individual to look directly at schedules and fares twenty-four hours a day. Most individual consumers currently do not have the necessary modem and subscription to a network to book their own flights, accommodations, car rentals, and so on. Moreover, the task of making one's own arrangements could appear onerous to the consumer. In addition, the travel agent has experience and clout in dealing with providers. Consumers may feel that the travel agent can negotiate advantageous prices and accommodations. Under deregulation, when prices can change quickly, agents may negotiate volume arrangements for their customers. Bigger agencies have greater negotiating power than smaller free-standing ones. Corporate clients and even individual ones can expect direct rebates from the travel agents.[6]

Computerization offers other benefits to the consumer. An example is computerized ticketing at such traveler frequented locales as airports, hotels, and (particularly in Europe and Japan) train stations. This is especially appealing to individuals who possess credit/charge cards like American Express. There is the distinct possibility that businesses such as supermarkets will compete with travel agencies, too. Another development is that the Official Airlines Guide and ABC World Airways Guide have started offering their timetables as data bases to teletext services.[7] This process is no more compli-

---

[5]Robert Cullen, Ruth Manshall, and Ken Pottengen, "The Minitel Revolution," *Newsweek*, April 7, 1986, p. 75 G.
[6]Mary J. Bitner and Bernard H. Booms, "Trends in Travel and Tourism Marketing: The Changing Structure of Distribution Channels," *Journal of Travel Research*, 20, Spring 1982, pp. 39-44.
[7]"Travel Agents," *The Economist*, July 5, 1986, p. 59.

cated than the one in establishing the software and codes necessary to permit access to large-scale data bases, like Dialog, and automatic billing. It might also appeal to the American consumer's preference for personal control, flexibility, and decentralization.

The New Marketing Mix

Distribution

All major reservation systems will interconnect. Britain has introduced Travicom, an on-line method for accessing the booking systems of more than 44 airlines throughout the world.[8] American Airlines' EAASY SABRE accesses more than 650 airlines worldwide. So many systems will likely lead to mergers and combinations among them. Pan Am and American Airlines are already discussing sharing their data processing capabilities.[9] This trend will probably continue.

Product

The expansive use of the computer in travel arrangements is virtually infinite. The integration of provider services makes it possible for the travel agent to offer customers wider choices of routes and accommodations and greater benefits. Even Amtrak has forsaken its antiquated reservation methods and is moving to tie into the air carrier systems.

Pricing

A consumer is always looking for the best value—frequently the lowest price for highest quality and greatest quantity. Computer search and retrieval custom tailor the traveler's trip. If electronic funds transfer (EFT) keeps pace with travel industry developments, then point of sale (POS) billing and payment wil be direct and immediate.

Promotion

Desktop publishing is in the offing. More and more software packages are being introduced for the personal computer and their prices have already dropped appreciably. Good quality laser printers will enable agents to produce their own promotional material to supplement brochures produced by suppliers. Individual newsletters for distribution to customers are eminently feasible as a promotional vehicle. Customers who possess their own modems and printers can be accessed directly for special sales, discounts, and other incentives.

[8]*Ibid.*
[9]David A. Ludlum, "Pan Am Exploring DP Sharing with American Airlines Group," *Computerworld*, May 5, 1986, p. 2.

The Future in Store

What will the travel agent of the future look like? Even though there will be more outlets, there will be fewer agencies per se. Consolidation will continue apace through merger, acquisition, and franchising. Larger agencies will dominate the industry. Select smaller ones will survive as specialists meeting simpler, limited, travel needs unprofitable for full-service agencies.

There will be potential competition from individual consumers with the expected widespread possession of microcomputers, if networks develop as in France. Similar American systems, like Viewtron, have not been successful so far. To see whether consumers are likely to make their own reservations on a large scale, it would be prudent to observe the French Minitel and the British Prestel systems. New hardware enables French customers to make their own reservations and charge them through smart credit cards. Already, the introduction of PC software eliminates the need for the specialized hardware like the Minitel equipment. On the one hand, as pointed out earlier, the individual consumer may not have the inclination to make all of these arrangements on his own without expert guidance. On the other hand, the do-it-yourself movement is firmly entrenched in home maintenance and improvements. This could carry over into the travel area. The agent's response is the complete one-stop shopping approach, allied with personal service and attention to the consumer. In this connection, the computer enables the travel agent to seek the best arrangement for a traveler. It is possible for an agency to contact other agents, to interface with more reservation systems, via Airlink, to tap into CruiseNet, and so on. At present, a final airline booking often involves a personal contact through an 800 number. It is common knowledge that all travel suppliers hold back a certain number of accommodations that cannot be accessed through computer contact. This will probably continue since it represents the provider's final control that would be lost through total automation.

All of this computerization, consolidation, and integration are adumbrations of the future direction of the industry.

Chapter 26

Marketing for the Travel Agency

Phil and Doris Davidoff
*Belair Travel
Consultants*

Phil and Doris Davidoff are leading travel industry professionals who are also active in travel and tourism education and training. They are the co-founders of Belair Travel Consultants in Maryland, and have served as travel and tourism educators for more than thirteen years. Both are Certified Travel Counselors and both own and operate the Capital Area Travel Academy in Maryland. Mr. Davidoff is First Vice President and Secretary of the American Society of Travel Agents.

The travel agency industry has come of age in the deregulated 1980s. Before deregulation, travel agency owners and managers were travel-oriented people who happened to be in business. Today, agency owners and managers are primarily business-oriented people who happen to be in travel.

More than any other part of the travel industry, travel agencies are independently owned small businesses. The vast majority of the 28,000 travel agencies in the United States are single-office operations or part of small (four locations or fewer) local organizations. Very few are part of true national chains. A number of independent agencies have joined cooperatives and consortiums to increase buying power and income.

Characteristically, the agency manager or owner/manager must wear many hats to run the agency properly. Marketing is only one function of the job. In addition to market planning and direction of sales efforts, the manager is personnel officer, operations supervisor, and senior salesperson as well. Only the largest agencies can afford full-time marketing personnel.

According to the 1986 Louis Harris survey sponsored by *Travel Weekly*, 72 percent of the more than $54 billion of travel sales generated by travel agencies was sold by agencies with sales less than $5 million. Only 28 percent was generated by the larger agencies. The median number of employees in a single travel agency location was five according to a 1984 study, further supporting the characterization of most travel agencies as small businesses.

The Marketing Mix in Travel

To understand how successful marketing is conducted in modern travel agencies requires an understanding of the marketing mix concept within the travel industry. Use of this mix shows the position of the travel agency within the total travel industry and provides general parameters for the development of agency marketing activities. The marketing mix in travel consists of four separate sub-mixes. Each sub-mix interacts continuously with the other three. The four sub-mixes are product and service, distribution, communications, and terms of sale.

A travel agency manager developing a marketing plan creates a marketing mix for his or her agency; but the mix is not a stagnant one. Because of continuous changes, the manager using the mix is like a juggler keeping four balls in constant balance and motion. Changes in one sub-mix usually affect the other sub-mixes.

In the travel industry, the product and service mix comprises the various components of tourism. To the travel agency, this is the total range of services provided to clients. Number one is air travel which accounts for more than 60 percent of sales generated by travel agencies. Some agencies that specialize in business travel concentrate 80 to 90 percent of total sales in the air travel product.

Hotel reservations, car rentals, tours, and cruises are also major products of most travel agencies. Rail travel, travel insurance, and travelers' checks are also part of this sub-mix in many agencies. Some agencies have small boutiques that sell maps, guidebooks, and travel related sundries such as cosmetic bags and electric current converters.

For many years, most travel agencies tended to sell virtually all the travel products available for sale. Selective selling is a newly emerging trend among better-managed agencies. Agencies are developing preferred supplier lists and directing sales as much as possible to specific operators. Override income, marketing support, and assistance with problems are the main advantages of a selective sales policy.

Within the broad travel industry, the travel agency serves as a primary retail distribution channel. The travel agency is the main link between the travel product supplier (for example, airline or tour operator) and the traveler.

More than 70 percent of domestic air sales and more than 85 percent of international air tickets sold in the United States are generated by travel agencies. The travel agencies' share of the cruise market is even higher, approaching 100 percent on many lines. Package tour sales are also dominated by travel agencies. While hotel and car rental sales by travel agencies are significant and growing, the majority of sales of these travel products come from direct sales by the hotel and car rental companies themselves.

The communications mix is the marketer's tool kit, providing a variety of ideas and means of informing potential clients about the variety of travel products offered, the benefits of the products, and a call to action for purchasing. The primary communications tools are personal sales, advertising, and public relations/publicity.

The travel agency budget is much smaller than almost all other travel suppliers. As a result, all but the very largest agencies have very limited advertising budgets. Personal sales, therefore, becomes the most critical form of communication.

Whether handled over the telephone or in person, in response to inquiries, or as outside sales, the personal sales effort is the major method for securing commitments from prospective customers. A strong, well-organized sales effort is essential to the marketing program of the modern travel agency.

Before deregulation, the only application of the terms of sale sub-mix in the travel agency was the determination of payment terms for commercial accounts. Most well-managed agencies limit credit extended to accounts and few agree to thirty day billing arrangements because of the requirements of the weekly Airline Reporting Corporation (ARC) sales report requirements. Agencies must pay ARC the net amount due for sales (total cash sales less commissions earned on cash and credit card sales) ten days after the end of each sales week. The airlines absorb the credit card company charges for tickets paid for by credit cards.

Today the terms of sale sub-mix have become a full pricing sub-mix. Agencies must consider the full range of pricing strategies including rebating commission income and adding service charges on low income-producing transactions.

Identifying a Target Market

The application of the marketing mix concept to a travel agency cannot be accomplished in a void. The choices of products and services, communications tools, and pricing strategies must be made with a specific target market in view. Like the archer and the shooter, the travel agency marketer must keep an eye on the target when creating the appropriate marketing mix. An agent with multiple target markets should create separate mixes for each target.

Agency target markets can be defined in several ways. The most common segments are commercial, vacation or leisure, group, and ethnic markets. Within each of the above categories are a wide variety of targets demographically definable in terms of size, economic level, and geographic boundary. In addition, new types of agencies have developed by defining their target market in terms of specific product or through unusual pricing strategies.

Agencies can serve a single market or aim at several. Since deregulation there has been great growth in agencies specializing in commercial travel which, according to the 1984 Harris survey, constituted 53 percent of travel agency sales. Commercial sales have apparently stabilized as the 1986 Harris survey reports no change in percentage of business travel sales.

Much of the travel by largest companies is handled on a centralized basis by a small number of large, very high-volume travel agencies often called *mega-agencies*. Yet, most business travel is purchased by small companies that can be served well by small, local travel agencies.

The mega-agencies can offer large corporations specialized reports and economic savings of centralization that cannot be met by competing smaller local agencies. The local agency can provide personalized service to the small company at a level that cannot be matched by the mega-agency.

The leisure market is the historical base of the travel agency industry. While this segment was somewhat neglected during the great growth of the commercial market, vacation travel is reemerging as the core market segment for the small- and medium-size travel agency. As smaller agencies see national companies centralizing their travel with mega-agencies, they are recognizing the vulnerability of local branch commercial accounts and are redirecting their marketing efforts toward leisure targets.

Agents Must Be Trained to Sell

Advertising and promotion create interest and inquiries. Trained sales agents convert shoppers into buyers. Since travel agencies are paid in direct proportion to what they sell, it follows that — no sale, no income. A travel agency manager can develop the best marketing plan, apply the marketing mix concept perfectly by choosing the right products and communications tools for the target market, and still have major problems if the sales staff does not know how to sell.

Most agents are capable of properly qualifying clients. They easily determine where the clients want to go, making expert recommendations when necessary. Clients then say, "Thank you, we'll call you next week," and leave. Next week comes and goes and nothing happens. The agent failed to close the sale.

Lack of knowledge of closing techniques is characteristic of too many travel agents. Agents must recognize that their basic goal in a sales situation is to get the client's commitment to purchase a trip. Without this commitment, all the time and effort invested in qualifying the clients, selling recommendations, and overcoming objections is for nothing. No commitment, no sale, no job, no travel agency! All efforts, from the initial stages of the conversation, must be directed toward the close.

Closing the sale means that the agent must ask for the business. Agents rarely ask for business because they fear rejection. They are afraid that the clients will say no.

It is important that agents recognize that it is the sellers' responsibility to close the sale. The ability to close sales and gain commitments separates the sales professional from the order taker. In today's competitive environment, travel agencies must have qualified, professional salespeople in order to survive and prosper.

Selective Selling Breeds Strong Relationships

Travel agents are finding that both service levels and profits benefit from an established, preferred supplier and product policy. Concentrating selling efforts on specific products and suppliers helps agents develop relationships with travel suppliers that will both help solve problems when they occur and bring important recognition to the agency and its clients.

Developing a preferred supplier list gives a travel agency manager control over what is being sold in the agency. The staff is less confused because they know the operators and programs with which they are expected to be thoroughly familiar. Since the agents know certain products more thoroughly, they can match products to clients' needs more effectively. Thus the clients benefit as well. Of course, the choice of preferred suppliers must be based upon a full analysis of the travel needs of target market segments.

Concentrating sales as much as is reasonable within a preferred suppliers list can often provide substantial override commission income. When standard product commission is 10 percent, earning 12 percent or 14 percent commission is actually a 20 percent or 40 percent increase in income on a transaction without additional sales effort.

Many small- and medium-size travel agencies have joined consortiums and cooperatives. These organizations have negotiated override commissions for their members from certain suppliers. Other operators will provide overrides directly to individual agencies based upon sales volume or number of passengers booked, usually on a yearly basis. Through consortiums, overrides are often paid from the first booking.

The marketing question today for the smaller travel agency is not whether to join a consortium, but which consortium is best for the agency. An analysis of suppliers participating in the consortium judged against the clientele and target markets of the agency is required for a sound decision.

Recognition and clout are among the most important reasons for dealing with preferred suppliers as much as possible. By concentrating bookings with fewer operators, volume increases with the chosen suppliers. As volume grows, recognition from the operators should increase as well. Sales support for special promotions or groups becomes more readily available. Agents who concentrate their business are more likely to be invited to special seminars, familiarization trips, and other special recognition functions.

Problem solving will also be easier. Accumulated clout, used judiciously, will help clear wait-listed space when other agents cannot. Clients from agencies with clout will be the last to be walked when a preferred supplier hotel is oversold. If a client does have a problem or if an agency employee receives poor treatment from a preferred supplier's reservationist, the agency will have achieved the recognition with supplier management to assure satisfactory solutions.

Relationship marketing, while not in fact new, is one of the most modern marketing concepts. The crux of the concept is that, given relatively equal situations, buyers will purchase from the companies with which they have developed the strongest relationships and which they believe will provide the highest support levels.

Nowhere is this theory more true than in travel agency sales situations — both between agent and supplier and agent and client. Travel service is clearly an intangible. The agent is in the middle, bringing supplier and traveler together. The agent secures from the supplier a confirmation of services to be provided to the traveler. Often the confirmation is only verbal. Most often it is an electronic message received via computer terminal. The traveler pays large sums of money to the travel agency and receives only paper (for example, tickets and vouchers) in return. Strong relationships among the three parties are clearly critical to successful operations.

Diversification versus Specialization

The decision to diversify or specialize has always been a difficult one to make in any business. Should an agency handle a broad range of products or specialize in just a few? Should it become known as a commercial, vacation, or group specialist, or does it develop expertise in all facets of the industry? Should the agency specialize in one or two destinations or should it sell the world?

For some strange reason marketing comparisons are often made between travel agencies and inventory-based businesses such as dress and grocery stores. How many times has the question "Do you want to be a supermarket or a boutique?" been asked?

The deck is automatically stacked if the travel agency is viewed as either a supermarket handling a broad variety of products or a boutique specializing in just a few. Everyone knows the vast financial and human resources needed for the successful operation of supermarkets. There have also been successful low-budget boutiques. As a result, as basically small businesses, travel agencies often opt for the boutique approach.

The comparison of boutique versus supermarket is not valid in the travel agency industry. Grocery stores and dress shops depend on prepurchased inventories. The amount of money (or credit) and space required to purchase and house inventory for a supermarket or department store is vastly different from that required for a convenience store or boutique.

Certainly the staff skills and knowledge required for a broad-based travel agency are more varied than for a specialized agency. However, since the travel agency is not in an inventory business, there are no goods to prepurchase or store.

A travel agency is affected by many factors outside its control. Perceptions of terrorism and the effects of a declining dollar damaged the European market in 1986. Declining domestic airfares directly affected travel agency commission income as well.

The more an agency depends upon a single type of business, the more it will be hurt by negative forces affecting its chosen specialty. Conversely, an agency with a broad product and service base will not be hurt as much by declines in any one product or service. There is some truth to the old cliche, "Don't put all your eggs in one basket."

Most agencies are suffering from an overdependence on the air travel product. The double whammy of lower domestic fares plus the loss of the European market had a major effect on profit. Those agencies with a strong cruise market were in better shape in 1986 than those who concentrate almost solely on air tickets or Europe.

An agency that specializes in a single destination can claim to be an expert in that area. However, can that agency make needed marketing changes when destination popularity abruptly shifts?

The great growth of commercial business since deregulation has created many agencies totally dependent on this market segment. Small agencies handling local branches of national accounts have lost large portions of their business, through no fault of their own, when these accounts centralized their travel.

Diversification is the best method of protection a travel agency can develop. While specialization may provide higher short-term profits, the diversified travel agency will be stronger over the long haul. The pitfalls of specialization are highly unpredictable.

A final thought on this issue. When determining the value of a travel agency, most experts will give additional credit for a diversified business mix. Thus, a diversified agency has a higher sales value than a specialized agency of equivalent size, age, and profitability.

A Word about the Future

The future is bright for the travel agency industry. In contrast to the predictions of many so-called experts, the industry will not be dominated by a few mega-agencies. The travel industry is driven by client needs and different marketing strategies meet differing client needs, thus assuring the future of virtually all types of agencies.

Any travel agency that defines its market or markets clearly and serves it or them well will survive. Those that are well-managed, properly apply marketing concepts, and are flexible to meet market changes can prosper.

Promotion for Travel & Tourism

PROMOTION IS THE FOURTH "P" IN THE marketing mix. Its elements generally include personal selling, advertising, public relations, and promotional activities. In short, promotion consists of all the things a company has to do to persuade people to buy its products or services.

Personal Selling

Personal selling undoubtedly qualifies as the most effective form of promotion. Its role in the travel and tourism industry is paramount. Several contributors to this book have dealt with its importance and specific techniques at length. Whit Hawkins, in his article on Delta's marketing strategy, discussed the expanding role of the airline marketing representative. Originally the marketing representative simply provided service. But, as Hawkins pointed out, the airlines recognized the need for personal selling and that task has fallen to their field representatives.

Amtrak, too, depends heavily on personal selling. Robert Gall talked about its need for educated sales professionals because as he puts it, "Selling vacations and recreational travel is a task highly suited to a one-on-one selling situation."

Bob Tisch pointed out in his article on New York City that in order to market the destination successfully, the first objective was to turn all 8 million New Yorkers into salespeople for the city, and thus the Big Apple campaign was born!

June Farrell and Howard Feiertag devoted their entire articles to personal selling in the hospitality industry, and the importance of the travel agent's ability to close the sale was emphasized again and again. Phil and Doris Davidoff, in their article on travel agencies, unequivocally said that "the personal sales effort is the major method for securing commitments from prospective customers."

Advertising

Despite all its advantages, the value of personal selling is severely limited. When we are dealing with mass markets we need mass marketing techniques and that is the role assumed by advertising and direct response techniques. Advertising is a substitute for the personal salesperson. It attempts to talk to all of the prospects who, for one reason or another, will never see a personal salesperson, as well as those who won't see one until they are ready to make a purchase. In the case of the airline, car rental, and hospitality industries a great deal of the advertising is expected to make the final sale. This fairly new role is still emerging and is due in a large part to the impact of new technology.

There is another aspect to advertising and collateral material (a form of advertising) in travel and tourism. Until after the sale is completed, what we are selling in most cases is an intangible product. Our customers have no way of sampling, testing, or even looking at what we have to offer. All they have to depend on besides the advice of their travel agent is brochures and advertisements. Thus, in a way, the ads and brochures become a part of the product or service itself, or at least a surrogate for it. This is especially true in products in which a large degree of uncertainty and anticipation exists because of unfamiliarity with the product. When a consumer buys a cruise or a European tour, he or she puts down money and all he or she has in return, often for several months, is a brochure full of enticing photographs and tantalizing copy.

In his article, Tony Wainwright, President of The Bloom Companies, ranks travel and tourism advertising campaigns from great to disappointing and tells why. His article is must reading for anyone involved in advertising decisions.

Several of our contributors have commented on the need for advertising and promotion targeted to the women's market in travel. Robert Shulman's earlier article noted that more women are traveling on business than ever before and "smart marketers are looking to see what they can do to make the whole experience more pleasant." In his chapter on advertising, Tony Wainwright comments that "it's curious that very little has been done to address this segment (women) or the specific benefits offered to professional women."

Jane Maas, President of Muller Jordan Weiss, tackles that problem. She discusses marketing to women — what works, what doesn't, and why. Maas is the coauthor of *How to Advertise*, one of the really good books on this business and also of *Adventures of an Advertising Woman*.

Public Relations

No enterprise in travel and tourism can succeed without a successful public relations program. Because of the nature of the marketplace, public relations is almost a mandatory activity. Consumers demand information; indeed, many have said we are in the information age. Destinations, for example, can encourage travel editors to develop new stories. These stories, when published, can significantly influence visitor demand.

Public relations programs have many different objectives and degrees of sophistication. Some public relations programs simply strive to attract attention.

Others use PR to educate and achieve understanding. Although public relations covers a wide scope of activities including financial, internal relations, and public affairs, we are only concerned here with those that support marketing.

Originally the emphasis in public relations was on words, not deeds. Ivy Lee, an early pioneer, stressed the importance of supplying news to the media. "I believe in telling your story to the public," he said. Later practitioners such as Edward Bernays saw that deeds could shape and influence public opinion as well. Thus, today's practitioners utilize a combination of words and deeds to attract attention and influence the various publics they deal with. Bill Ruder, a well-known public relations consultant and founder of Ruder & Finn told me when I worked for him, "I believe the best way to get news is to do something newsworthy."

With that principle in mind, almost every destination stages a series of annual events as a means of attracting attention and visitors. You can celebrate the Queen's Birthday in more than a dozen countries, attend chili cook-offs, independence celebrations, anniversaries, centennials, dog shows, golf tournaments, and yacht races. All of these are public relations activities. Airlines have inaugural flights, hotels stage grand opening extravaganzas, and there is a celebration of some kind going on almost all the time at Disney World.

Even when nothing is going on, public relations is an essential tool to disseminate information that travel editors, travel agents, and the trade press feed on. Without press releases, thousands of travel writers and columnists would join the ranks of the unemployed. Newspaper Sunday travel sections would shrink in size and *Travel Weekly* would become *Travel Monthly*. There are always new destinations, new resorts, new cruise ships, and new air fares, and before anyone can buy or sell them, they need to first learn about them.

Richard Weiner, President of Richard Weiner Associates, has written a chapter on how to get publicity that attracts favorable attention for your product or service. Weiner has a vast background in all phases of public relations and *Time* magazine credited him with putting Cabbage Patch Dolls on the map. His guidelines are simple but practical and important, and his examples are very relevant.

Sales Promotion

Sales promotion has taken on an important role in travel and tourism. While it has many meanings, it is most often a direct incentive to travel agents and consumers to create an immediate sale! It includes such techinques as special seasonal pricing and packaging, sweepstakes, overrides, and rebates. In the travel agency business, free or discounted fam trips, airline passes, cruises, and tours are frequently regarded as sales promotions designed to motivate agents. In dollars, spending on sales promotion has far outstripped spending on media advertising in recent years.

Besides using sales promotion techniques to stimulate its own sales, the travel business has been one of the leading recipients of growth of sales promotion techniques in other industries. In the incentive business alone *Advertising*

Age reported that in 1985 American companies spent nearly $1.6 billion on travel incentives. Insurance and electronics industries are the number 1 and 2 users, respectively, of travel incentives according to a survey conducted by *Incentive World*, a trade publication. Other big participants, in order of use, are auto parts and accessories, autos and trucks, farm equipment, heating and air conditioning, office equipment, electric appliances, toiletries and cosmetics, and building materials.

Top incentive destinations include Arizona, California, Florida, and Hawaii in the United States and the Bahamas, Bermuda, the Caribbean, Europe, and Mexico abroad. Cruise lines are benefiting enormously from incentive travel. (See Howard Fine's article for more on this.) Even Intourist has expressed an interest in making the Soviet Union an incentive destination.

Consumer products and services of all kinds have found travel to be one of the most popular prizes in sweepstakes and contests. A recent new wrinkle has been for mail order direct merchandisers to sell coupons for discounted airfares or upgrades to catalog purchasers.

No one knows more about the sales promotion industry than Bill Robinson. His company leads in its field and Robinson's books and writings on sales promotions are classics. Robinson examines the best promotions in travel and tourism in his article.

Putting It All Together

The final article in this section is written by Peter Rickard, a noted hotelier who has spent his lifetime opening and promoting hotels. His most recent assignment was General Manager of one of Florida's most successful resorts, the Pier House in Key West. Rickard gives specific advice on advertising and promotion based on his own highly practical experience.

Chapter 27

Effective Advertising in the Travel Business

C. Anthony Wainwright
President, The Bloom
Companies, Inc.

C. Anthony Wainwright has been the President of The Bloom Companies, Inc., and CEO of The Bloom Agency since 1980. Prior to working for Bloom, Mr. Wainwright served as the Executive Vice President/General Manager of The Marschalk Company/New York, where he directed the growth of A1 Steak Sauce, Minute Maid, and Stroh's. Other work in advertising included being Vice President/Account Supervisor for Grey Advertising in Chicago, copywriting for Leo Burnett's "Green Giant" account, and founding and running his own agency, Wainwright, Spaeth & Wright.

A irline deregulation in 1978 changed the way the travel industry competes. The intensity of airline competition affected other aspects of the industry. Hotels, resorts, cruise ships, railroads, buses, and car rentals have all adjusted their advertising and marketing programs accordingly.

Prior to free competition, less-intensive image advertising prevailed. United Airlines created "Fly the Friendly Skies," American Airlines prided itself on "doing what we do best," and Greyhound said "leave the driving to us." In the past eight years, however, price has become the dominant factor. The customer base for travel has broadened as more people have the opportunity to fly to their chosen destinations. Travel packages have become more important. Now an airline, hotel, and rent-a-car are included in a single rate.

Targeting has been critical. Business travelers represent the highest return. These are frequent travelers who have less concern for price. Schedules, amenities, and special treatment all evoke positive responses. American Airlines' AAdvantage program did more for locking in the frequent traveler than any program to date.

In examining the travel market, there are two broad categories: mainline travel activities and ancillary activities. Mainline activities include advertising/marketing for airlines, hotels, and other aspects of travel. In 1985, direct media spending totaled over $725 million.

Ancillary activities include such categories as cameras, liquor brands, automobiles (*not* rent-a-cars), insurance, books, traveler's checks, and electronic equipment to name a few. These companies' spending exceeded $1 billion in 1985.

The most consistent, quality advertising campaign has been Leo Burnett Company's work for United Airlines. In the mid-1960s, Burnett introduced the concept "Fly the Friendly Skies of United." The overall feeling conveyed by all media was one of confidence and care. The highly emotional print and television executions showed a little girl who left her doll on the plane (it was returned); a tired, young serviceman on his way home (the flight attendant wakes him at his destination); and a hardworking businessman trying to unwind after a difficult day (he meets another businessman and makes a sale). The photography, casting, and direction were and are outstanding. All of United's creative efforts are excellent. A comfort level prevails in them. United's advertising is like a visit from an old friend. In today's somewhat frenetic environment, it continues to be refreshing and reassuring.

American Airlines had for years a smart, single-minded campaign: "We're American Airlines. Doing what we do best." The work done by the Doyle Dane Bernbach agency was clearly directed to the business traveler. It evoked confidence. American had a well-deserved reputation as the airline that took care of the frequent traveler. The airline led the way with such innovations as the AAdvantage Program (the first frequent flyer reward system); Sabre, for computerized researching, the Airpass offering unlimited mileage for one initial price; and the Admiral's Clubs in major airports.

American's image was reflected in warm, yet highly professional ads and commercials. Then, American moved from New York and made its new headquarters in Dallas. In doing so, American switched advertising agencies. As is too often the case, the new agency (Bozell & Jacobs) wanted to put its own stamp on the creative. After some time, the new theme was introduced: "Something special in the air." The look was changed, and the image that was so finely tuned for years, was lost.

Still another example is the long-running campaign for Delta Airlines: "Delta is ready when you are." It was a simple and persuasive thought offering convenience (*very* important for the business traveler). Further, in annual passenger polls, Delta has always ranked near the top as the airline offering the best service. Proud of its nonunion, employee-motivated service, Delta simply "tried a little harder." But while American and United pushed ahead in marketing, routes, and innovation, Delta seemed to stand still. Its advertising, while never inspired, drifted into a nondescript mode with a new line: "Delta gets you there." It's disappointing to observe an airline with so much potential not having a marketing focus.

My company, the Bloom Agency, handled Southwest Airlines for more than 10 years. We were their first and only advertising agency until we made the decision to attempt the turnaround at Braniff International.

Southwest began as a small Texas-based commuter carrier. Our positioning was one that appealed to the business commuter after a long hard day: *Fun!* Our theme was "Love is in the air." All of our promotional materials played on this love theme (drinks, candies, giveaways). Our flight attendants were dressed in hot-pants and boots (this was before the women's movement) and the total experience (from gate to gate) was one of enjoyment. Advertising was bright with a lot of color and verve. By the early 1980s, Southwest was the most profitable airline in the country.

One other example of airline innovation is worth noting. Although it is a somewhat dated case history, the creative efforts for Braniff through their agency, Wells, Rich, Green, were outstanding.

Who could forget "the end of the plain plane?" Mary Wells attempted the daring. She convinced Braniff to fill the skies with color. "The Air Strip" depicted flight attendants changing from one specially designed Pucci outfit to another.

What Braniff did was to reach out and try new concepts. Today, there is less innovation and more emphasis on price/destination.

Prior to deregulation, the airline industry ran to form. Three-year plans were developed and implemented with minor changes; pricing seldom went down; airlines were a respectable, predictable business. Image was everything.

Eastern Airlines did its takeoff from the film *2001* in the introduction of "The Wings of Man."

National Airlines named its planes after women saying, "I'm Sue, Fly Me."

Southern Airlines depicted the difference between itself and other airlines by showing the extremes in coach and first-class. The funny commercials were among the first done by Joe Sedelmaier. First-Class showed a Roman orgy; just a curtain away, Coach showed debris, passengers with chickens, and a steamy atmosphere. The message was that Southern offered better service in both of its classes.

TWA used dramatic music ("Up, Up and Away") and scenes of wonderful meals being served around the world.

No airline was crass enough to discuss price advantages.

Now, more than $30 million of People Express's media is price (comparative) oriented.

Price also dominates in the rent-a-car industry. The wonderful humor of the Hertz "Lost Soul" and the innovative positioning of Avis as "We're only number two, we have to try harder" are memories.

Today, the big three (Hertz, Avis, and National) have continuing battles over price and merchandise. Current Hertz ads say, "A small price to pay for great service." The price ad does have a logo line, "You don't just rent a car, you rent a company," but it's not developed in the advertising. Avis, too, depicts its prices, calling them Super Value Rates. Their new logo line is "Avis. So Easy." National now says, "When you rent one-way from some companies, you've got to keep both hands on your wallet." Their advantage is a fixed, added $10.00 for one-way service. National's logo line is "You deserve National attention."

These companies, plus Dollar, Alamo, and others, are *all* uninspired. Advertising in this category has hit an all time low. Because there is a sameness throughout the industry, the opportunity for a creative break-through has never been better. Obviously, all the companies are nervous and reacting to each other's price and merchandise deals.

Conversely, the credit card/traveler's check categories are wonderfully innovative.

American Express is clearly the leader. The "Do you know me?" long-running campaign for their card is breakthrough creative. And their Karl Malden traveler's check advertising is equally persuasive. Finally, their classic logo line, "Don't leave home without it," says it all.

Lately, Visa has been revitalized. A new advertising agency has devel-oped the highly intrusive visits to places that don't accept American Express. The photography, places, and people are charming. Visa achieves its objec-tive. The advertising is convincing. It makes you want their card.

Mastercard is disappointing. After a straight celebrity campaign (featur-ing James Coburn), MasterCard now simply talks about "the possibilities" that its card offers. It is a nondescript campaign.

More interesting is the rebirth of Diner's Club. With CitiCorp behind Diner's, the company is making a bid for credibility. Interestingly, CitiCorp is also promoting its own card (Citibank with either Visa or MasterCard). The campaign features Vincent Price with the line "CitiBank gives me power I've always longed to possess." An application is an important part of the ad.

The card customer is a powerful asset. The American Express mailing list is one of the best. Their ancillary sales of various items continues to grow. Overall, we're looking at an intense marketing battleground. It's more and more likely that heavy usage card users will utilize only one major card.

The use of media is interesting. The major cards use network and spot television, and radio. The print budget goes primarily to magazines. It is generally divided between image and direct response. All of the competitors also have healthy co-op budgets. The cards select retailers and restaurants by market and feature them in listings. Special campaigns are used for corporate accounts, college-age cardholders, and extra cards for spouses (of business cardholders).

One of the travel categories that offers the greatest creative opportunities is marketing a country or city. For the past year, Jamaica has used the theme, "Come back to Jamaica." The players are a variety of friendly natives in different roles. The objective is twofold: to convince tourists to "come back again" (undoubtedly, their research has shown that many travelers have been to Jamaica), and to overcome the perception that the islanders are unfriendly (even dangerous).

Ten years ago, Jamaica was recognized for its award-winning advertising. Then, the commercials showed many quick-cut sequences of the beauty, excitement, and diversity of the island. There was no copy. Just exciting, driving music. The close-ups made you feel the pulse of the people. And at the end of the commercial, in giant letters, was the name "Jamaica."

Different times, different executions. It's always important to remember that the objective of advertising is to solve problems and achieve sales objectives. Too often, especially in a category like travel, the aesthetics overwhelm the objectives. For years, travel advertising was among the winners in the major travel awards. This can be gratifying. But *only* if the advertising works.

In most of the countries' executions (France, Holland, Italy), the emphasis is on the people with secondary attention given to tourist sites, food, and entertainment. Certainly one of the overriding concerns has been that Americans may have been mistreated in the past. The nagging fear of being shortchanged or verbally abused or having possessions stolen has been a growing problem. With terrorist activities, more Americans have changed their travel plans.

Hawaii has become the hottest overseas vacation destination. Airlines and hotel/resorts on all the islands are vying for the consumer dollar. Separate inviting campaigns attempt to lure the visitor past Oahu/Honolulu to the out islands. The issue of safety is never mentioned; instead, the appeals are friendly people, lush scenery, sports, deep sea fishing, and wonderful accommodations, all with favorable package prices.

It is important to note that the mindset of the vacation traveler has been dramatically modified. There are still older people (retirees) who select carefully organized tours. And there are still the wealthy who travel without regard for prices, timing, or destination. But the big market encompasses all other people with special emphasis on young professionals.

These people were brought up traveling. Distances are no concern. Comfort and pleasure are necessities. The young professionals are independent. They make good incomes. And they feel that travel and relaxation are important life-style components. This market is of most interest and concern to the travel industry. If these travelers have positive experiences with airlines, hotels, and destinations, they not only will visit repeatedly, but they become missionaries spreading the word among their contemporaries.

One of the important positionings for a travel-related company would be a direct appeal to this group. Even though many companies currently appeal to the business traveler, the young professional represents a growing subsegment.

As an example, professional women represent an important new travel segment. They have special needs, and special concerns. It's curious that very little has been done in advertising to address this segment or the specific benefits offered to professional women. I believe that segmentation is a key component of each company's marketing plan, but often the pieces aren't translated into specific advertising campaigns.

Overall, I'm disappointed in the lack of direction and innovation in travel agency advertising. Prices have become a blur. So much emotion is involved in the travel decision, I think the opportunity for compelling imagery is significant, but being lost.

Chapter 28

Marketing to Women Travelers

Jane Maas
President, Mueller
Jordan Weiss
Advertising

Jane Maas is president of the New York Advertising agency Mueller Jordan Weiss. She is an expert in travel and tourism marketing, having directed the "I Love New York" tourism program for five years while at Wells, Rich, Greene. Prior to that, as a creative director at Ogilvy & Mather, Mrs. Maas headed the American Express and Cunard accounts. She is the co-author of the classic How to Advertise *and author of* Better Brochures *and* Adventures of an Advertising Woman.

Women are very different from men, especially when they travel. If this fact intrigues you, read on.

In 1986, women accounted for 36 percent of frequent travelers, a figure that has *tripled* in just five years. Women are worth $2 billion in annual sales to airlines.

Women are an increasingly important target audience for all ages of the travel industry, but in order to sell to them, you must know what they want, what they don't want, and what motivates them.

So . . .

16 Guidelines for Tapping the Profitable Women's Market

1. Understand Your Target Audience.

Of 120 attitudinal measures, the woman traveler differs significantly from the male traveler on six major attributes.

Women say they like to be pampered, want to read lots of brochures, enjoy planning for a trip, prefer packages, and delight in all the excitement of big city visits, including quaint restaurants, shopping, and cultural events.

Women are also more likely than men to want to see new places, try different hotels when returning to the same city, make reservations further in advance, and take a vacation with a purpose. Leading the list of "far less interested in than men are" are vacations featuring outdoor sports.

2. *Women Who Travel on Business Have a Higher Self-image.*

A study pointed out important contrasts between women who travel on business versus those who travel only for pleasure. The business travelers rated themselves almost 50 percent higher in creativity and intelligence. They also consider themselves more efficient, refined, and style-conscious; less economy minded and less easily persuaded than nonbusiness women.

3. *Flag the Single Woman Traveler.*

Remember that at least 40 percent of the full-time working women's market is single — unmarried, widowed, divorced, or separated. Even among the married group, 45 percent approve of separate vacations.

The woman traveling domestically on business is almost 50 percent more likely than the average woman to be single and to be in the 18 to 34 age group.

4. *Call Attention to the Travel Agent in Your Advertising.*

Women, far more than men, rely on travel agents, and are likely to return to the agent who gives them special service. They also tend to spread the word about their favorite agents to friends.

Advice to travel agents: Let her know you have a "Star File" on her, that you are aware she likes the nonsmoking section, a window seat, and the seafood salad when she flies; and prefers a hotel room near the elevator. Blow your own horn.

5. *Advertise Your Good Security Systems.*

A recent study showed that 12 percent of women listed security as the prime reason for selecting one hotel over another.

The new Burnsley Hotel in Denver held a seminar for regional travel agents to discuss marketing to women. Owner Joy Burns told the group about her state-of-the-art security, including closed circuit television that follows guests from the time they park their cars until they check in at the front desk.

6. *If You Offer Suites, Put That Benefit in the Headline.*

Laventhol & Horvath, an accounting firm that tracks the travel industry, states that there were some 350 all-suite hotels in the United States in 1986. It predicts the number will *triple* by 1990. Women are largely responsible for this boom. They like to conduct business meetings and social events in a room apart from their bedroom.

The headline of every advertisement for the Lombardy calls attention to its key consumer benefit: apartment living and location. "Rent a Park Avenue pied-a-terre for a night, a week or a year."

Women are also leading the trend toward preference for smaller, European-style hotels. Security is one reason; extra personal attention and pampering is another.

7. *Don't Be Patronizing.*

In the 1970s when women first emerged as an important segment of business travelers, some hotels created special rooms with touches like pink color schemes and canopied beds designed to appeal to female guests. They flopped.

> A few hotels still offer women-only floors. However, 92 percent of business women surveyed say they do not like being segregated. Concierge floors that cater to executives are steadily increasing in popularity among men and women.

Another way to cater to women without segregating them is "the captain's table." These tables, set aside for single travelers who don't want to eat alone, appeal to both sexes.

8. *Be Helpful, Not Clever.*

Instead of witty copy and gimmicky layouts, give practical information: what your climate is, what clothing to bring, and what attractions are in your area. And don't neglect that grand old word, *free*. It is still one of the most powerful persuaders in advertising. If your destination doesn't charge for visits to the wildlife sanctuary, if your hotel offers free transportation to the airport, say so. Loudly.

9. *Always Include a Response Device in Your Advertising.*

Print advertisement should contain a coupon and a telephone number. The coupon should look like a coupon, and be placed so the consumer can easily tear it out. If possible, use a toll-free telephone number in television commercials. All advertisements aimed at travel agents must contain a telephone number; it is the single most important element in any trade ad.

> Research shows that more than 75 percent of travel agents found it helpful to have CRT access codes in addition to a telephone number.

10. *It Pays to Include Several Pieces in a Mailing.*

Include a personalized letter with your brochure. At the very least, attach a business card.

> South Carolina's "Trip Kit" includes an accommodations directory, state map, specialized brochures on camping, golf, tennis, and points of interest, a calendar of events, and a thank-you note.

11. *Put News in Your Headline.*

Your product or service will only be new once. It pays to announce it with a loud bang. If necessary, invent news. A new menu that features a few reduced calorie dishes is news — especially for women.

12. *"Loyalty" Programs Add Value to Your Product.*

Women are slightly more likely than men to look for added value. More destinations (and tourism-related attractions such as theme parks) should study the success of the frequent-flyer and frequent-guest airline and hotel programs.

13. *Women Make 90 Percent of Vacation Decisions.*

The couple will decide together on the amount of money they want to spend. Then, 90 times out of 100, the woman decides on the destination. Win her over when she visits you on business and she may return to you for pleasure.

14. *Don't Neglect the Increasingly Important "Mature" Consumer.*

Americans over 50 account for 80 percent of all money spent on pleasure travel. As noted earlier, women are an important constituency.

Eastern Airlines appeals to the 50+ consumer in a commercial that portrays an attractive older couple enjoying themselves on a holiday. The man says, "When we were young, I promised you the world. Now we are here."

15. *Tell the Truth.*

It's not only a legal necessity. Being truthful, even about some of your negatives, makes you credible to potential customers.

American Express pioneered a brochure program that not only gave complete facts to potential travelers, but disclosed possible drawbacks. They described one tour, for example, as not suited for people unable to walk long distances. A flood of letters told them such advice made the rest of their statements extremely believable.

16. *Don't Be Afraid of Long Copy.*

When you are selling a big-ticket item like a vacation, people are hungry for facts. Make the copy inviting to read by breaking it up with subtitles.

A magazine advertisement for "I Love New York" theater packages used more than 2,000 words of body copy. It was the most successful advertisement in the campaign.

Seven Tips for Selling Packages to Women

1. *Your Package Must Tie In with Your Basic Positioning.*

If your destination is positioned as the utmost in luxury for affluent adults, don't market packages that offer inexpensive vacations to families.

The Parker Meridien is positioned as "the luxurious French hotel in New York." It offers weekend packages that stay with this strategy, such as "Le Weekend Francais."

2. *Try to Create a Package Unique to You.*

There is more me-tooism in packages than in any other area of the tourism industry.

The Vista International took advantage of its unique location on New York Harbor to offer "Statue of Liberty" packages during The Lady's centennial. They included free trips to Liberty Island. The headline was "No one's closer to Miss Liberty than we are." No other hotel in New York could have run that advertisement.

3. *Women Prefer Packages with Frills.*

Of course they know you are building in the costs for theater tickets or a champagne breakfast, but packages that offer these extras appeal more than those that simply offer reduced rates.

4. *Include Features That Appeal to Women.*

Remember that women enjoy pampering, cultural events, and quaint restaurants. They also enjoy shopping, yet few package tours take advantage of tie-ins with stores or outlets.

5. *Watch the Trends.*

If you know what women are doing, you can create packages that will appeal to them. Physical fitness is in, for example. Offer a package that gives them free exercise facilities, a reduced rate on massages and aerobic dance classes, and a list of jogging trails and walks.

More than 65 percent of Americans go on at least one picnic every year. If you have the appropriate surroundings and the right climate, include a romantic picnic basket excursion. You could change a woman's attitude toward a rugged, rural destination from negative to positive.

6. *Be Aware of Psychographics.*

The working woman is exhausted much of the time, pulled by her responsibilities to her career, husband, and children. Advertising that shows you understand her problems can work wonders. Doesn't she deserve a "Breakfast in bed" weekend?

7. *Don't Ignore Your Own Backyard.*

The "I Love New York" program discovered that 60 percent of the New York City packages were bought by people living within the 100 miles of the city. Women, especially working women, love the idea of leaving the children with a babysitter and escaping for a romantic tryst — even if the destination is just a few miles away.

We noted earlier in this chapter that women are the package tour purchasers. Because they are doing their homework, they are undoubtedly comparing your package to your competition's. Build in innovative and unique elements that your competition is not offering.

Guidelines for Better Brochures

Travel industry brochures must learn to work harder to appeal to women. These sales promotion pieces are one place where you have the time to woo them, either visually or verbally.

1. *Put a Message on the Cover.*

The cover of a brochure works just like the headline of a print advertisement: four out of five readers never get beyond it. So it follows that if you do not put a message on the cover, you are wasting 80 percent of your money.

The Sagamore puts a great deal of important information on its cover, including its location, the fact that it is an Omni Resort and Conference Center, and the positioning line "A private island resort surrounded by pleasures."

2. *Use One Illustration on the Cover.*

Research says that one large illustration is more effective than several smaller ones. And photographs, on the cover or inside the brochure, are 26 percent more effective than drawings.

3. *Avoid Clichés and Travelogues.*

The travel industry is riddled with clichés. The smiling chef. The smiling pilot. The smiling married couple in the hotel room. Look for photographs that set you apart.

The Eden II hotel has a daring postioning expressed in its headline: "For lovers only." Instead of showing the expected photo of a young couple, they show a closeup of intertwined bare feet.

A famous photographer said that the secret of his success in creating arresting visuals was simply taking small details and blowing them up.

4. *Always Caption Photographs.*

Next to the headline, captions are the most-read element in a brochure or advertisement. The best captions are actually little advertisements in themselves; yet, after studying hundreds of travel-related brochures, I have found that almost none use captions.

Kiawah Island Hotel has captions that are packed with information and benefits. "Historic Charleston — just 21 miles away." "Plan a crabbing or fishing safari."

5. *Demonstrate Your Point of Difference.*

Women respond to television commercials that make believable points with demonstrations. This successful packaged goods technique is one the travel industry should borrow.

A Del Webb hotel directed a brochure to meeting planners. Instead of merely showing floor plans and giving the square footage of their convention space, they drove huge trailer trucks into the hall and showed that photograph. It made a dramatic visual.

6. *Spotlight the Important Facts.*

One of the chief complaints heard from women about brochures is that they do not give facts or they make the facts hard to find. Maps are not only a way of giving important facts but can be a welcome graphic element. You might want to indicate where your resort is located in a certain area and how close it is to other attractions.

The Bristol Hotel in London always includes a map showing it just around the corner from Piccadilly. The Hay Adams Hotel of Washington, DC never forgets to tell consumers it has a view of the White House.

Other devices that help to call attention to important facts are bullets, bold type, and easy grids to list prices. Women resent mice type that buries essential information.

7. *Sell Romance and Special Attention.*

I am making this point again because it is a key in effective marketing to women.

The brochure for the Kahala Hilton is a wonderful example of copy that appeals to women. "Our luxurious accommodations are complete with his and her dressing rooms, where you can slip into a yukata robe and slippers provided for your comfort. A freshly cut Hawaiian pineapple in your room is our traditional welcome. An orchid on your pillow each evening is our way of wishing you pleasant dreams."

Finally, the two most important rules of all for marketing to women: They are moving targets, so you must know where she is going to be tomorrow; and, once you know the rules, you can break any and all of them for a reason.

Chapter 29

How to Use Public Relations as a Marketing Tool

Richard Weiner
President, Richard
Weiner & Co.

Richard Weiner heads Doremus/Richard Weiner, one of the world's largest public relations agencies. His travel and tourism experience includes Barbados, the Gallapagos Islands, Marco Island (Florida), Marriott Hotels, Mexican National Tourist Council, New York Air, and St. Lucia. The author of seven public relations books, he teaches a public relations course at Fordham University Graduate School of Business Administration. Awards include five Silver Anvils from the Public Relations Society of America, including the 1983 introduction of the Cabbage Patch Kids.

B ad news travels fast. It always has a greater impact than good news. Just ask the folks at Tylenol and Gerber baby foods. And everyone in the travel industry knows the impact of terrorism.

What everyone in the travel industry does not know is the role of public relations as a marketing technique. Whether the marketing operation is for a major country or airline, or limited to a small hotel, the emphasis in marketing generally is on advertising.

Advertising is essential in the marketing of consumer products and services and has many advantages, notably that the complete and exact text of the advertisement will appear whenever and wherever the advertiser wants it, if you buy the time or space. Advertising thus has predictability and frequency; however, even the largest advertisers cannot advertise in all the media that they would like, particularly with the very high cost of local, regional, and national radio and television commercials, as well as large-space advertisements in national magazines.

Therefore, the basic technique used by most marketers in the travel industry consists of booklets and other materials that are distributed via direct mail, at trade shows, and in person to the travel trade and directly to consumers.

The key area of marketing is public relations. Surprisingly, even sophisticated marketers who make use of public relations techniques generally do not do as good a job in this area as they do in advertising and producing their own publications. In fact, most case studies and articles about travel promotion really are about advertising.

Actually, public relations consists of all forms of communication, so technically, advertising is a public relations technique. *Public Relations News*, one of the leading newsletters in the field, defines public relations as "the management function which evaluates public attitudes, identifies the policies and procedures of an individual or an organization with the public interest, and plans and executes a program of action to earn public understanding and acceptance."

So, public relations includes all forms of communication, such as advertising, exhibits, publications, as well as such offbeat techniques as skywriting. For the purpose of this chapter, I'll concentrate on publicity, since it can be an invaluable technique for all organizations in the travel business and can be particularly useful to travel agents, proprietors of individual hotels, and others with very limited promotion budgets.

Publicity sometimes is called free advertising; it isn't, though it is true that publicists do not purchase the time and space as do advertisers. Publicity consists of news and feature articles in newspapers, magazines, and other print media, news reports and interviews on radio and television programs, and other material that is not purchased as advertising. Readers, listeners, and viewers generally pay more attention and have a greater respect for news reports as compared to advertisements.

The goal of travel publicists is to convince editors and broadcasters that they should utilize the material that we provide free to them. It is not the obligation of the media to use our material since we are not buying the time or space. Thus, it is necessary for publicists to be as proficient in communication skills as journalists employed by the media.

As with advertising, the first step in a public relations campaign is to determine who you (that is, your company or organization) are and who your major prospects are. This research phase is essential in an advertising campaign, yet is often neglected by public relations people who frequently do not have the staff, resources, and budgets for focus groups and other research. As proficient as many public relations people are, it is imprudent to work too quickly and it is essential to have a plan.

Following is a description of eight major areas of a public relations program that can be particularly useful to someone in the travel industry who does little or no advertising.

Research

Find out by studying past data and conducting interviews who your target audience has been, is, and will be in the future. You don't have to hire a market research firm to determine the demographics of your customers and prospective customers. What is essential is that you put on paper a description of your image. What do people think of your organization and its reputation, and who is likely to be attracted to you?

Beam your message to past customers as well as prime prospects. This research phase, which can consist of a professional audit, should result in the development of a credo. This strategy statement should be based on a situation analysis, and not simply a random list of goals or wishes for fanciful objectives.

The Message

Based on the research, you can develop a major theme and secondary themes. These may involve slogans or other statements (in advertising, they are called *copy points*), so that the program is targeted to your major prospects and emphasizes the message you want, not just incidental, trivial, or irrelevant publicity.

When we opened the Marco Beach Hotel in Florida a few years ago, our research suggested that one of the property's biggest benefits was that it was not on Miami Beach, which had a lot of negatives associated with it. The tropical ambience of Southwest Florida and the hotel's island location were pluses. The message stressed that Marco was "a tropical island you could drive to." We also recommended that the talent in the hotel's night club, particularly for the opening, not be entertainers typically associated with Miami Beach. Our choice was David Frost, the English author and comedian, who at that time was hosting a TV network talk show.

Materials

It is not necessary to prepare an elaborate press kit, though it is essential that the materials be in a format to which media people are accustomed. Therefore, if you are not familiar with publicity materials — and how to write and produce them — obtain a collection from one of the travel organizations or visit a local newspaper and ask to see a batch of news releases. The most common form of publicity material is the news release. Become familiar with the style and formats of various types of news releases.

You will be overwhelmed to discover that a major daily newspaper receives hundreds or thousands of unsolicited news releases and other publicity materials each day. Almost all of them are skimmed quickly and most are thrown away. Thus, it is important that you prepare your materials in such a way that they are likely to be read and utilized.

Perhaps the first piece of publicity material should provide background information about your organization. It can range from one page to many. Generally this should be sent to a large number of media people annually, as they sometimes keep information of this type as reference material.

You also should invest in good quality photography and have a variety of photos. Most newspapers prefer 8″ × 10″ glossy black and white photos, so you generally do not have to pay for color photography and prints, because media that utilize color photos generally take their own.

If you have sales promotion material or advertising specialties prepared for travel agent trade shows or sales calls, consider sending them to important editors. Whether they are colorful posters, postcards, or something as offbeat as coffee cups, they will help to focus more attention on your news releases.

One elementary textbook which is also used by many professionals is *Professionals Guide to Publicity*, written by Richard Weiner (Public Relations Publishing Company, 888 Seventh Avenue, New York 10106, $9.50). Of course, I'm not objective about this book, since I'm the author, though I'm proud to note that the book is in many libraries and is a textbook at dozens of colleges and universities.

Media

The next step is to prepare lists of media people who may be interested in your publicity material. Your marketing plan should indicate the geographical areas of your prime prospects and your publicity materials should be sent to media that cover this area.

If you draw 90 percent of your clientele from an area spanning 350 miles, there's no sense in sending materials to media which do not reach customers within that area. Many publicists feel that the wasted money, which is relatively small in terms of printing and postage, is inconsequential and they therefore make large mass mailings. However, the small operator should be frugal in everything, including publicity.

Do not limit your media list to the travel press. While travel pages of Sunday newspapers are extremely important, you often can obtain greater impact with feature editors, such as those who write for the life-style pages, as well as food, fashion, business, and other sections of newspapers, magazines and broadcast media. For example, we publicized St. Lucia on the personal business pages of such influential publications as *Forbes* and *Business Week*.

Almost everyone in the travel industry is competing for space in the travel media, which is another reason to look elsewhere, where the competition for time and space may be less intense.

Communication

Your publicity materials should be sent to the media, accompanied by a letter, phone call, or personal visit.

Again, it is important to understand that media people are not required to utilize publicity material and are deluged with it. Therefore, your letter should be limited to one page and should utilize underlining or other techniques to make it easier for the salient points to pop out.

Similarly, when you phone an editor or broadcaster, rehearse what you want to say, particularly in the first 30 or 60 seconds of the conversation. Think about communicating to the media as you would in a direct marketing campaign beamed to prime prospects.

With regard to news releases, they generally should be no more than two or three pages long. The most important part of the news release is the beginning of the first page. I strongly recommend that every news release have a headline. It can be one or more lines, and should simply highlight or summarize the news release.

If your destination or resort is located outside of the United States, there is another technique you can use to gain attention for your news releases. Use picturesque commemorative stamps if they are available. Even though the envelopes will arrive with hundreds of other letters, these authentic appeals can make your mailing stand out. We tried this with news releases for our client, Delsey Luggage. Although they are France's largest luggage manufacturer, they were unknown to many editors in the United States. Our press releases were written in New York for the American audience and then sent to France for mailing back to the States!

Interviews

If you are fortunate, your publicity materials will result in an interview of you or your spokesperson, either over the phone or in person. One of the most common types of interviews, which is ideal for people in the travel industry, is the radio talk show. Often, you will be interviewed for 30 minutes or more and then answer questions called in by listeners.

Many sophisticated travel agents and other small operators in the travel industry find that they can get exposure on local radio and television programs simply by writing and calling the media and suggesting newsworthy subjects. For example, if there is an event in the news, such as terrorism, you can turn it to your advantage by contacting the news assignment director of a radio or TV station, or the producer of a radio or TV program, to suggest that you be interviewed.

Obviously, you should prepare for the interview by rehearsing. This means extra work but it can pay off because you can think about answers to questions you are likely to be asked. The next time you watch the "Today Show" or "Good Morning America," notice the proficiency of some of the authors and others who are interviewed. They have replies that almost always include the name of the book or whatever else they are promoting. You can do the same thing; it merely requires rehearsal.

Keep in mind that a television interview often consists of only a few seconds or a few minutes, so it is important that your answers be relatively brief, such as 15 to 30 seconds, and that you include the name of your organization and other salient points. Again, refer to your public relations plan, with its key points.

Here's an offbeat tip. It is obvious that you should bring your press kit, booklets, and other materials with you to a newspaper interview. Bring these same materials with you to a TV interview, even if they have been sent to the producer prior to the program. In fact, you should discuss with the producer whether you can provide slides, videotapes, or other visual materials.

However, you may not be aware that you should also bring visual materials with you to a radio interview. Many radio interviewers are facile conversationalists who conduct studio interviews with relatively little preparation. You can help the interviewer and yourself by bringing booklets and other materials with you so that they can be referred to by the interviewer, as well as by you, during the interview.

When you are interviewed, request a videotape or recording of the interview from the station. This may prove invaluable in obtaining other interviews. When we were hired to promote Cabbage Patch Dolls, many people felt that the product just appeared from out of the blue. That was not true. Xavier Roberts, the creator, had been getting his own local publicity since the early 1970s and we sent this published material to all of the national media. It gave the product credibility and a history and helped land it on such programs as the "Today Show."

Continuity

Once you commence your publicity campaign, you must continue it. If successful, you will become known as a resource to media people. Whether or not you are successful initially, you must continue to initiate contacts with media people. Whenever possible, try to arrange for visits with them so they can get to know you. And when you visit with them, ask them for the types of materials or subjects they like, including examples of excellent publicity materials which have been sent to them by others in the travel industry. As with all of your marketing activities, it's not easy. The winners generally are those who persevere.

Special Events

The best way to generate news is to conduct races, contests, concerts, art exhibitions, fashion shows, and other events at your facility. This often requires time and money well beyond most budgets; however, offbeat events can often be created on shoestring budgets, and because they are novel, they are often more newsworthy. For our client, Lone Star Beer, we created Texas Armadillo Races. We recruited "professional" armadillo racers and had them compete against one another. The cost was miniscule but it got Lone Star on "Mike Douglas" and other network TV shows!

For additional help on this subject, you should subscribe to an unusually useful newsletter, *Special Events Report* (213 W. Institute Place, Chicago 60610, $240/year). A subscription includes a directory of Special Events & Festivals.

There is one more point to this eight-point public relations program and that is that you must be a believer. You must truly believe in your organization and its message. You must have confidence in yourself or whoever else is the publicist and the spokesperson. And you must believe in and appreciate the power of publicity. Of course, it has to be good publicity, not publicity about terrorism, strikes, accidents, or other negative occurrences.

So in the final analysis, the believers succeed. Another way to believe is to pray. Indeed, there is a cathedral in New York that has a special pew for publicists. I've been there often, but I'm sorry that its location is the one secret I must withhold.

Chapter 30

Proven Sales Promotion Techniques

William A. Robinson
President, William A.
Robinson, Inc.

William A. Robinson, President and Founder of William A. Robinson, Inc., is keenly aware of the power of effective marketing and promotion techniques in generating trial, gaining distribution, helping to create new product images, inspiring a sales force, and setting new sales records. Robinson's column on sales promotion appears regularly in Advertising Age. *Having taught courses in sales promotion at Northwestern, Michigan State, and Florida State Universities, Mr. Robinson has written* Best Sales Promotions, *and co-authored* Sales Promotion Essentials *and* Sales Promotion Management.

Sales promotion in the travel and tourism industry has increased dramatically. Most of this increase has occurred since 1973, due primarily to two major economic factors: the meteoric rise in fuel prices resulting from the oil crisis of 1973 and again in 1978, and the deregulation of the airline industry in 1978.

Consumers in love with Detroit's gas guzzlers were suddenly facing shortages at the gas pumps and skyrocketing prices throughout 1973. Hotels and motels, car rental agencies, and destination marketers all felt the impact. Americans simply couldn't afford to travel as before.

The 1978 airline deregulation prompted another change in the way Americans traveled, and a fiercely competitive pricing climate emerged. The pressure of airlines competing for the same passengers to fill their seats was enormous. Only those who could win the inevitable fare wars would survive.

Marketing within the newly deregulated environment caused airline marketers to begin looking for new ways to build brand loyalty. What they found were old-fashioned continuity programs. Remember those supermarket promotions? Get a full set of dishes—one piece at a time? This tried and true promotional technique kept customers coming back. And although it had never been used by a service industry before, it was the right idea at the right time. Loyalty programs were created to meet the airlines' objectives of filling seats, persuading passengers to switch airlines, and ultimately improving bottom-line performance. As a result, the frequent-flyer program was born. Let's take a closer look at how this type of program works.

Loyalty Marketing

American Airlines, with its AAdvantage program, started loyalty building. Preemptive in the industry, the AAdvantage program was simple. It offered valuable rewards to people who travel frequently. American not only rewarded its frequent flyers with free travel, depending on how many miles they logged with American, but it also gave them special services on the ground and in the air. In other words, American showed these frequent travelers that they were important and rewarded them for their business.

Very simple, but very effective, frequent-flyer programs are perhaps the ultimate continuity program for this target market. According to Stevan A. Grosvald, Continental's Staff Vice President of Marketing, "frequent-flyer plans are the strongest and most effective marketing progam in place today."

American's inaugural frequent-flyer program, now with more than 4.5 million flyers on its rolls, also tied-in additional benefits from its travel-related affiliates addressing the same audience. With American Express, Hertz, and Hyatt Hotels initially involved in the AAdvantage program, American was able to up the ante in rewards to the consumer.

American's AAdvantage program worked so well that competitors immediately jumped on the bandwagon to offer their own programs. Today, all major U.S. and most foreign carriers have some kind of a loyalty marketing program. And most smaller regional carriers, which can't afford their own programs, have joined a major carrier's program to remain competitive. As a result, mileage bonuses have become as familiar to the airlines as the "Fasten your seat belt" signs.

Why was the AAdvantage program so successful? First and most important was—and still is—its genuine appeal to the frequent flyer. The recognition that there's a beach in Hawaii waiting for you after countless trips through O'Hare. That someone is finally paying you back for the nights away from home and the meals on the run. That's better than a discount fare any day!

Another reason for the continued success of this concept is its extendability. New dimensions can easily be added to the program. Sometimes it's bonus points for flying special routes or for staying in a new hotel. Other times it's a special free ticket just for flying a number of miles and segments in a certain time period. Or, it's special recognition because you're a member of the program. Incentives like first-class upgrades, special check-in lines, unlisted telephone reservation numbers, even advance seat assignments can go a long way towards maintaining brand loyalty, sustaining participation in the program, and keeping airplanes filled with paying passengers.

The successes realized through loyalty marketing have given rise to identifying niche audiences, such as frequent flyer programs targeted to travelers 65 years of age and older. Several of the major airlines have developed programs that offer special reduced fares and/or companion passes for the senior traveler. These programs are effective in increasing passenger load, particularly during off-peak periods.

After 1981 the entire travel and tourism business was stimulated by people traveling on low-rate fares and participating in continuity programs. Soon travel marketers, such as hotels and car rental companies, also created continuity promotions to capture a larger share of frequent travelers and strengthen brand loyalty.

National Car Rental's "The More You Rent, the Greater Your Reward" is just one of several continuity programs created for frequent car renters. Designed to stimulate trial and encourage switching, this promotion offered escalating car rental awards ranging from a free rental car upgrade for two rentals to a free round-trip coach ticket for any domestic Republic Airlines flight after seven rentals. This promotion was not only easy to monitor and execute, but also boosted sales and residually increased National's market share.

Hertz, on the other hand, created a promotion designed to keep its current customers and counter competitive switching by offering a mileage incentive on the frequent-flyer programs of United, Eastern, Pan Am, or TWA. Frequent travelers could rent a car from Hertz and earn up to 2,000 bonus miles depending on the carrier they chose. This is a good idea that resells the interdependence of air travel and auto rental and makes Hertz an easy choice when the frequent traveler needs to rent a car.

The value of loyalty marketing and promotion has also been demonstrated in the hotel industry. In addition to participating in airline frequent traveler programs, some hotels have created their own continuity promotions independently.

One example of hotel continuity is the Radisson Frequent Guest Awards program. To stimulate repeat stay among frequent business travelers, the

Radisson Hotels developed a program that offered 14 award levels. Award points earned for every dollar spent, not only for lodging, but for food, beverage, room service, telephone, laundry, and dry cleaning are an excellent way to boost occupancy and increase sales within the hotel.

Tie-Ins

Teaming up marketers of diverse products can create awareness and generate sales for both parties. An excellent tie-in was the "Buy a Polaroid 600, Fly Delta Free" promotion.

In this promotion, Polaroid joined with Delta Airlines to increase the sales of Polaroid Series 600 cameras at Christmas and generate purchase among affluent air travelers and college students.

In exchange for a proof of purchase from the Polaroid 600, customers received an air travel certificate on Delta airlines, good for a free roundtrip ticket to anywhere Delta flew when they bought a ticket of equal or greater value. This trade-for-mention promotion offered Delta free advertising exposure and incremental revenues, and generated incremental sales for Polaroid. In fact, this effort was so successful it represented Polaroid's biggest Christmas sell-through in more than 10 years!

AT&T and United Airlines went together for another successful promotion, the "AT&T Buy and Fly Offer." Consumers purchasing an AT&T phone could receive up to $200 worth of free travel on United Airlines. From a marketing perspective this translated into a high-perceived value incentive for AT&T plus low-cost participation and incremental revenue potential for United. The high-quality standards of both partners made for a good promotional fit.

Another example of a tie-in brought peanut butter, airplanes, and hotels together. Although they are not traditional partners, this promotional effort allowed consumers to get half-price certificates good for air travel on American Airlines with any roundtrip coach fare and save 50 percent on a three-consecutive-night stay at Sheraton Resorts and Hotels, after purchasing five jars of Skippy Peanut Butter.

The key thing to remember about tie-ins is they can add more muscle to promotional efforts for fewer dollars, since the tie-in companies often share the cost of the program.

Leisure-time marketing efforts offer another opportunity for promotional tie-ins. TWA's "Spend a Free Weekend in the Country" promotion offered TWA passengers the opportunity to get free weekend use of a Dollar Rent A Car plus weekend accommodations at a Holiday Inn. To earn the free weekend, TWA passengers had to book a Dollar Rent A Car for two weekdays, earning them use of a Dollar Rent A Car free for the prior or following two weekend days when they presented their TWA ticket and boarding pass. Passengers could get the same free deal at participating Holiday Inns by booking two weekday nights and presenting their TWA ticket and boarding pass. TWA's tie-ins offered a strong incentive for consumers to choose TWA over other carriers without having to make deep fare cuts.

To promote their new non-stop service from New York to Manchester, England, British Airways created a "Free and Easy" promotion. In this case, passengers received a free rental car with unlimited mileage for seven days when they flew the newly established New York—Manchester route. A simple yet effective tie-in that created awareness of the route and a good reason to fly it immediately.

In order to get people to try their new service, Amtrak offered business travelers "An Invitation to Experience Amtrak's Metroliner Service." Through direct mail, passengers received a special incentive offer when they rode the Metroliner service between New York and Washington, D.C. Just one trip between the two locations entitled rail travelers to their choice of a free six-month subscription to *Fortune* or *Discover* magazines. In addition, those travelers who stayed at participating Sheraton Hotels received free gifts and certificates good towards a "Free Getaway Weekend."

"Ship Out! Cash In!" That's what Royal Viking Lines urged consumers to do when they booked a Royal Viking Mexico and Panama Canal cruise. The incentive to cruise passengers: A special land package. Passengers on a five- or ten-day cruise could get a pre- or post-cruise Acapulco land package, with airfare, for a special low price of $99. Optional land incentives for cruise passengers included free two-night land packages in San Francisco or Los Angeles and free airfare. This promotion effectively asked the question "Why not take that cruise *now* while you can get so much more for your money?" This promotional tie-in made a lot of a sense for the target market and helped convert prospects into paying passengers.

Travel marketers can also utilize promotional tie-ins with destination marketers. American Airlines hopped on the "I Love New York" campaign bandwagon by sponsoring special marketing activities and offering special tour packages that worked in conjunction with the promotion.

Special Fares

The promotional technique that can be the most effective in the short-term, and yet the most dangerous in the long-term, is price cutting. Special fares enable marketers to counter special market situations and create short-term sales incentives.

Upon settlement of a 1985 employee strike, United Airlines looked for a way to get customers back in the friendly skies—fast. The solution: Offer passengers a one-week, 50-state rebate.

Passengers who flew any United flight between July 1 and July 7 could receive a 50 percent cash rebate from United when they sent in a copy of their ticket along with the rebate form they received in flight.

Savings of 50 percent on flights to 50 states accomplished three of United's important objectives: fill seats, regain United passengers who had been forced to fly other airlines during the strike, and create top-of-mind awareness of United's service to all 50 states.

In the spring of 1986 Pan Am developed a promotion to counter the falloff in overseas traffic due to increased terrorist activities. By offering passengers a $150 Eurocash coupon to be applied to any transatlantic Pan Am flight during the peak summer travel season, Pan Am provided a powerful incentive for U.S. tourists to stop worrying and pack their bags for a money-saving summer vacation in Europe.

Of course, a special fare promotion can be as simple as "American's Summer Seat Sale." This market-specific promotion offered travelers special low fares with advance reservations and purchase of airline tickets to any of American's destinations. Of course, this type of promotion is only effective if limited to a specific time period; otherwise the promotional costs become prohibitive.

Fare savings can be used by marketers to speed booking decisions and fill carriers. Sitmar Cruises' "Book by New Year's Eve and Save Up to $800" promotion offered great savings on 1987 cruises booked in 1986. Limiting the life of the offer boosts response and increases the inherent value of the offer, by cancelling the discount at the end of a specified promotional period.

The Holiday Inn Crowne Plaza in Miami had a different reason for promoting a price cut—a new hotel in a highly competitive market. To encourage frequent business travelers to stay at their new property, the Crowne Plaza offered them "The Date is the Rate" room tariffs for one month. This promotion offered room rates that corresponded to the date of the month. For instance, guests who checked in on September 2 paid just $2.00 for their room. Check-ins on September 3 paid $3.00, and so on through the end of September. And while those who checked in on the 20th paid ten times the rate on the 2nd, their bill was still only $20, less then one-third of the actual room rate!

Crowne Plaza created a unique way to generate trial, repeat business, and awareness in a crowded market that resulted in more than a 20 percent occupancy boost after the promotion.

Sweepstakes

Probably the most exciting and potentially rewarding sales promotion devices for the consumer are contests and sweepstakes. Everybody likes to dream a little—to imagine that they've won a million dollars or a trip around the world, a chance to escape the daily grind and live their fantasy. That's the strength of special event promotions and their use by travel marketers.

In the spring of 1986, British Airways needed something to force decreasing transatlantic ticket sales due to America's fear of increased European terrorist activities. The big idea: British Airways' "Go For It, America" sweepstakes.

Launched with sweepstakes entries, newspaper-delivered in the airline's 15 U.S. gateway cities, British Airways offered readers 5,200 free roundtrip tickets for two to London with free first night's lodging. July's sweepstakes offered a chance to win 100,000 British pounds sterling for a shopping spree. In August, a 5-year London townhouse lease. September offered a Rolls Royce, and October's big prize was a British Investment Portfolio worth 100,000 British pounds sterling.

By creating a promotion that carried through the peak travel season and giving away exciting prizes, British Airways stimulated ticket sales and ultimately filled those empty airplane seats by generating readership and participation in their sweepstakes. The British Airways "Go For It America" sweepstakes was an exciting, successful solution to a difficult market situation the airline had little control over.

While generating excitement with consumers, British Airways didn't forget their most important ally, the travel agent. By creating an opportunity for travel agents to win fantastic prizes every time they booked a passenger on their airline, British Airways added insurance to the success of this promotion.

Special Event and Cause Marketing

Although not widely used, corporate-sponsored philanthropic efforts have made an entry into the travel industry. These efforts have significant value in creating awareness and goodwill. Joining in an all-American charitable effort, for example, American Airlines was among the sponsors of the Tall Ships Bicentennial event and the Statue of Liberty-Ellis Island Foundation restoration project.

Locally, Chicago-based United Airlines sponsors many civic organizations, cultural events, and major sports teams in the Chicago area. These sponsorships help enhance United's prominence in Chicagoland. One example is the strong helping hand United has provided to public television stations' fund-raising efforts by providing certificates good for $50 worth of United Airlines travel when a person donates $75 to the participating PBS station.

American Airlines generated goodwill in the Chicago community through support of Chicago's public school system. In their American Educational Challenge program, American donated $1.00 to the school system for every person who flew American out of O'Hare. They also gave recognition to top students in Chicago area schools. In addition to generating a half-million-dollar donation to the Chicago public schools, the program was successful in creating visibility and goodwill for American Airlines.

American generated additional goodwill in Dallas by offering cash contributions to the Dallas Symphony for each passenger who boarded the then-new daily 747 flight from Dallas to London. By joining with the Business Committee for the Arts, Inc., American was able to realize increased ridership and bottom-line benefits.

Trailways Corporation earned a busload of goodwill with its "Operation: Home Free" program, which offered runaway minors a free ride home from anywhere in the United States—with no strings attached. In the program's first seven months, Trailways gave free rides to more than 2,000 runaways, uniting them with their families.

Distribution Channel Communications

As you can see from the British Airways sweepstakes detailed previously, involving the distribution channel in the promotional efforts is important. In fact, the trade's support and enthusiasm for promotion can make the difference between a mediocre sales effort and an overwhelmingly successful one.

Short-term promotions offer travel agents a reason to book more passengers on one parity carrier over another, push special consumer promotional offers, and keep a brand at top-of-mind awareness.

When Tour Alaska faced a shortfall in bookings, they turned to the trade to help them fill their remaining vacancies. Their offer to travel agents: "Send us a booking and we'll send you a fur. Free!"

This incentive is highly appropriate to the cruise line brand image, and highly attractive to the largely female travel agent target. It was a great promotion that generated excitement and involvement.

With KLM, travel agents were invited to celebrate KLM's 65th anniversary and enter the Amsterdam Connection sweepstakes. Weekly prizes were awarded ranging from a grand prize vacation for two to exotic destinations like Bangkok or Egypt. Lower-level prizes offered travel agents even greater odds of winning something.

KLM made it easy for travel agents to learn more about their Amsterdam connection and enter the sweepstakes through programmed learning with weekly questions and correct answers programmed into the agent's computer. When travel agents found the correct answers in their system, they mailed them to KLM, and their name was automatically entered in the sweepstakes.

Programmed-learning sweepstakes are, as KLM quickly realized, an effective involvement technique that both motivates and informs KLM's most important non-staff sales representatives — the travel agents.

The variety of potentially lucrative promotion techniques available to travel and tourism marketers is vast. What I've attempted to give you is a broad overview of some of the most successful promotional techniques being used today, how they met the marketing objectives, and what they accomplished.

Overall, travel marketers will find the greatest effectiveness in their future sales promotions when their programs are part of a cohesive, overall marketing strategy, consistent with the reinforcing brand imagery, and addressing appropriate promotion objectives.

Chapter 31
Promoting a New Hotel

J. Peter Rickard
Former General
Manager,
Pier House, Key West
Florida

Born in Yorkshire, England, and trained in the West End of London, J. Peter Rickard has been in the hotel business, including his years at Hotel School, for 24 years. He has managed hotels in England, Jamaica, Barbados, Bermuda, the Far East, Canada, and the United States, among them the Sandy Lane in Barbados, the Elbow Beach and Belmont Hotels in Bermuda, the Lyford Cay Club in the Bahamas, the King Edward in Toronto, and the Regent of Kuala Lumpur in Malaysia.

The advertising and promotion decisions you make during the year prior to, and the year after, opening will have a profound effect on your hotel's level of success for many years.

The old adage that you never get a second chance with a first impression is particularly true in the opening of a new hotel. You are only new once and you must use that advantage to its fullest to carve out your market share.

I will leave it to the professional marketers to explain the minutiae of marketing plans and advertising schedules and will confine myself in the next few paragraphs to some practical observations from the viewpoint of a general manager.

Marketing Plan

No doubt the developer of the hotel will have commissioned a feasability study from an accounting firm specializing in hotel accounting. Included in such a study will be market breakdowns, occupancy, and average rate information for your competitors. You should however make your own assessment. Collect information from the Chamber of Commerce, relevant Tourist Authority, Convention Bureau, Hotel Association, and last but most important, your future competitors. Usually you will be pleasantly surprised at how much information most of your competitors will divulge. From this information you will have a breakdown of where business comes from in your area, whom your competitors attract, and from where. You can then make a comparison with the physical attributes of your hotel, its facilities, location, and level of service, so as to position yourself within the market and achieve your financial goals. You will have a clear picture of where you fit in, what level of services you will need to provide to attract a clientele consistent with the rates you will need to achieve financial success.

Pricing

After establishing your position within your market, it is advisable to set your rates in the first year a little lower than your main competitor. You will need to offer some incentive to gain customer loyalty. Occupancy, not average rate, must be your goal for the first year. It is also a good idea for a short period during your soft opening—the period when perhaps not all your rooms are complete or all your facilities available—to offer "preopening rates" at a reduction. Your staff will need the guinea pigs, and you will avoid any complaints about unfinished facilities. It will also help overcome the customers' initial reluctance to stay at such a newly opened property.

If business is less than you had anticipated during the first year, you are in a position to offer "introductory" rates for the first year without demeaning at all your position in the marketplace.

Sales Goals Can Now Be Established

Because transient business tends to be very short lead, your sales efforts are likely initially to be directed at group and meeting business. Since lead time with groups can be anywhere from three months to three years, you will need to be booking business today for the same time next year, if you want to be successful. Specific room/night goals booked per month are therefore essential and must be adhered to. If your sales staff merits it in terms of numbers, the various markets should be broken down and each salesperson assigned an area and a room night goal.

It is all too easy to allow your Director of Sales to become immersed in paperwork or take on roles during the preopening period that are not strictly related to sales. It is very exciting to show prospective clients around the construction site, but that function can be carried out by somebody further down the line, leaving the Sales Director to close the sale.

Having established where your business is coming from, you now have to lay out a plan of action, which will include at least the following:

1. Advertising
2. Public Relations
3. Direct Mail
4. Sales Trips
5. Brochure and Collateral Material
6. Trade Show Participation

Advertising

First, you need to cover the basics. Make sure that you appear in the appropriate trade directories and meeting planner guides. It is very worthwhile during this initial period to take out large display boxes in these publications; later, when you are established, you can reduce the size of your insertion. Also, do not forget to contract for your yellow page insertion well in advance of the opening. Trade advertising in travel trade papers and magazines is also essential depending upon your reliance of travel agent business. The balance of your advertising dollars will basically be split between direct selling advertisements — normally newspaper ads selling a rate or package, but could be such vehicles as billboards — and image ads normally placed in magazines. This situation is always a dilemma. You will never have enough dollars for advertising everywhere you want, and while image advertising is needed, it is long-term, and in the opening period your needs are immediate. A solution is to concentrate your image advertising in the preopening stage in a few select magazines aimed at your target markets. Move to direct selling newspaper ads after opening, maintaining at that time a small image ad campaign.

Remember, a newspaper ad has a life of no more than 24 hours and should be selling something specific, such as a special rate or program. The ads should be eye catching and not verbose; buying a hotel room is not a high-risk item and a potential customer just doesn't have the time to read all that you really would like to tell.

Magazines have a longer life and can better reflect your image. Your advertising campaign will result directly from your marketing plan, as a support to your sales strategy in your primary markets. Better to penetrate one or two markets well than to scatter your advertising dollars across a broad spectrum of markets and gain no recognition at all.

Public Relations

I cannot emphasize sufficiently the vital role a good public relations program plays in the marketing of a new hotel. Do not think that you can do it yourself; you will have far too many other demands on your time and will not have access to the right members of the press. Develop your program with a professional agency at least a year prior to the opening.

Your aim is to reach your target market with the image you wish to portray by building excitement and anticipation so that by the day you open your propsective clients know you exist and are eager to try you out. There are three main opportunities to do this — the Groundbreaking when the construction starts, the Topping Out when the final roof is on the building, and the Opening Ceremony. However, to maintain interest during the preopening period, other events and story lines must be developed. Do not miss a single opportunity. For example, even when doing the mass hiring, get the press in to photograph the queues of applicants; in an area of high unemployment, this may be a newsworthy item and will help both your community image and your recruitment drive.

I remember in one hotel I opened, we had a full article in a construction magazine published on the other side of the country—and we actually got some business through this article. Another technical magazine published an article on the latest technology in fire alarm systems, which we were installing. The possibilities are endless, but it is up to you and your P. R. Agency to develop the opportunities.

If You Don't Want It in Print, Don't Say It

With the assistance of your agency, compile a media kit containing a fact sheet, providing statistical information about the hotel, biographies of the key members of the management team, and press releases providing general stories on the hotel and special interest stories, for example, on food and beverage outlets or special services and facilities the hotel will provide. As the hotel's construction progresses this kit can be updated with photographs and additional story lines. While your agency will compose these press releases, it is vital that you check them closely; nobody knows the facts better than you and it is important that you maintain honesty and credibility with the press.

Do not make grandiose statements you cannot live up to. If you don't want to see a specific point utilized as a story headline, then don't include it in your releases.

When opening the King Edward in Toronto we made the mistake of including in one story the fact that our Royal Suite rented for $1,365 per night; the fact that this included four sittings rooms, five bedrooms, a dining room, and a butlers kitchen, and would normally be rented as four separate suites, except when the Saudis were in town, was omitted! The result—newspaper headlines read "King Edward suites at $1,365 a night."

It certainly positioned us a top-of-the-line hotel, but it took us months to get the message across to our prospective clients that our preopening rates started at $85.

Opening Night

Here is your chance to announce to the world that you have finally arrived, and to do so in spectacular way. The purpose of the opening party is to obtain the maximum press possible and expose the hotel to as many potential clients as possible.

Since you want to make the best possible impression, it is not necessary or indeed advisable to coincide the opening party with the actual opening of the hotel. Two or three months after opening is fine, depending of course on the level of completion at soft opening. No matter how hard you try, the hotel will not be 100 percent when you open and there will usually still be bugs to iron out. For your opening debut, however, they should be as minor as possible.

In the late 1950s, the British company Ind Coope, which was a major brewing company, opened a hotel in Manchester, the first such to be built outside London since the war. In view of the occasion, a member of the Royal Family was the guest of honor at the opening banquet. Just as she entered the banquet room, with the television cameras zooming in, a section of the ceiling paneling crashed to the floor due to hasty last minute installation. Nobody was hurt, but for years after the hotel was known as the place where the ceiling fell in on opening night. It is worthwhile, therefore, to lose two or three months while you run up to full gear to make the right impression. While you obviously want to make the best impression possible, you should not take on more than you can cope with. If a full formal banquet is a little more than you can handle, then organize a floating buffet, showing off the foods of your restaurant with buffets spread throughout the public areas of the hotel, and a dance band occupying the main function room where the actual ceremony can take place at an appointed hour. If you wish your hotel to be the center of the social activities in your area, you should tilt your opening toward the social end of the market. This is best achieved by combining with a charity organization known for its high social aspect. Allow the organization to sell tickets to the event, donating the funds to the charity. It is likely in this way that you will be able to attract the attendance of top officials, who might act as offical openers and may not perhaps have otherwise attended a purely commercial affair. If your markets are not on the social side, you may prefer a business breakfast with a high profile speaker.

Whatever you do you have to provide angles for the press. The opening of the hotel may not be newsworthy in itself in a large city.

Get Involved

Henri Manassero, the general manager who built up The Pierre in New York to what it is today, once told me that "there is no truly long-term successful hotel anywhere which is not regarded as such by its local community." To achieve this end, you must become involved in your local community. Let them know you are there and that you are community minded; in short, that you are an asset to their area. Needless to say you also have to provide the quality of service and facility consistent with your chosen position. Not only should your management staff become involved in local organizations, but you should encourage your staff to participate in community events. If there is a suitable parade, for example, encourage and support your staff in a tangible way. For example, have them purchase costumes. This action will maintain morale among your staff and give them a sense of pride, as well as let the community know that you are part of it.

During training periods, when you are simulating the service of food and beverage, invite some local dignitaries and prospective clients to act as "guinea pigs." They will know that you are still in training so will excuse any faux pas and will feel especially important to be in at the beginning.

If you have empty meeting rooms during the opening period, contact some of the local charitable associations and offer to host their meetings at no cost, with the understanding that they will have to be flexible regarding date and place. Such gestures will reap their rewards in food and beverage business.

Don't forget those people who may never use your hotel, but may have considerable impact on your business—the taxi drivers and the local tour operators, for example. Coin holders and key rings customized with the name of the hotel can be obtained at very little expense and make excellent giveaways when you ask taxi drivers to call by the hotel for a free box lunch.

How to Handle Comps

If the destination is a popular or upcoming one you will not be short of requests for rooms from travel agents or from meeting planners for site inspections. You will need as much exposure as you can get for your new product, so don't alienate them—you need them. You can, however, regulate the flow, and you can charge if you need to, at least to cover your cost of making up the room. Most worthwhile agents will understand that you cannot accommodate them during peak periods, but go out of your way to encourage them when you are likely to have empty rooms. In the initial months when you are unlikely to be operating at full capacity all the time, announce special agent introduction periods at low or complimentary rates. At the same time, with the willing help of an airline serving your area, you can organize familiarization trips. The airline will have good knowledge of the best producing agents for your area, and putting on a full program of tours of the area, meals in your restaurants, and such will maximize the exposure. The same applies to meeting planners and the press.

Remember Your Staff Is Part of Your Marketing and Sales Team

During the preopening and training period you and your management team will be able to pick out those staff members with a vibrant enthusiastic attitude who are full of ideas. Utilize these people and their ideas. Form an ad hoc marketing group and bounce your plans and programs off them and listen to their ideas. This exchange will stimulate your own thinking and make them feel part of the effort.

Particularly in a small community, where word spreads quickly, let your staff know what is happening—which ads you are placing and why. This can be done cheaply and simply through a pasted and duplicated news sheet. Often immediately after opening there is somewhat of an anticlimax, the rush of the preopening period is over, the training mostly complete, and because you may not be running 100 percent, there is a sense of letdown. The staff will wonder what is being done to attract business. Tell them, show them, explain. They are on your team and play a huge role in the salesmanship of your hotel.

A hotel is only so much bricks and mortar without a dedicated, caring, committed staff. After all, what are we selling? Service. And the staff members cannot give all-out service and attention unless they know what it is you are trying to achieve. Telling them how you are marketing the hotel is all part of the process of involvement.

Looking Ahead

WE MAY NEVER BE QUITE SURE WHICH IS the oldest surviving profession, but there is no doubt that oracles are high on the list. The very earliest writings of the Egyptians depict oracles predicting the future for monarchs and priests — the managers of those early societies. In ancient Greece the Delphic Oracle played a key role in planning both love and war.

The situation has not changed greatly in the last 3000 years. The Delphic Oracle has merely been replaced by Alvin Toffler and John Naisbitt. As a nation, we are obsessed with a concern for the future. Peter Drucker writes about *Managing in Turbulent Times* and Kiplinger sells advice on how to cope with *Changing Times*. Strategic planning, which is simply a plan for survival in the future, has become an emerging new and important business discipline.

Whatever scenario of the future you subscribe to (and there are as many scenarios as there are futurists), there are profound implications for tourism's future.

Some micro-trends are already clear, such as the consolidation of airlines and the segmentation of consumer markets, but there are far more unknowns than knowns to cope with. Technology is changing the way we live and the way we behave. Ultimately, political, economic, and environmental forces will shape our future. They will determine the accessibility of travel, the safest and most attractive destinations, consumer demand, and the size of the marketplace. We cannot predict, with confidence, any of these factors for more than a few years ahead. We have learned through experience that even our best forecasts can be rendered meaningless by a terrorist attack or an act of Congress.

This closing article by Bill Marriott needs no further introduction. The Marriott Corporation has demonstrated time and again its ability to cope with new consumers and new trends in almost every sector of travel and tourism. Marriott does not speculate on the future, but he does tell how the company intends to cope with it. His lesson in survival tactics is also a good place to start thinking about marketing for travel and tourism in the years ahead!

Chapter 32

Managing Change in the Travel Industry

J. W. Marriott, Jr.
Chairman, Marriott
Corporation

J. W. Marriott, Jr. began work in his father's restaurant chain while still in high school and college. Two years after receiving his degree in banking and finance, he joined his father's company. Moving up through the ranks of executive vice president, member of the Board of Directors, and President, J. W. Marriott, Jr. succeeded his father as CEO in 1972. In 1964, when he became president, the company grossed $84 million in sales and employed 9,600 people. In 1985, sales exceded $4.2 billion and more than 160,000 people worked for Marriott.

Managing change has become, I believe, the greatest challenge we in the busines community face today.

As I look back over the nearly 60 years of Marriott Corporation's growth, it becomes apparent that the history of our company is really a history of change in the restaurant and hotel industries. Our succes is due, in large part, to the fact that we have been able to foresee change and adapt to it. As *Megatrends* author John Naisbitt pointed out, "Trends, like horses, are easier to ride in the direction they are already going." We certainly are testimony to that axiom. By anticipating and even encouraging change, we have grown from a single root beer stand to a multibillion dollar international lodging company.

The driving force behind our company for so many years was its founder, my father, J. Willard Marriott. A true entrepreneur, he began as a small businessman with little more than his family behind him, a strong vision to guide him, and the burning desire to succeed. He viewed change as opportunity. Realizing the potential of the automobile and the effect it would have on people's lives, he opened the first drive-in restaurant on the East Coast in 1927. Thirty years later, he continued to act on his vision and opened the world's largest motor hotel—Marriott Twin Bridges in Arlington, Virginia, the first of more then 160 hotels we now operate around the world.

In the years that came between he found additional opportunities. He pioneered in-flight catering by providing box lunches to airline passengers.

World War II brought a need to provide meal service to defense plants and government installations and he created our food service management division.

Not every businessperson has my father's penchant for action. Too often we meet people who tell us all the reasons why things can't be done, rather than why they can happen. To succeed in today's highly competitive business environment, we can't accept that negative attitude. We must be open to change and we must learn to manage and create change or change will manage or confine us, and we may not like the results.

Our Industry Is Challenged on Many Fronts

Today we are faced with prevailing undercurrents that challenge the very nature of our industry in terms of marketing systems, changing consumer values, and the multiplicity of available options. Everywhere we look we see an industry in flux—in some cases, the result of deregulation; in others, the result of federal tax policies that once encouraged the construction of hotels that may not have been as well thought-out as they should and could have been.

We see consolidation and mergers; and automation of the marketing system that sometimes seems to be progressing faster than any of us can comprehend and with far-reaching results that few of us can imagine.

We see a consumer who is increasingly discriminating in terms of what he or she wants to buy and how much he or she is willing to pay; yet, at the same time, we see a consumer who is also bewildered by the many travel options now available, not to mention all the alternatives that mitigate against travel.

We hear many prognosticators characterize our industry as mature with little room for growth or future opportunity. To prove their point they note the intense competition for market share now occurring among all components. They cite the proliferation of experienced customers in the marketplace and the industry's need to concentrate on containing cost and providing superior service. They point to the fact that many suppliers who are caught in the middle are being squeezed out of the game. They predict a big shakeout in the airline, lodging, and travel agency components. And some say the recent tax reform legislation will have dire effects on business travel and future hotel expansion.

Survival Depends upon Being Innovative

While many may recieve these predictions with alarm, I believe—as in the past—the best, most flexible, innovative, action-oriented, and most entrepreneurial operator will view these challenges as opportunities and consequently will prevail.

Every challenge is different. To respond to the challenges we face today, we must learn to think with an open mind. Be ready to ask, "Why not?" Welcome the challenge of change and make it work to your advantage.

How do we welcome change? We begin by recognizing that as our economy becomes more service-oriented, the services in greatest demand are those related to travel: hotels, airlines, restaurants, cruise ship companies, motor coach lines, sight-seeing tour operators, rental car firms, and so forth. This simple fact offers tremendous potential for success.

We welcome change by truly learning the business we're in. I don't think anyone can run any business today unless he or she really understands it in detail. This fact has been shown in the studies of why many mergers don't work. When companies buy other companies that they are not familiar with and when executives with no experience in the acquired businesses try to run them, they often find they simply don't know what to do.

For this reason, I believe the future will see more chief executives cultivated and promoted from within rather than hired from without. I also believe that business schools will begin to change what they teach, shifting their emphasis from developing strategists, financial experts, and consultants to developing middle managers who want to learn the business from the bottom up.

When my father founded our company, he spent at least half his time out of the office in the operations. I try to do the same thing. Managing "by walking around" really does work. The best managers use the knowledge they get in this manner to improve their products and, most importantly, to learn from and about their customers. It surprises me how few of today's managers subscribe to this practice. They too quickly isolate themselves from their revenue source in the process.

We welcome change by accepting the fact that the entire basis of our capitalistic system lies in the delicate relationship between the customer and the product provider. More than selling hotel rooms, airline seats, car rentals, theme park visits, and sight-seeing tours, we're really in the business of satisfying customer needs—in terms of service and product.

As Bob Crandall of American Airlines noted in his address before the 1986 Discover America International Pow Wow, "It takes only a relatively few unhappy travelers talking to their friends and acquaintances . . . to persuade people that they should stay home and buy a new car or new golf clubs or another club membership or a new boat or something besides the travel experience which you and I want to sell."

That's why it's so important that we hire the right people and train and treat them well. My father used to say, "Treat your people well and they'll take good care of the customer." A well-trained, motivated, happy employee will enthusiastically see that your customer's needs are met. Almost everyone wants to do a good job and I believe, in most cases, when something goes wrong, it's not the employee who fails, but his or her manager who failed the employee by not providing the proper environment that leads to success.

While providing exceptional service is one-half of the customer-need equation, the other half is designing the right product and offering it at a price that creates the perception of value. Some people call this market segmentation. Everywhere we look today, we find a proliferation of hotel brand names and different travel options in a response to the plurality of today's marketplace. Whereas a single product like the traditional, full-service Marriott hotel may have been considered satisfactory by a diverse group of guests in the past, each of today's customer groups has a specific image of the type of hotel they want to stay in, what kind of services they want available, and how much they are willing to pay.

Today's travelers are not equal anymore. They are better educated, more well-trained about the mechanics of traveling, and less likely to accept standardization in what they consume. They're not interested in having their needs and expectations met nearly; they expect that their needs and wants will be met exactly.

As a result, we see many travel companies, big and small, now involved in what may well be the biggest gamble in the industry's history — as we all scramble to attract the discriminating traveler. For some, segmentation could bring great payoffs. Others, meanwhile, will quietly withdraw. Some firms simply won't play the game at all.

We welcome change when we really know our competition. It astounds me how many of today's managers are oblivious to the environment in which they're operating. At Marriott, we emphasize it, talk about it frequently, and have our people shop the competition to see what they are doing differently — what they're doing that we're not doing. I stay at competitive hotels three or four times a year to learn about new things plus to see what they could do better and to think about those things we could do better.

We welcome change by accepting the fact that we have to operate differently. Automation has already revolutionized internal information processing systems and back-of-house operations, freeing our people to really concentrate on providing service. It now has become a dominant force in our industry's entire distribution network, giving companies and their travel agencies the ability to track their travel and entertainment costs, and suppliers a greater opportunity to better track where their business is coming from. This ability will place more emphasis on the need to negotiate — on price and service elements — and to more clearly identify who one's best customers are.

There is no easy road to success, but opportunites abound if you are open to them. I firmly believe that by offering quality products at every price level, treating your employees well, providing good service, listening to your customers and acting on their suggestions, displaying a spirit of goodwill, and maintaining great perserverence, we all will achieve greater satisfaction and a fulfilling return on investment in the years to come.

OTHER TITLES OF INTEREST FROM
NTC BUSINESS BOOKS

Contact: 4255 West Touhy Avenue
Lincolnwood, IL 60646-1975
800-323-4900 (in Illinois, 312-679-5500)

Successful Direct Marketing Methods by Bob Stone

Successful Telemarketing by Bob Stone and John Wyman

How To Create Successful Catalogs by Maxwell Sroge

Best Sales Promotions by Bill Robinson

New Product Development by George Gruenwald

Opportunities in Marketing Careers by Margery Steinberg

Opportunities in Travel Careers by Robert Scott Milne

Opportunities in Transportation Careers by Adrian Paradis

Opportunities in Hotel and Motel Management Careers by Shepard Henkin

Opportunities in Airline Careers by Adrian Paradis